4.95

# THE DEVELOPMENT
## OF THE EARLY
## CHRISTIAN CHURCH

A STUDY BASED ON THE
ACTS OF THE APOSTLES
AND
THE EPISTLES

# THE DEVELOPMENT
# OF THE EARLY
# CHRISTIAN CHURCH

BY CHRIS B. HARTSHORN

Reorganized CHURCH OF JESUS CHRIST
of Latter Day Saints
1967

# PREFACE

The spread of the gospel throughout Palestine and beyond is religiously significant. This biblical history is summarized in the book of Acts, with many details of the events elaborated in the Epistles. Students of Christianity have found it helpful to follow this development of the church in a chronological order as nearly as possible.

The story begins with the ascension of Jesus from Mount Olivet. It really has no end; but for the purpose of this course, it will be limited to the events included in the New Testament. The time and place of these events, though significant, will not be given primary importance. The meaning and value of the Christian message for us today is enhanced by a knowledge of the conditions under which that message was originally written.

Some valuable history has been lost, but it was not the primary purpose and plan of Paul, Peter, John, and James to write history. They were so close to the events and to the society of that day as to make it difficult for them to anticipate the value of that history to distant generations. These church leaders were promoting Christian doctrines and striving to establish the kingdom of God. This course has kept that same purpose uppermost and used the historical background as connective tissue.

Since the four Gospels are covered in other church school study texts, and the apocalyptic book of Revelation has little historical connection with Acts and the Epistles, these five books will receive only incidental mention.

History always involves geography, and it will help class members to grasp the reality of the people and places if wall maps of the areas discussed are before them. Each member should be continually urged to bring his own Bible or New Testament to class each Sunday. The basic text of this course is the Inspired Version. The Revised Standard Version, indicated herein by the initials R.S.V., and other versions will be indicated when used. In studying and teaching these lessons one should have the scriptures open before him and read the context of the chapter under consideration as indicated in the lesson text. A better understanding of Christ's mission and the kingdom of God will result from a greater knowledge of the book of Acts and the Epistles.

# CONTENTS

# 1 OVERVIEW OF "ACTS OF THE APOSTLES"

## INTRODUCTION

The exact time and place of the church's beginning in Palestine is not known, and speculation on such matters is not profitable. There is abundant testimony that a fellowship of believers, an organization of disciples, or, as we commonly say, a church was brought forth and established through the labors of Jesus and his followers aided by the Holy Spirit.

Mark affirms that "Jesus came into Galilee, preaching the gospel of the kingdom of God; and saying, The time is fulfilled, and the kingdom of God is at hand; repent ye and believe the gospel" (1:12, 13). The purpose and mission of the Son of God in coming to earth was to set up the kingdom of the Father to save men from sin and death.

After Jesus asked John the Baptist for baptism in the Jordan River where there was "much water" (John 3:24), he at once began making converts and choosing apostles. On one occasion he turned to his disciples and asked, "Whom do men say that I, the Son of Man, am?" Peter answered correctly, "Thou art the Christ, the Son of the living God." From this dialogue Jesus announced, "I will build my church, and the gates of hell [powers of death—R.S.V.] shall not prevail against it" (Matt. 16:14-19).

This was a prophetic affirmation. The church would be built. Satanic powers could not frustrate God's purpose by closing gates or through martyrdom. It would be a mistake to emphasize the pronoun "I." Jesus was not planning to present the world of that age or any other with a ready-made church. He invited his disciples to help; in fact he was depending on their help: "Seek not the things of this world but seek ye first to build up the kingdom of God, and to establish his righteousness, and all these things shall be added unto you" (Matt. 6:38). Jesus presented the gospel plan for the kingdom; they were to build it up and establish it. There is a great difference in building a thing and "to build up and establish."

## The Church Is Basic

The existence and strength of the church was then and is today of great importance in God's purposes for man's welfare. It was not a temporary mold or scaffold for a living organism. It was an essential part of God's eternal plan. Jesus left no doubt of this when he said, "I have not spoken of myself; but the Father which sent me, he gave me a commandment, what I should say, and what I should speak. . . . Therefore, even as the Father said unto me, so I speak" (John 12:49, 50).

## Small Beginnings

The book of Acts indicates that this church was not fully established, nor did it consist of large groups of believers, when Jesus had finished his work and ascended into heaven. His crucifixion was not the public exhibition of a failure nor the sad end of a noble plan. It was a crowning achievement of divine grace. It was the fulfillment of an essential phase of the plan of salvation made "in the beginning" before the world was, and before man's creation.

This is made clear in the last recorded prayer of Jesus:

I have finished the work which thou gavest me to do. And now, O Father, glorify thou me with thine own self with the glory I had with thee before the world was. . . .

And now come I to thee; . . . as thou hast sent me into the world, even so have I also sent them into the world. . . . And the glory which thou gavest me I have given them; that they may be one, even as we are one; I in them, and thou in me.—John 17:4-23.

The work of the apostles, as presented in the book of Acts, traces the development of the kingdom of God, commonly called the church of Jesus Christ. We shall not only note its structure and progress but the power that made it go and grow against great odds. There need be no discussion of the church in competition with Christ. They are inseparable and complementary. Paul wrote, "Christ also loved the church, and gave himself for it" (Eph. 5:25).

As Jesus faced the completion of his mission, he must have startled his apostles when he declared, "He that believeth on me, the works that I do shall he do also; and greater works than these shall he do; because I go unto my Father" (John 14:12). Could weak men, as they knew themselves to be, do "greater works"?

## Wait for the Promise

Luke starts this historical book of Acts of the Apostles by identifying himself with the Gospel which carries his name. "The former treatise have I made, O Theophilus, [Luke 1:3] of all that Jesus began to do and teach."

Paul identifies Luke as "the beloved physician" (Col. 4:14). He was Paul's counselor and traveling companion (see II Timothy 4:11 and Philemon 1:24). It seems likely that Luke wrote Acts about A.D. 80.

In one of his last recorded discussions, Jesus told his disciples "that they should not depart from Jerusalem, but wait for the promise of the Father" (v. 4). This waiting was a conditioning and seasoning process. After the crucifixion the apostles seemed stunned and uncertain. When Peter announced that he was going fishing, the others decided to follow (John 21:3). They fished all night but caught nothing. Their risen Lord stood upon the shore in the morning and directed them to cast the net on the right side of the boat. They caught so many fish that they could not lift them into the boat, but dragged the net with the fish to the shore. Jesus had a fire waiting there and soon they dined together. Before leaving them on this occasion, Jesus said, "Tarry ye in the city of Jerusalem, until ye be endued with power from on high" (Luke 24:40-48).

Jesus continued by reminding them, "John truly baptized with water (v. 5), but ye shall be baptized with the Holy Ghost not many days hence." As further evidence that these apostles were not ready to launch out on the Great Commission, "Go . . . teach all nations" (Matt. 28:18, 19), Luke records that they asked, "Lord, wilt thou at this time restore again the kingdom to Israel?" (v. 6). The tradition of centuries that a great king should again sit on David's throne was still on their minds.

Jesus brings them back to reality by declaring, "But ye shall receive power, after that the Holy Ghost is come upon you; and ye shall be witnesses unto me both in Jerusalem, and in all Judea, and in Samaria, and unto the uttermost part of the earth" (v. 8). This verse sets forth the threefold historical structure of Acts of the Apostles:

1. The gospel preached in Jerusalem
2. The message taken to the rest of Judea and Samaria
3. Christ preached to the Gentiles

## THE ASCENSION

Maturing in devotion and in judgment takes time. James said it this way: "The trying of your faith worketh patience. But let patience have its perfect work, that ye may be perfect and entire, wanting nothing" (1:3, 4). No longer would the apostles have the daily companionship and wisdom of Jesus to lean on. They must stand on their own feet. Only as some of us are stricken by sickness or financial reverses do we learn that man cannot lean upon the arm of flesh (Jer. 17:5). It is sometimes good for such persons to have reverses so that they will look up to God the omnipotent.

Paul reminds us that, "God is faithful, who will not suffer you to be tempted above that ye are able; but will, with the temptation also make a way to escape, that ye may be able to bear it" (I Cor. 10:13). This relief from the temptation to go back to fishing and to forsake their covenants of ordination came to the apostles on Pentecost, the fiftieth day after the Passover which in this instance coincided with the crucifixion. This Pentecost was only ten days after Christ's ascension. It was then that the Comforter as promised by the Father came to the church and the apostles became "born of the Spirit."

The final act of Jesus' ministry in Palestine occurred near Bethany, the home place of his friends Lazarus, Mary, and Martha (Luke 24:49). It was a little south and east of Jerusalem[1] on Mount Olivet (v. 12). The record is very simple and direct, "While they beheld, he was taken up; and a cloud received him out of their sight" (v. 9). Out of the cloud, or at least above them,

Two men stood by them in white apparel[2]; which also said, Ye men of Galilee, why stand ye gazing up into heaven? this same Jesus, which is taken up from you into heaven, shall so come in like manner as ye have seen him go into heaven.—Verses 10, 11.

It must be assumed that these two were heavenly messengers. They could not have been so positive about Jesus' destination by natural means. Moreover, a very significant prophecy was added: Jesus was to return in like manner; that is, out of the clouds of heaven.  (See Matthew 16:30; 24:4, 27, 38; 26:65.)

---

1. The return from the place of the Ascension to Jerusalem (verse 12) is "a Sabbath day's journey." This is about 2,000 cubits or five-eighths of a mile (see Num. 35:5; Exod. 16:29).
2. White garments are the garb of angels (Mark 16:3).

## QUESTIONS FOR DISCUSSION

1. To what extent was Jesus' declaration, "I will build my church," achieved before his ascension?
2. What was the purpose of an assembly or the body of believers (*ekklesia*) organized as a church?
3. What is the relation of the church to "the kingdom of God" which we pray "shall come; and thy will be done on earth, as it is done in heaven"?
4. What was the primary purpose of Christ's coming to earth?
5. Why did Jesus demand baptism in Jordan by John?
6. If we grant that there were only between one and two hundred disciples by the time Jesus prayed, "I have finished the work thou gavest me to do," can we be sure that any more members were needed or that the organization was to be enlarged?
7. What "greater works" than Jesus had done were the disciples to achieve?
8. Have someone prepared to give an assignment on the life of Luke.
9. What are the three major divisions in the book of Acts?
10. Where was the missionary work of the apostles to start and how far were they to reach out?

# 2

# THE COMING OF THE HOLY SPIRIT

(Acts 1:13 - 2:41)

While Luke is the only writer who gives the details of Jesus' return to the Father, there are numerous references in the Bible to the plan of the Savior's temporary sojourn here. The scriptures which follow clearly indicate Christ's preexistence with God and show that his return was anticipated.

John records Jesus' answer to the Jews, "Your father Abraham rejoiced to see my day; and he saw it, and was glad" (John 8:56).

Paul wrote, "But when the fulness of the time was come, God sent forth his Son" (Gal. 4:4).

Peter declared, "Searching what time, and what manner of salvation the Spirit of Christ which was in them did signify, when it testified beforehand the sufferings of Christ, and the glory which should follow" (I Pet. 1:11).

John wrote that Christ said, "I am he that liveth, and was dead; and, behold, I am alive for evermore" (Rev. 1:18).

"I will prepare a place for you; and come again, and receive you unto myself; that where I am, ye may be also" (John 14:3).

"I came forth from the Father, and am come into the world; again, I leave the world, and go to the Father" (John 16:28).

15

The Book of Mormon supports this view. (See Mosiah 1:104, 105; Jacob 3:4; III Nephi 5:9-17.)

## Worship in the Upper Room

The apostles returned from the ascension to Jerusalem and assembled in an upper room. Luke gives their names: Peter; James and John (sons of Zebedee, Matt. 4:20); Andrew (Peter's brother, John 1:40); Philip; Thomas ("the doubter"); Bartholomew (perhaps the same as Nathaniel); Matthew; James (the son of Alpheus); Simon Zelotes; and Judas (the brother of James). These were all Galileans (v. 11). Judas Iscariot had killed himself before this (Matt. 27:6) and is not mentioned (v. 13).

These eleven continued in prayer "with the women, and Mary the mother of Jesus, and with his brethren" (v. 14). This is significant history. Luke's writing is unusual for that age in that it accorded women a particular and respected place. This may stem from the fact that he was a Gentile of Greek culture. Jesus did not share the traditional view that women were the chattels of or inferior to men. The Mosaic code[1] gave to the man only the right of divorce (Deut. 24:1-4). Girls could be sold (Exod. 21:7; Neh. 5:5). A son was more desired than a daughter (Lev. 12:1-5). Wives were to be submissive to their husbands (Col. 3:18). The women were to keep silent and not rule in the churches (I Cor. 14:34); neither were they to teach (I Tim. 2:12).

The name of only one of the women in the upper room was given—Mary, Jesus' mother—but it is considered likely that the group also included Mary Magdalene, Joanna, Susanna, Mary the mother of James, and Salome,[2] since Luke mentions them in his Gospel (8:2, 3; 23:56; 24:9).

Even more significant is the statement that Jesus' brethren ("brothers," R.S.V.) were also there (v. 14). They did not accept his Messiahship during his ministry (John 7:5). Their names were James, Joses, Judah, and Simon (Mark

16

6:4). It seems likely that the events surrounding the crucifixion and ascension convinced them that he was more than a brother in the flesh.

## THE TWELVE REORGANIZED

"Peter stood up in the midst of the disciples" (v. 15) indicates that he had overcome his despair and was ready to speak out. There "were about 120" in this upper room. The idea that there were no more disciples in the church at that time is false, for Paul records that after the Resurrection "he was seen of above five hundred brethren" besides the apostles (I Cor. 15:5, 6). The disciples were reminded that Judas, who "was guide to them that took Jesus," (v. 16), had fulfilled a prophecy of David. Judas had shared with them as an apostle (v. 17). After Jesus was condemned to death, Judas suffered remorse and committed suicide. One account says he hanged himself (Matt. 27:6). It may be that he broke the rope or garment used in the hanging and rolled over a cliff thus mutilating his body (v. 18). Matthew records that it was not lawful to put the thirty pieces of silver which Judas returned in the treasury, so they bought a parcel of ground where they buried him. It became known as "the field of blood" (v. 19). The reference to the Psalms (v. 20) is likely inferred from Psalms 69:25 and 109:8.

Peter suggests that the successor for Judas be one who had "companied with us all the time that the Lord Jesus" had been with them (v. 21, 22). Two men were named, Joseph and Matthias, who seemed qualified. The sacredness of this act, described as "gave forth their lots" (v. 26), was recognized. The disciples made it the specific subject of prayer that the Lord would guide them (v. 23-25). The "casting of lots" (R.S.V.) was a traditional method of choosing. *The Interpreter's Bible* says the original text could be interpreted as saying, "they gave their votes."

Most significant is the fact that they recognized it to be important that the council of twelve be not diminished in number. It was not intended that it should be a temporary body; its work had scarcely begun. As we shall see, other apostles were chosen later as vacancies arose.

## ENDOWMENT OF THE HOLY SPIRIT
(Acts 2)

The Jewish day is from sundown to sundown of the next day. Pentecost was fifty days after the Passover. "When the day of Pentecost was *fully* come" (v. 1) would refer to the next sunrise (Lev. 23:15). This would be Sunday morning, sometimes called "the Christian Sabbath," but appropriately known as "the Lord's day."

"They were all with one accord in one place" (v. 1) indicates unity of spirit in the meeting. "Be one; and if ye are not one, ye are not mine" (D. and C. 38:6 a). The coming of the Holy Spirit could even be heard as a wind, but it was also visible as a halo of fire resting upon each of them (v. 2, 3). This gift of power manifested itself by their speaking "with other tongues, as the Spirit gave them utterance" (v. 4).

Every faithful Jew was to return to Jerusalem once each year. This was later limited to those living within fifteen miles of the city. That there were devout Jews "out of every nation" who gathered, as word of the endowment spread in the neighborhood (v. 5-8), indicates that Jews of the diaspora joined the assembly, for "every man heard them speak in his own language" (v. 6); yet those who spoke were all Galileans (v. 7-12). Some unbelievers explained the gift of tongues as caused by drinking too much wine (v. 13).

Peter and his brethren of the Twelve denied this, for it was only the third hour of the day (9:00 A.M., v. 14, 15), but they said it fulfilled the prophecy of Joel (2:28-31).

## PETER PREACHES OF CHRIST

Addressing himself to the Israelites, Peter spoke forthrightly: "Jesus of Nazareth, a man approved of God among you by miracles and wonders and signs . . . being delivered by the determinate counsel and foreknowledge of God, ye have taken, and by wicked hands have crucified and slain" (v. 22, 23).

The plan of salvation was determined in heaven before man's fall. He was "the Lamb slain from the foundation of the world" (Rev. 13:8).

God's approval of this man of Nazareth had been manifested not alone in the wisdom of his teaching and the many wonderful miracles performed; he is the one "whom God hath raised up, having loosed the pains of death" (v. 24). The quotation credited to David is from Psalm 16:8-11 and emphasizes Christ's resurrection from the tomb (v. 25-28). The word "prison" comes from a Greek term meaning the "unseen world," also translated "hell" or "hades" in other versions of the Bible.

Peter reminded his hearers that, "the patriarch David . . . being a prophet, and knowing that God had sworn with an oath to him, that of the fruit of his loins, according to the flesh, he would raise up Christ to sit on his throne" (v. 29, 30). This is a reference to Psalm 110:1, 2. Isaiah also prophesied of this event when the Prince of Peace should be on "the throne of David" (Isa. 9:6, 7).

"Let all the house of Israel know assuredly, that God hath made that same Jesus whom ye have crucified, both Lord and Christ" (v. 36). The term "Christ" is from the Greek word meaning "anointed" and hence the Messiah, or one who would be anointed as Israel's king. Later the name "Christ" came to be used as a proper noun. This stinging indictment reached them: "They were pricked in their heart" (v. 37), and cried out, "Men and brethren, what shall we do?"

"Repent, and be baptized every one of you in the name of Jesus Christ for the remission of sins, and ye shall receive the gift of the Holy Ghost" (v. 38), said Peter. "Save yourselves from this untoward [crooked—R.S.V.] generation" (v. 40). Those who "gladly received his word were baptized . . . about three thousand souls" (v. 41).

---

1. God meets people's needs on the level of their development. The gospel given to Adam and Abraham seemed above the reach of Israel after four centuries of bondage in Egypt. Therefore, "He took Moses out of their midst and the holy [Melchisedec] priesthood also" (D. and C. 83:4 c). Paul said, "The law was added" (Gal. 3:8, 19, 24).

2. Salome was the mother of James and John. There is a strong inference that she was a sister of Jesus' mother (Mark 15:45; John 19:25).

## QUESTIONS FOR DISCUSSION

1. Give reasons why Jesus' death was due to more than Jewish persecution.
2. Which of the twelve apostles was not a Galilean?
3. What was the social and personal status of women among the Jews and the heathen nations?
4. How long did the meeting in the upper room last?
5. What significance is attached to the mention that Jesus' brothers were present?
6. How large do you think the church was at this time?
7. Why do you suppose Jesus committed his mother to the care of his cousin John while he was dying on the cross instead of to his brothers?
8. Which day of the week was the pentecostal blessing bestowed?
9. Who were those persons that were most amazed when the apostles spoke in tongues?
10. What is the original meaning of the term "Christ"?

# 3 REBORN APOSTLES AT WORK IN JERUSALEM

(Acts 2:42 - 4:7)

As a concluding statement of the last chapter we learned of a great number who were added to the church. They must have followed Peter's advice (v. 38) and were baptized. Some have pointed out the difficulty of immersing "about three thousand" in one day. As was pointed out, the membership was over five hundred, and the record does not say that only the Twelve performed the ordinance. Luke wrote, "The Lord appointed other seventy also, and sent them two by two before his face, into every city and place where he himself would come" (Luke 10:1). Dr. J. Vernon Bartlet declared, "While such large numbers embraced on that very day the conviction 'Jesus is the Christ,' they need not all have been actually baptized then and there."[1]

## A COMMUNITY OF BELIEVERS ESTABLISHED

"They continued steadfastly in the apostles' doctrine and fellowship, and in breaking of bread, and in prayers" (v. 42). In this young church and with little if any written instructions, there must have been great need for continued teaching and association. "Breaking of bread" might mean the eating of the common meal (v. 46), or it could refer to the sacrament

21

of the Lord's Supper. In Corinth the two were not sharply separated, and Paul wrote them about certain abuses of eating and drinking too much (I Cor. 11: 20-30). Some observed the Lord's Supper daily (v. 46); others weekly (Acts 20:7). Paul indicates that there was no fixed time: "As often as ye eat this bread, and drink this cup" (I Cor. 11:26). Latter-day revelation gives much the same counsel (D. and C. 119:5 a, b).

"Fear came upon every soul" (v. 43) refers to reverence or awe. See Hebrews 12:28; Revelation 14:7. "Many wonders and signs were done by the apostles" were the miracles they performed through the Holy Spirit.

The statement that they "had all things common" has often led Christian people to try to practice a type of communism. We need to distinguish the difference here between history and doctrine. The disciples "sold their possessions and goods, and parted them to all men, as every man had need" (v. 45). From a common pool they received their daily sustenance. Their expectation of the prompt return of Jesus doubtless stimulated their enthusiasm for this type of communal life. Some saints in Thessalonica were carried away by a similar enthusiasm, and Paul had to admonish them against it (II Thess. 2:1, 2; 3:8-11). "Sold . . . as every man had need" seems clearly to indicate a continuing process. Barnabas retained land, for he later sold it and made a consecration (Acts 4:36, 37). Ananias and Sapphira did the same thing, but were punished because they lied "to the Holy Ghost" (Acts 5:1-4). Mark's mother retained her home (Acts 12:12).

Jesus taught stewardship, not communism (Luke 12:34-48; Matt. 25:14, 15, 29; Luke 11:42; D. and C. 42:9; 72:1). The Essenes had a common table, but there is no scriptural support for such practice. Joseph Smith, Jr., was asked about this practice in the early days of the Restoration. He condemned "having all things in common" after some unhappy experiences with it. On October 30, 1835, in Kirtland, Ohio, Joseph Smith, Jr., said:

We had no common stock business among us; that every man enjoys his own property, or can, if he is disposed, consecrate liberally or il- liberally to the support of the poor and needy, or the building up of Zion.—*Church History*, Vol. 1, page 593.

Was Jesus' teaching specifically responsible for the experiments mentioned in III Nephi 12:11 and IV Nephi 1:4, 28?

## PETER AND JOHN VISIT THE TEMPLE
(Acts 3)

Note the author's literalism in narrating this event. The apostles "went up together into the temple" (v. 1). The temple was situated on Mount Zion (Moriah) which was the highest point in the city. Then high steps and porches had to be ascended to reach the temple court.

"The ninth hour, for prayer" (v. 1) would be at 3:00 P.M. People were going and coming at all hours of the day; hence this would be a good place for the lame man to get alms as he lay at the gate "which is called Beautiful" (v. 2). When the invalid called out to Peter and John, they responded by saying, "Look on us" (v. 4). "Silver and gold have I none," said Peter, "but such as I have give I thee; in the name of Jesus Christ of Nazareth rise up and walk" (v. 6).

The Hebrews attached great significance to the use of a name. See Genesis 32:27, 29; Judges 13:17, 18; Luke 9:48; 10:18.

No doubt the lame man was startled by such a command. But Peter suited action to his words by taking him by the "right hand" and helping him. "Immediately his feet and ankle bones received strength" (v. 7). The word used here for "ankle bones" is a medical term such as Luke, the physician, would use. Feeling this power come into his limbs, the

23

man leaped up, stood, and walked (v. 8). Then he entered the temple with the apostles "leaping, and praising God."

This man was a familiar figure to the worshipers who had used the gate Beautiful. As he held to Peter and John he gave praises to God and a crowd gathered (v. 10, 11). Peter took advantage of this situation and preached his second sermon:

Ye men of Israel, why marvel ye at this? . . . The God of Abraham, and of Isaac, and of Jacob, the God of our fathers, hath glorified his Son Jesus; whom ye delivered up, and denied him in the presence of Pilate . . . and desired a murderer to be granted unto you; and killed the Prince of life, whom God hath raised from the dead.—Acts 3:12-15.

Peter strikes hard in trying to get his hearers to sense their guilt, and calls on them to repent "and be converted, that your sins may be blotted out" (v. 17-19). Next he tells them that God will send this Jesus whom "ye have crucified, whom the heavens must receive until the times of restitution of all things" (v. 20, 21).

Peter calls attention to Moses' testimony, "A Prophet shall the Lord your God raise up unto you of your brethren, like unto me; him shall ye hear in all things" (v. 22, 23; see also Deut. 18:18). Then Peter cites the covenant God made to Abraham in 1921 B.C., "And in thy seed shall all the kindreds of the earth be blessed" (v. 25). See Genesis 12:1-3; 22:22. Paul capitalized on this prophecy in writing the Galatians. The promise was not "to seeds, as of many; but as of one, And to thy seed, which is Christ" (Gal. 3:16, also 3:8).

## THE APOSTLES ARE ARRESTED
(Acts 4)

Peter closes his sermon by emphasizing the Resurrection. It was God who "raised up his Son Jesus" whom he had sent "to bless you, in turning away every one of you from his iniquities" (Acts 3:26). By this time the officials of the temple got together. "The priests, and the captain of the temple, and the Sadducees, came upon them" (Acts 4:1). The sect of Jews known as Sadducees were the aristocrats and rulers. They were liberal in religion, but strong on politics. They rejected the doctrines of resurrection of the dead (Matt. 22:23), immortality, and angels (Acts 23:8).

The sermon antagonized these people, and particularly were they grieved about Peter's claims that Jesus had been raised from the dead (v. 2). "They laid hands on them, and put them in hold unto the next day" (v. 3).

"The captain of the temple" had charge of the police force of the temple who were made up mainly of Levites. He stood next to the high priest in temple rank. "The hold" is a place of confinement, or a jail. It was now evening, and there was no desire to try the apostles until the next day.

As a result of the miracle and the sermon, about five thousand believed (v. 4). This is quite in contrast to the labors to establish the kingdom before the endowment of the Holy Spirit at Pentecost. The witness of Jesus' resurrection and ascension had a magic effect, and the gospel net gathered in great numbers. Truly the apostles had become "fishers of men."

Under the Romans the high priests were appointed by the Herods or procurators. Josephus tells us that there were twenty-eight between 37 B.C. and A.D. 68. They wore gorgeous attire (Exod. 28:4-29:9). They presided over the Sanhedrin or ruling body of Jews. They were supposed to be lineal descendants of Aaron, and they held the office for life. Annas was the ex-high priest. Caiaphas, son-in-law of Annas, was the high priest who presided at the trials of Jesus (Matt. 26:56, 57). John and Alexander were doubtless members of the family of Annas, "kindred of the high priest" (v. 6). Mention of their being "gathered together at Jerusalem" likely indicates that they functioned in jurisdictions outside the capital city.

As the trial opens the prisoners were set "in the midst." "By what power, or by what name, have ye done this?" (v. 7) they asked. By "power" they meant magical power or name in violation of Deuteronomy 13:1-5.

---

1. *New Century Bible*, "The Acts," p. 151.

## QUESTIONS FOR DISCUSSION

1. It has been said that three thousand people could not have been baptized by immersion in one day. Why do you agree or disagree?
2. When and how often should the Communion be served?
3. Did Jesus or his apostles teach the doctrine of having all things in common? Give reasons for your answer.
4. What evidence is found in the miracle at the gate Beautiful that the writer of the account was Luke?
5. What action led to the arrest of Peter and John in the temple?
6. Give some points in the sermon in the temple and the results of it.
7. What was the covenant made to Abraham and how was it fulfilled?
8. Tell something of the high priest and the captain of the temple.
9. What was the Sanhedrin and its function?
10. Why were the apostles asked at the trial about the name by which they performed miracles and preached?

# 4

# THE CHURCH ADVANCES THROUGH TRIAL

(Acts 4:8-5:29)

Peter and John had been in the "hold" overnight because of the excitement and the crowd which gathered as the healed alms beggar praised God in the temple. Brought before the high priests, the apostles were asked to explain by what magic they had done this miracle. This gave Peter the setting for his third sermon.

## IN THE NAME OF JESUS

This sermon was started a little differently than the other two: "Ye rulers of the people, and elders of Israel" (v. 8), which indicated that the apostles and the man who had been healed were before members of the Sanhedrin. It was the highest Jewish court, consisting of seventy members and the high priest who presided. The Jews usually trace this council back to Moses' day (Num. 11:16), though it more likely goes back only to the Greek or Persian period (312-550 B.C.). Its authority was limited to the reaches of Judaism. Rome did not permit it to inflict the death penalty until the Roman court had reviewed the case. "It held its sittings inside the outer wall of the temple, and twenty-three constituted a quorum."[1]

Peter said that if they were being examined for "the good deed done to the impotent man" (v. 9), he wanted it known to all Israel that "by the name of Jesus Christ of Nazareth, whom ye crucified, whom God raised from the dead . . . doth this man stand here before you whole" (v. 10).

He then paraphrased Psalm 118:22 and applied it to Jesus. He is the "head of the corner" you builders rejected (v. 11). Only in this name is there salvation and in "none other name under heaven" (v. 12).

Jesus told his disciples, "Whatsoever ye shall ask in my name, that will I do, that the Father may be glorified in the Son" (John 14:13). Again he said, "Whosoever shall give you a cup of water to drink, in my name, because ye belong to Christ . . . he shall not lose his reward" (Mark 9:38). Paul declared of Jesus, "God also hath highly exalted him, and given him a name which is above every name; that at the name of Jesus every knee should bow" (Phil. 2:9, 10). He also directed, "Whatsoever ye do in word or deed, do it all in the name of the Lord Jesus" (Col. 3:17). This counsel is also given many times in latter-day revelations (16:4 c-g; 17:6 a; 59:2 a).

## They Spoke with Boldness

Members of the Sanhedrin were impressed by the outspoken manner of Peter and John. The rulers saw that they were not trained in the rabbinical schools. Neither was Jesus (John 7:15). They were not "ignorant" in the sense of being illiterate, but the sermon was not in the language of Galilean fishermen. The council sensed that they had been with the Master Teacher (v. 13). The evidence of the miracle they had done stood before them, so there was no question of deception. They could think of no further charge on which to hold the prisoners, and so asked them to step outside that the council might consider what action to take (v. 13-16).

Something had to be done lest the message they declared and the power they exercised stir up all Jerusalem. They decided to threaten them, so they called them back "and commanded them not to speak at all nor teach in the name of Jesus" (v. 17, 18). The record indicates that John joined in the reply made to this decision: "Whether it be right in the sight of God to hearken unto you more than unto God, judge ye" (v. 19, 20). To inflict any severe punishment in the face of this defiance was to be avoided for two reasons: "because of the people; for many glorified God for that which was done" (v. 21), and further it was difficult to find any wrong in what the apostles had done. Therefore the three were released and "went to their own company" (v. 23).

When the rest of the disciples heard their report, they praised God and cited a statement of David (Ps. 2:1, 2). This was applied to the persecution of Herod[2] and Pilate in Jesus' trial and the subsequent mocking and crucifixion of Jesus by the Gentiles (non-Jews, here particularly the Romans) and the people of Israel (v. 27). Then they prayed the Lord to notice the threatenings and to give them boldness to "speak thy word" (v. 29, 30). As though it came in answer, the house "was shaken . . . and they were all filled with the Holy Ghost" (v. 31).

## Of One Heart and Mind

The solidarity and unity of the church members assembled are emphasized by the statement, "Neither said any of them that aught of the things which he possessed was his own; but they had all things common." They had individual possessions to give as needed, but did not stress ownership (v. 32). As a result of this unity and love, the apostles were given great power to "witness of the resurrection of the Lord Jesus" (v. 33-34). "Distribution was made unto every man according as he had need" (v. 35). A Levite of Cyprus sold his land and laid the money "at the apostles' feet" (v. 37).

The incident of Ananias and Sapphira shows that the saints are weak when left to themselves, for God has said, "My Spirit shall not always strive with man" (Gen. 8:5; Luke 13:24; R.S.V. Gen. 6:3). Only when under the influence of the Holy Spirit are they "of one heart" (4:32). This man and his wife were overcome *by their own greed.* "Why hath Satan filled thine heart to lie to the Holy Ghost, and keep back part of the price of the land? . . . After it was sold, was it not in thine own power"? (Acts 5:3, 4). They were at liberty to consecrate as much or as little as they wished. Both of these church members were stricken and died immediately (v. 5-10).

As this tragedy was noised among the saints, "Great fear came upon all the church" (v. 11). The lesson of this event should not be lost on the church today. In our stewardship we are asked to tithe our increase as the Lord's rightful share. The nine-tenths remaining is ours to use as wise stewards. We are held accountable whether we have ten, five, or only one talent. But in rendering our account to God through the bishopric (D. and C. 72:1) we should be both fair and honest. We can save ourselves only at the price of our selfishness. Cheaters and deceivers die spiritually at the time they let Satan fill their hearts with a lying greediness.

The apostles continued to minister to the sick and needy among the people. The record indicates that the gathering was "in Solomon's porch" of the temple, but of the rulers "durst no man join himself to them; but the people magnified them" (v. 12, 13).

## The Apostles Imprisoned but Escape

The church continued to grow in numbers and influence, and the apostles grew bolder in their ministry. "Multitudes both of men and women" became believers (v. 14). They brought their sick and those "vexed with unclean spirits; and they were healed every one" (v. 16). But success always attracts attention and often opposition. The high priest and "the Sadducees . . . were filled with indignation" (v. 17). This resulted in the apostles being put in the common prison (v. 18).

That night "the angel of the Lord" came to their rescue and "opened the prison doors, and brought them forth" (v. 19). It was not sufficient for this agent of God just to open the doors. He had a message for the apostles. So he brought them out and commanded, "Go, stand and speak in the temple to the people all the words of this life" (v. 20). They did as directed early in the morning.

The high priest assembled the Sanhedrin that morning and sent officers to the prison to get the apostles. They returned and reported that the prison was shut and the keepers standing guard, but none of the prisoners were inside. This only added to the seriousness of the work of the council. About this time a man came and reported that the apostles were again teaching the people in the temple (v. 21-25).

The captain of the temple police and his officers went and brought the apostles "without violence; for they feared the people" (v. 26). The high priest reminded them that they had been forbidden to teach in this name, and "ye have filled Jerusalem with your doctrine, and intend to bring this man's blood upon us" (v. 28). The apostles replied, "We ought to obey God rather than men" (v. 29). This was a direct challenge to the authority of the Sanhedrin to control them. Their prison would not hold them, and the decision of the council was defied. Something more drastic had to be done.

---

1. E. E. Stringfellow, *Acts and Epistles,* William C. Brown Co., 1945, p. 26.

2. This Herod was known as Herod Antipas. He was appointed by Rome and was tetrarch over Galilee and Perea from 4 B.C. to A.D. 39 (Luke 3:1).

## QUESTIONS FOR DISCUSSION

1. What was the Sanhedrin, who were its members, and what were their powers?
2. How was Jesus "head of the corner" and the "stone the builders had rejected"?
3. The council took note that these "ignorant" fishermen had been with Jesus. What gave evidence of this?
4. What was the decision of the Sanhedrin and the response of Peter and John? Reconcile your answer with D. and C. 58:5.
5. Why are not the Saints always of one heart and mind? Comment on, "Once in grace, always in grace."
6. How does the tragedy of Ananias and Sapphira apply to the Saints of our time?
7. Why were the apostles put in the common prison and how were they released?
8. Where do angels come from and what is their work?
9. Why did the captain of the temple police fear to use force to take the apostles before the Sanhedrin?

# 5

# THE CHURCH IS SPREAD
# BY PERSECUTION

(Acts 5:30-7:7)

The apostles were again brought before the Sanhedrin when they were found teaching in the temple in defiance of the council's orders. Their defense was that they preferred "to obey God rather than men." They believed that the angel spoke for their heavenly Father and commanded, "Go, . . . speak in the temple."

## GAMALIEL WARNS THE SANHEDRIN

As another crisis arose and the apostles were permitted to speak, they bore witness for Christ. They were eye witnesses that this "Jesus, whom ye slew and hanged on a tree" had been made alive by the power of God (v. 30). While this placed the blame for the crucifixion on the council, the apostles had some good news to offset this charge. "Him hath God exalted . . . to be a Prince and a Savior, for to give repentance to Israel, and forgiveness of sins" (v. 31).

This bold accusation cut the council to the heart and they "took counsel to slay them" (v. 33). They had succeeded in destroying Jesus, and this seemed the best way to rid themselves of his chief disciples. One member, a Pharisee named Gamaliel who was a doctor of the law, interceded.

This is the first mention of the sect of Pharisees in Acts. The word means "separatists" because they withdrew from everything which was non-Jewish, even from tax collecting which supported Rome. Josephus said they numbered six thousand in the first century after Christ. Their chief tenets were (1) devotion to the law and the mass of traditions, (2) a bodily resurrection, (3) belief in angels and spirits (Acts 23:8), (4) the coming Messianic reign on David's throne, (5) and a middle ground between predestination and absolute free will; that is, every event is not absolutely determined in advance but is modified by group behavior.

This sect was often in active opposition to Jesus, and he condemned them for hypocrisy (Luke 11:39-55). Their attitude, however, was not as violent against the early Christians. This may be due to the common belief in a resurrection, angels, and spirits, which became more apparent following Pentecost.

Gamaliel was a grandson of Hillel, a famous rabbi, the first among seven teachers to receive the higher title, "Rabban." He was a teacher of Paul (Acts 22:3). Because of his reputation, the council took notice of what he had to say.

He asked that the apostles be withdrawn while he made his talk (Acts 5:34). Then he called attention to movements led by Theudas, who had four hundred followers, and Judas of Galilee[1] who "drew much people after him" (v. 36, 37). Both of these men perished, and their work came to naught.

And now I say unto you, Refrain from these men, and let them alone; for if this counsel or this work be of men, it will come to naught; but if it be of God, ye cannot overthrow it; be careful, therefore, lest ye be found even to fight against God (v. 38, 39).

The council gave heed to his words. Instead of slaying the apostles, they beat them and commanded them not to speak the name of Jesus. The brethren left, rejoicing that they were able to "suffer shame for his name" (v. 41). But

34

they had no intention of observing the council's order. In fact, they went daily to the temple and from house to house "to teach and preach Jesus Christ" (v. 42).

## GRECIAN WIDOWS; STEPHEN ACCUSED

The church was spreading fast. Many of the Jews spoke the Greek language and were called "Hellenists" or "Grecians" (*The Interpreter's Bible*, Acts, p. 88). Jews who had once lived abroad were especially inclined to use Greek. The common vernacular of Palestine was Aramaic.

Some disciples alleged that the Greek-speaking widows among them were being neglected in favor of the Hebrew widows (v. 1). The term "disciples" means learners and is used frequently in the Gospels. The title was quite appropriate as they needed to be taught by the Master Teacher while he was with them. This is the first of twenty-eight times it was used in Acts. It is not found in the epistles and Revelation. In earlier chapters of Acts they are called "brethren" or "believers." Later Acts uses the names "Christians" and "saints" for them.

The apostles, as church leaders, took the complaint under advisement as to the best course of action. They talked among themselves, "It is not reason that we should leave the word of God, and serve tables" (v. 2).

The twelve selected seven men who were honest, spiritual, and wise "whom we may appoint over this business" (v. 3). The plan was presented to the body of the church and approved by them. Not much is known about these seven, who are often referred to as "deacons" because of the nature of their task, though Acts does not use the term. From their names it is said that three were Hebrew, three Greek, and one "a proselyte of Antioch" (v. 5). It may have been only a temporary committee.

The church in Jerusalem continued to grow, and Luke mentions that "a great company of the priests were obedient to the faith" (v. 7).

A young man named Stephen, one of the seven, in addition to helping the widows, was blessed with spiritual power and "did great wonders and miracles among the people" (v. 8). While he taught in the synagogue, some Jews from abroad began to dispute some of his teachings; but they soon found that they were no match against his wisdom and the Spirit which attended him (v. 9, 10). So they resorted to bribing ("suborned") men to bear false witness: "We have heard him speak blasphemous words against Moses, and against God" (v. 11).

This stirred up the "elders and scribes"[2] who brought him before the council. Here they added to their false accusations that Stephen had blasphemed against "this holy place, and the law" (v. 13). This referred to the temple where the Sanhedrin held its meetings and to the Law of Moses. Doubtless they were connecting him with Jesus' prediction of the destruction of Jerusalem, including the temple, under the siege of Titus and his Roman army in A.D. 70 (Matt. 33:38; 24:1-4).

"Change the customs which Moses delivered us" (v. 14) suggests Jesus' statement, "Think not I am come to destroy the law, or the prophets; I 'am not come to destroy, but to fulfill" (Matt. 5:19). When Jesus talked about divorce he cited the Law of Moses which provided that if one "put away his wife, let him give her a writing of divorcement" (Matt. 5:35, 36). Jesus changed this by making the grounds only that of fornication. On the matter of using oaths, under the law the prohibition was against swearing falsely (forswear). "But I say unto you swear not at all" (Matt. 5:38).

36

## STEPHEN'S DEFENSE
(Acts 7)

The high priest asked Stephen if these accusations were true (v. 1).

He addressed the council as "Men, brethren, and fathers" (v. 2). Then he cited them to Abraham's call (1921 B.C.) in Mesopotamia (a word meaning between the rivers Euphrates and Tigris). Genesis relates that the birthplace of Abraham was "Ur of the Chaldees" (11:19; 12:1-4). He stopped in Haran in Mesopotamia, sixty miles north of the Euphrates on Belikh River and six hundred miles northwest of Ur, on his way to Canaan. He lived in Haran (also spelled Charran) until after the death of his father Terah. Abraham was seventy-five years old when he moved to Canaan (v. 2-4).

"He gave him none inheritance in it" (v. 5) refers to Canaan. From Genesis 23:1-15 we learn that Abraham did not have title to any part of Palestine. When his wife, Sarah, died he bought a field in Machpelah for four hundred shekels in which to bury her. God had promised Canaan to his seed and that he should become a great nation, but nothing more (Gen. 12:2, 6). History shows that they were far from becoming a great nation then. His seed was to "sojourn in a strange land" and be in bondage four hundred years, then they would "come forth, and serve me in this place" (v. 6, 7).

---

1. This Judas was the son of Hezekiah. Following Herod's death (4 B.C.), he plundered Sepphoris, and sought to make himself king (*Josephus,* Ant. 17:10, 5). When Quirinius tried to have the Jews register (A.D. 6), he urged the Jews not to pay tribute to Rome, but to recognize God only as ruler (*Ibid.,* 18:1:1; B.J. 7:8, 1).

2. Scribes originally meant those who copied the law, but in time they were the interpreters of the law. Acts 23:9 refers to them as "scribes that were of the Pharisees." Luke 5:17 refers to them as lawyers or "doctors of the law." They were members of the Sanhedrin (Mark 15:1), and may or may not have been priest-

37

hood members. See the *New Standard Bible Dictionary*, p. 814, Funk and Wagnalls Co., 1936.

## QUESTIONS FOR DISCUSSION

1. Who was Gamaliel and in what way did he serve the apostles?
2. Why were the Pharisees less antagonistic to the early Christians than they were to Jesus?
3. What caused the conflict about widows between the Hellenists and their brethren?
4. What terms are used in Acts to refer to members of the church?
5. How were "the seven" chosen and what were they to do to relieve the apostles?
6. What is the significance of the statement that "a great company of the priests were obedient to the faith" (6:7)?
7. What was the specialty of the scribes and what other names were given to them?
8. What did Stephen say about Abraham and why did he bring this in his defense?
9. What reason had the witnesses for accusing Stephen of blaspheming the temple?
10. Cite evidences from the Sermon on the Mount that the "customs of Moses" were being changed.

# 6 STEPHEN'S MARTYRDOM; THE GOSPEL GOES TO SAMARIA

(Acts 7:8-8:40)

Stephen was permitted to answer his accusers before the Sanhedrin. He related the story of Abraham's coming to Canaan and the delay in making of them a great nation as God had promised. They had to become slaves in Egypt, where they sojourned four hundred years. Exodus 12:40 says "four hundred and thirty years," which probably includes the journey in the wilderness of Sinai.

## ISRAEL IN EGYPT

The account of the covenant of circumcision is given in Genesis 17:1-14. It had to do with both health (purification) and fertility. Originally the father was to perform the surgery (Gen. 17:30), but later "it was more common either to call a physician or to regulate the duty altogether to a special official (the mohel)."[1] It was performed on the male child when he was eight days old. There is evidence that it was practiced by Egyptians and the "Semitic peoples generally, except Assyrians and Babylonians."[2]

Stephen told of Jacob and his twelve sons getting into Egypt through the jealousy of eleven of the sons over Joseph whom they sold. He recounted the part Joseph performed,

39

as Pharaoh's governor over Egypt, in saving the Hebrews from famine. Jacob's family alone then numbered seventy-five (v. 9-15). He included in his narrative Jacob's death and burial in land purchased in Sychem, also spelled Shechem (Gen. 33:18), which was in Palestine between Mount Ebal and Gerizim.

The Hebrews "grew and multiplied in Egypt" (v. 17). Then "another king [Pharaoh] arose, which knew not Joseph" (v. 18) and dealt cruelly with the Israelites, compelling them to expose "their young children, to the end they might not live" (v. 19). He told of the fair child Moses being adopted by Pharaoh's daughter and reared as her son. Thus he became "learned in all the wisdom of the Egyptians" (v. 20-22).

When Moses was forty years old, he "smote an Egyptian" in defense of a Hebrew who was being abused, and he had to flee out of the land to Madian (also spelled Midian) which was in northwestern Arabia near Mount Sinai. Here he married Zipporah, the daughter of Jethro (also called Raguel in Numbers 10:29 or Reuel in the Revised Standard Version) who bore him two sons, Gershom and Eliezer (Exod. 18:1-4). After living here forty years he had a remarkable experience which changed his whole career. While in the wilderness of Mount Sina (also spelled Sinai and Horeb), an angel of the Lord appeared "in a flame of fire in a bush" (v. 30). As Moses drew near, the Lord spoke, "I am the God of thy fathers . . . Abraham . . . Isaac, and . . . Jacob" (v. 31, 32). The Lord said to him, "Put off thy shoes from thy feet; for the place where thou standest is holy ground" (v. 33). "I have seen the affliction of my people which is in Egypt . . . and am come down to deliver them. And now come, I will send thee into Egypt" (v. 34).

## ISRAEL DELIVERED FROM EGYPTIANS

Stephen then recounted the steps of the deliverance of the Israelites "with wonders and signs in the land of Egypt," the Red Sea, and the forty years in the wilderness of Sinai (v. 36). He quoted Moses as saying to his people, "A Prophet shall the Lord your God raise up unto you of your brethren, like unto me; him shall ye hear" (v. 37).

"The wonders and signs" included the ten plagues narrated in Exodus, chapters 7-12 and 16 and 17. This probably occurred in the thirteenth century B.C. Deuteronomy 18:15 ff. gives the prophecy mentioned and may have referred to Moses' successor, Joshua (Num. 27:18-20). The Greek form of Jesus is Joshua (v. 45).

Stephen called attention to the rebellious nature of the Israelites who disobeyed God and whose "hearts turned back again to Egypt" (v. 39). He also recalled their worship of the idol they had made in the form of a golden calf. While Moses was up in the mount communing with God and getting the tablet containing the Law, the people persuaded his older brother Aaron (Exod. 6:20), who was Moses' spokesman and assistant, to make the idol. The Egyptians worshiped living bulls as the incarnation of their god Osiris and the sun-god. Aaron also built an altar and told his people, "These be thy gods" (Exod. 32:1-5).

"It is written in the book of the prophets . . . ye offered to me slain beasts and sacrifices by the space of forty years in the wilderness" (v. 42). The "book" refers to the minor prophets, all those books following Daniel in the Old Testament which were in one scroll. The quotation is from Amos 5:25, 26.

Stephen also mentioned the building of the tabernacle in David's time and the temple Solomon built (v. 44-47). "The Most High dwelleth not in temples made with hands. . . . Heaven is my throne, and earth is my footstool" (v. 48, 49; Isa. 66:1, 2). The Jews looked upon both the tabernacle and the temple as the dwelling place of God (II Sam. 7:5; Ps. 132:1-5).

## The Sanhedrin Is Enraged

Addressing the members of the council directly, Stephen said, "Ye stiffnecked and uncircumcized in heart and ears, ye do always resist the Holy Ghost; as your fathers did, so do ye. Which of the prophets have not your fathers persecuted?" (v. 51, 52). They had even slain them, and of "the Just One . . . ye have been now the betrayers and murderers" (v. 51, 52). This was more than the council could take. "They were cut to the heart, and gnashed on him with their teeth" (v. 54). The Revised Standard Version says "ground their teeth against him." It is likely they made grimaces rather than committed mayhem.

Stephen's remarks may seem impetuous, for he was a young man addressing a high court. However, since he was "full of the Holy Ghost," we cannot safely charge him with being intemperate. Under this power he saw a vision of heaven and "the glory of God, and Jesus standing on the right hand of God" (v. 55). Stephen exclaimed, "Behold, I see the heavens opened, and the Son of Man standing on the right hand of God" (v. 56). Ephesians 1:20, Colossians 3:1, and Hebrews 1:3 picture Jesus as sitting on God's right hand.

This testimony was considered blasphemous (Lev. 24:16, 23) by the members of the Sanhedrin. They stopped their ears, began shouting, and rushed him outside the walls of the city and stoned him (v. 57, 58). The witnesses laid their clothes at the feet of a young man whose name was Saul. The Hebrew law required that there be two or three witnesses to the death penalty and that these witnesses cast the first stones (Deut. 17:6, 7).

Saul was born about the same year as was Jesus. The term "young man" might apply to anyone twenty to forty years old. Josephus applied it to Herod Agrippa I (Acts 12:1) when he was about forty-five (Ant. 18:6, 7). Saul was born in Tarsus of Cilicia and was a strict Pharisee (Acts 22:3; 23:6). His Greek name was Paul. He was a member of the Sanhedrin (Acts 26:10). Tradition required that members of this council be married.

While Stephen was being stoned, he called on God, addressing his prayer to Jesus (v. 59). With a loud voice he cried, "Lord, lay not this sin to their charge." Then "he fell asleep" (v. 60). This description is an euphemism for "death."

## Philip Preaches in Samaria
(Acts 8)

Following Stephen's martyrdom "there was a great persecution against the church which was at Jerusalem" which scattered it "throughout the regions of Judea and Samaria, except the apostles" (v. 1). One wonders why the apostles were permitted to remain. They were the recognized leaders and had been imprisoned before. Of course, their success in getting out of prison may have caused the Jews to hold them in awe, but doubtless the apostles were less likely to antagonize than were the Hellenists.

After Stephen's burial, Paul went from house to house hailing men and women to court and prison. As his work was noised about, the Christians scattered abroad. They preached Christ wherever they went (v. 2-4). Philip, another of the seven, went down to "the city of Samaria, and preached Christ unto them" (v. 5). Samaria was about one thousand feet lower than Jerusalem. His preaching was well received, and the miracles he performed created "great joy in that city" (v. 6-8).

Simon, the sorcerer, had bewitched the city and they acclaimed him as "the great power of God" (v. 9-11). But when they heard about the kingdom of God and Jesus Christ, "they were baptized, both men and women" (v. 12). Even Simon was convinced and was baptized. He followed Philip about and was amazed by the "miracles and signs which were done" (v. 13).

When word of Philip's success reached the apostles in Jerusalem, they sent Peter and John who confirmed those who had been baptized (v. 14-17). "When Simon saw that through the laying on of the apostles' hands the Holy Ghost was given, he offered them money . . . that on whomsoever I lay my hands, he may receive the Holy Ghost" (v. 18, 19). Peter rebuked him "because thou hast thought that the gift of God may be purchased with money. . . . Thy heart is not right in the sight of God." He called on him to repent and ask God's forgiveness. Simon asked them to pray for him (v. 20-24).

Under divine direction, Philip went south on the desert road to Gaza. He met an Ethiopian official under Candace, the queen, who had charge of her treasury. The Ethiopian must have been a Jewish proselyte since he had come about twelve hundred miles to Jerusalem to worship. A eunuch is a castrated male employed by oriental monarchs who kept harems. When he met Philip he was "sitting in his chariot" reading from the prophet Isaiah 53:7, 8. Directed by the Spirit, Philip joined him and asked if he understood what he was reading. He invited Philip to sit with him and to guide him or explain the prophet's meaning. They rode along till they came to a stream or pond of water. The eunuch asked for baptism. Philip asked if he believed. The Ethiopian (the word means darkskinned) replied, "I believe that Jesus Christ is the Son of God" (v. 27-37).

After baptizing the man, Philip was caught away by the Spirit, and the eunuch went on his way rejoicing. Philip continued his missionary work at Azotus (the Greek for Ashdod) which was midway between Gaza and Joppa about thirty miles west of Jerusalem and near the sea. He preached in all the cities till he reached Caesarea. This probably included Lydda and Joppa (v. 40).

## Questions for Discussion

1. What was the covenant given to Israel which required the male babies to be circumcised? What was its purpose?
2. What gave Moses the opportunity to acquire the learning and wisdom of the Egyptians?
3. What convinced Moses that he was to be the deliverer of Israel from Egyptian bondage?
4. What caused Pharaoh to let the Israelites go?
5. Give reasons why the Israelites in Sinai would choose to worship a golden calf.
6. What prophecy did Stephen use to bring Jesus into his defense?
7. What accusations did Stephen make against the council members which enraged them?
8. Under what conditions did Stephen see a vision and what did he see?
9. What was the early background of Saul or Paul?
10. Who was Philip and what evangelistic work did he perform?

# 7 PAUL'S CONVERSION AND MISSION

(Acts 9:1-9:42)

Philip had carried the gospel into Samaria and many converts were made to Christ. Under divine direction he left the work there in the hands of Peter and John and went to Caesarea, the Roman capital of Palestine. on his way he met, instructed, and baptized the treasurer of Ethiopia and preached in the cities through which he passed.

## SAUL WENT TO DAMASCUS

The persecution of Christians in Jerusalem was systematically pursued by Saul and others with such success that the saints who could get away scattered abroad. But this did not accomplish Paul's purpose; he wanted to do away with this way of "heresy" completely. So he started out to pursue "the disciples of the Lord."

Arming himself with letters of authority from the high priest, Caiaphas, he started for Damascus in Syria about 170 miles northeast of Jerusalem. This is reputed to be one of the oldest cities in the world. Genesis 14:14 shows that it was a city back in Abraham's time. It was the capital of that land until 300 B.C. when Antioch was built.

The Sanhedrin had authority over the Jews in Judea, but could use only moral persuasion on the outside according to

46

the loyalty of each Jewish community toward the council. The letters he carried were to the rulers of the synagogues in Damascus. By some high-handed procedures, Saul planned to bind and bring these Jewish Christians back to Jerusalem where the council could use its authority on them (v. 1, 2).

As Saul "came near Damascus" he was struck to the earth by a blinding light from heaven. He "heard a voice saying unto him, Saul, Saul, why persecutest thou me?" He answered, "Who art thou Lord? And the Lord said, I am Jesus of Nazareth whom thou persecutest; it is hard for thee to kick against the pricks" (v. 3-5).

This light may have been similar to lightning. It came about noon (Acts 22:6). It was the voice which prompted Saul's inquiry. A voice from heaven is a challenging event. All the fight went out of the man of Tarsus. Kicking against the "goad" (R.S.V.) is an allusion to driving oxen and prodding them with a sharpened stick. Some goads had iron points on them. The oxen often would kick, only to get more jabs with the goad. It was Saul's conscience which was prodding him now. What he was doing was contrary to Gamaliel's counsel. A righteous man would not punish nor slay others for holding a belief different from his.

## Told What He Must Do

When Saul became convinced that he was helpless, and unsure of himself, he cried out, "Lord, what wilt thou have me to do?" Back came the answer, "Arise, and go into the city, and it shall be told thee what thou must do" (v. 6). Saul arose, but when he opened his eyes he could not see; he had been blinded by the light.

There is some confusion in the testimony recorded about the effect of this phenomenon on Saul's traveling companions. This chapter in the R.S.V. and King James Version reads that they heard the voice, but saw no man. The Inspired Version reads, "They . . . saw indeed the light . . . but they

47

heard not the voice" (9:7). This is the same wording as found in Acts 22:9 in the other versions.

"They led him by the hand, and brought him into Damascus. And he was three days without sight, and neither did eat nor drink" (v. 8, 9). The Jews used fasting frequently as a means of obtaining divine favor (Matt. 9:15; Luke 18:12).

In another part of Damascus was a disciple named Ananias. He is the first Christian outside of Palestine known by name. The Lord directed him in a vision to go to the house of Judas on Straight Street and ask for "Saul, of Tarsus; for behold, he prayeth" (v. 10, 11). This street runs east and west and is the main street of the city even today. Doubtless, word of the martyrdom of Stephen and the persecution in Jerusalem which followed had reached Ananias and the change in Saul who was now praying for help was to reassure this disciple. The Lord added that Saul had seen in a vision Ananias' coming and laying hands on him that his sight might be restored (v. 10-12).

Notwithstanding all of this evidence that God was intervening in this situation, Ananias protested, "I have heard by many of this man, how much evil he hath done to thy saints at Jerusalem" (v. 13). This is the first time that the disciples are called "saints" in the Acts though the term is used frequently in the epistles of Paul. The root word from which it came means "set apart," or the verb meaning "sanctify." Ananias added, "He hath authority from the chief priests to bind all that call on thy name" (v. 14).

The Lord directed, "Go thy way; for he is a chosen vessel unto me, to bear my name before the Gentiles, and kings, and the children of Israel" (v. 15). Saul was to carry an important ministry in Christ's church. He was foreordained to be a special witness (apostle) to the Gentiles (non-Jews). He was destined to suffer "for my name's sake" (v. 16). As the Lord's instructions were followed, Saul received his sight, was baptized, and "preached Christ in the synagogues" (v. 17-20).

## SAUL PERSECUTED BY THE JEWS

The Jews who gathered for worship were at first amazed: "Is not this he that destroyed them which called on this name in Jerusalem, and came hither for that intent?" (v. 21). There is no evidence that Saul actually "destroyed" the lives of any disciples. He was present at Stephen's stoning, but the only connection he had is revealed by the statement that the garments of those doing the stoning were laid at his feet (Acts 7:58). The word "destroyed" was used in the sense of persecuting or making havoc. (See Galatians 1:23.)

Saul increased in strength and was able to confound the Jews who questioned him about Jesus. The Jews became angry and plotted to kill him. They had the gates guarded so he would not slip away. Saul learned of the plot and he had the disciples "let him down by the wall in a basket" (v. 21-25). Paul wrote later in more detail that Aretus, the king, sought to apprehend him, but he was let out "through a window" (II Cor. 11:32, 33).

And when Saul was come to Jerusalem, "he assayed [attempted—R.S.V.] to join himself to the disciples, but they were all afraid of him" (v. 26). Note that this does not say he went immediately after his escape to Jerusalem, but "when Saul was come to Jerusalem." Paul reveals that he did not go directly to the apostles, but went into Arabia, then to Damascus and stayed three years. After that he went to Jerusalem to see Peter and "abode with him fifteen days" (Gal. 1:16-21).

Barnabas, a Levite from Cyprus (Acts 4:36), befriended Saul. He took him to the apostles and told them the story of his conversion and his subsequent preaching in the name of Jesus at Damascus, also of his recent witnessing in Jerusalem (v. 27-29). "When the brethren" learned that some

49

of the Hellenists[1] were lying in wait to kill Saul, they brought him to Caesarea where he could take a boat to Tarsus, his birthplace (v. 27-30).

## PETER BUILDS UP THE CHURCH
## OUTSIDE JERUSALEM

Peter had gone to Samaria to confirm those baptized by Philip (Acts 8:14-17). He continued his ministry in Samaria, Galilee, and parts of Judea outside of Jerusalem. The churches in these areas were edified and blessed by the Holy Spirit. Their numbers multiplied as a result.

At Lydda he brought a healing ministry to Aeneas who had been bedfast eight years with the palsy ("paralyzed"— R.S.V.). "All that dwelt at Lydda and Saron [Sharon— R.S.V.] saw him and turned to the Lord" (v. 33-35). Lydda was known as Lod in Old Testament times (Neh. 11:35). It now was one of the seats of rabbinical learning located ten miles southeast of Joppa. Sharon means "level country" and is the plain extending fifty miles south from Mt. Carmel. It was six to twelve miles wide and very fertile.

Peter's next miracle was performed in Joppa, a seaport thirty-five miles northwest of Jerusalem. The cedars of Lebanon used in Solomon's temple were shipped here and brought in from this port. It is now known as Jaffa and is the terminus of the railway from Jerusalem. Here lived Tabitha, a woman greatly loved for her "good works and almsdeeds," who became sick and died. Her body was bathed and put in an upper room. "In Jerusalem burial should be on the day of death, but outside Jerusalem three days might intervene."[2]

The disciples sent two men to Lydda for Peter who came back with them and went to the upper room where he found "all the widows . . . weeping." They showed him the coats and garments Dorcas (the Greek name for Tabitha) had made. Peter asked them to leave the room. Oriental women

50

usually vent their mourning with loud wailing which would make it difficult to concentrate in prayer. When he arose from praying, he turned to the body and said, "Tabitha, arise. And she opened her eyes; and when she saw Peter, she sat up." He assisted her to her feet and presented her alive to the "saints and widows" (v. 36-42). This miracle became known throughout Joppa and "many believed in the Lord."

1. Hellenists—see Chapter 5, page 2.
2. Prof. E. E. Stringfellow, *op. cit.,* p. 62, "Upper Room."

## QUESTIONS FOR DISCUSSION

1. What authority had Saul over the disciples who had gone to Damascus, and how did he plan to use it?
2. Describe two things which happened to Saul and his company as they neared Damascus.
3. In what way was Saul "kicking against the pricks"?
4. What plans did the Lord have for Saul's recovery and his future life?
5. After Saul's strength returned, in what ways did he demonstrate his conversion?
6. When did Saul return to Jerusalem, and how was he received by the disciples?
7. Tell of Peter's early missionary work in Samaria and Lydda.
8. What caused Peter to go to Joppa?
9. Why was there so much weeping at Dorcas' death?
10. Compare the miracle in the upper room in Joppa with the raising of Jairus' daughter (Luke 8:50-55).

# THE CONVERSION OF CORNELIUS
# THE CENTURION

## 8

(Acts 10:1-48)

The power exercised by Peter to teach, comfort, heal, and even to bring back to life one who lay at least a day prepared for burial caused many to accept his testimony of a risen Savior. Doubtless there would be "mass conversions" today under similar circumstances. When people are attracted to the Christ and unite with his church as a result of miracles or spectacular gifts of the Spirit, there is a likelihood that it will take continual demonstrations of such power to keep them happy and make them faithful members.

### ROMAN OFFICER HAS A VISION
(Acts 10)

Caesarea, the Roman capital of Palestine, was about thirty miles north of Joppa where Peter "tarried many days . . . with one Simon a tanner" (Acts 9:43). There are eleven "Simons" mentioned in the New Testament, so it was necessary to use descriptive terms to identify each one.

Rome kept a garrison of troops in Caesarea to quell any uprising which might develop in the Jewish province. "Cornelius, a centurion of the band called the Italian band" (v. 1) was one of six such officers, each having charge of a hundred soldiers. Although he was a Gentile and a Roman, he was "a devout man, and one that feared God . . . gave much alms to the people, and prayed to God always" (v. 2). The Romans usually worshiped Jupiter and other gods, but this man had forsaken polytheism and, under Jewish influence, believed in one God. There was a large group of Gentiles who had accepted the universal God and were known as "God-fearers." These Gentiles prayed to God and accepted the ethical precepts of the Jews but would not submit to circumcision, or keep the meat laws and other ceremonial rites.

"He saw in a vision . . . an angel of God coming in to him" (v. 3). The angel addressed him by name. This happened in broad daylight, about 3:00 P.M. Cornelius was afraid as he looked at the heavenly messenger and responded by asking, "What is it, Lord?"

The Greek term "lord" has five uses in Acts: (1) Referring to Jesus (1:6, 21; 7:59); (2) to God (1:24; 2:34); (3) to a person in the sense of "Sir" (9:5); (4) to an angel (10:4); (5) to an earthly lord as an emperor (25:26). "The context must determine who is meant."[1]

The angel replied, "Thy prayers and thine alms are come up for a memorial before God" (v. 4). Cornelius was then directed to "send men to Joppa, and call for one Simon, whose surname is Peter. He lodgeth with one Simon a tanner, whose house is by the sea-side; he shall tell thee what thou oughtest to do" (v. 5, 6).

## PETER INSTRUCTED BY VISION AND VOICE

Cornelius acted promptly to carry out the instruction, sending two servants "and a devout soldier" to Joppa. As they approached that city the next day, "Peter went up upon the housetop to pray about the sixth hour" (noon—v.7-9). "He became very hungry, and would have eaten; but while they made ready, he fell into a trance, and saw heaven opened" (v. 10, 11). The Greek word *ekstasis* here translated "trance" is our word "ecstasy" and literally means "standing out." The word is often used to describe "one who passes out of his normal self in a vision."[2]

In his vision Peter saw "a great sheet knit [bound or gathered] at the four corners" (v. 11). In it "were . . . four-footed beasts . . . wild beasts, and creeping things, and fowls of the air" (v. 12). A voice said, "Rise, Peter; kill, and eat." As a Jew he saw animals there which were forbidden (see Deuteronomy 14:3-20). He protested that he had "never eaten any thing that is common or unclean" (see Leviticus 20:25). Back came the reply, "What God hath cleansed, that call not thou common" (v. 14, 15). This vision was repeated three times to impress Peter with the importance of the moral over the ceremonial law. This reveals that Peter, and perhaps all Jewish Christians, were keeping the Jewish meat laws some ten years after they had been abrogated by Christ (see Mark 7:2-15).

While Peter was pondering on the meaning of this vision, the men from Joppa arrived at the house and asked for him. At the same time the Spirit told him, "Behold, three men seek thee . . . go with them, doubting nothing; for I have sent them" (17-20). He went down, introduced himself, and asked the reason of their visit. He was told that Cornelius "was warned from God by a holy angel to send for thee into [to come to—R.S.V.] his house, and to hear words of thee" (v. 21, 22). He invited the three in, lodged them for the night, and the next morning with "certain brethren from Joppa" accompanied them (v. 23).

When this group arrived in Caesarea, Cornelius and "his kinsmen and near friends" were together waiting for them. Cornelius went out and knelt before Peter and worshiped him. In mild rebuke, Peter said, "Stand up; I myself also am a man" (v. 25, 26). He added, "Ye know how that it is an unlawful[3] thing for a man that is a Jew to keep company, or come unto one of another nation; but God hath showed me

54

that I should not call any man common or unclean" (v. 28).
He then asked Cornelius to explain why he had sent for him.

Cornelius told of the experience he had received four
days previously. The time given here illustrates the ancient
method of reckoning time. The elapsed time was actually
three days (72 hours) as shown by Acts 10:3-23, 30. They
counted each fraction of a day as a day. In verse 40 Peter
affirms that Christ was "raised up the third day." Some
writers say he was in the tomb three days, which distorts the
facts. Peter described the angel who visited him thus: "a
man stood before me in bright clothing" (v. 30). He concluded the relating of his experience by saying, "Now therefore are we all here present before God, to hear all things that
are commanded thee of God" (v. 31-33).

## The Spirit Given to Gentiles

"I perceive that God is no respecter of persons,"[4] said
Peter, "but in every nation he that feareth him, and worketh
righteousness, is accepted with him" (v. 34, 35). He then
presents Jesus Christ as one sent to the children of Israel by
God to preach the gospel. The work began in Galilee, where
Jesus lived and chose his special witnesses, and spread throughout all Judea. This Jesus "went about doing good, and healing all that were oppressed of the devil; for God was with
him" (v. 36-38). Peter doubtless felt the need to emphasize
that Jesus was sent only to the house of Israel (Matt. 15:23).
But he was slain by Jews "and hanged on a tree; him God
raised up the third day, and showed him openly . . . unto witnesses chosen before of God, even to us, who did eat and
drink with him after he rose from the dead" (39-41).

"Showed him openly" refers to the times Jesus made personal contact with his disciples after his resurrection. Nine
are recorded in the Gospels: five on the resurrection day,
one the following Sunday, and three the following weeks.

Paul records six appearances, but only two are in addition to the list given, thus making eleven appearances in all.[5]

The detail Peter gave about eating and drinking with him (see Luke 24:41-43; John 21:12, 13) helps establish the testimony that the resurrection was not an apparition or docetic.

"And he commanded us to preach unto the people . . . that . . . he . . . was . . . to be the Judge of quick and dead" (v. 42). The Gospels give the Great Commission, "Go ye therefore, and teach all nations" (Matt. 28:18, 19; Mark 16:14, 15); but the rest of the command Peter cited is inferred or unrecorded.

"To him give all the prophets witness, that . . . whosoever believeth in him shall receive remission of sins" (v. 43). Chapter 53 of Isaiah is the best illustration of this witness of the coming Christ. The writings of both Peter and Paul emphasize Christ's power to forgive sins (see Luke 24:46-48; Acts 2:38; 13:38; 26:18).

While Peter was speaking, "The Holy Ghost fell on all them which heard the word. And they of the circumcision which believed were astonished" (v. 44, 45). Here is an instance where the Holy Spirit was received by believers before baptism and confirmation. The promise in the gospel is that "the gift of the Holy Ghost" is to follow repentance and baptism (Acts 2:38, 39), and it was promised as an abiding comforter by Jesus only to the disciples who kept his commandments (John 14:15-17).

The astonishment of the Jews was due to the belief that the gospel blessings were to Jews only. Matthew records Jesus' direction to the apostles, "Go not into the way of the Gentiles . . . but rather go to the lost sheep of the house of Israel" (10:5, 6). Only after his ascension and the endowment were they to go into all the world.

"For they heard them [the Gentiles] speak with tongues, and magnify God" (v. 45, 46). Paul wrote that "tongues are for a sign, not to them that believe, but to them that believe not" (I Cor. 14:22). However, in this case the Gentiles believed and the gift of tongues was given to them to convince the Christians that the gospel was for the Gentiles as well as for the Jews.

Peter was convinced, and being a man of action, asked, "Can any man forbid water, that these should not be baptized?" Then he commanded them to be baptized (v. 47, 48). The record is not completed, but leaves the inference that Peter baptized them "in the name of the Lord." He tarried with them a few days, to stabilize them in the duties of a Christian life.

---

1. E. E. Stringfellow, *op. cit.*, p. 12.
2. *Ibid.*, p. 60.
3. According to the traditions of the scribes, but not prohibited by the Law of Moses.
4. Upon the basis of birth, race, color, class, or outward condition. See Deuteronomy 10:17.
5. E. E. Stringfellow, *op. cit.*, p. 5.

## QUESTIONS FOR DISCUSSION

1. Illustrate how some of the eleven "Simons" mentioned in the New Testament are identified.
2. What was the function of this centurion and why should a Roman officer be in Palestine?
3. How did God convince Cornelius that He was God of the Gentiles as well as of the Jews?
4. What animals was Peter commanded in the vision to eat which were forbidden to Jews under the law?
5. What was the meaning and purpose of Peter's vision?
6. What reasons can be given for the Roman officer wanting to worship Peter?
7. Why did Peter tell the group in Caesarea that Jesus was sent to the children of Israel?
8. What evidence did the apostle offer to show that Jesus was now alive and active?

9. If the unbaptized believers can receive the Holy Spirit, why should they need baptism and confirmation?
10. Who spoke in the gift of tongues and what was the effect of exercising the gift?

# 9 PETER'S DEFENSE AND IMPRISONMENT

(Acts 11:1 - 12:17)

A new era began in church history when Peter took into the church of Christ uncircumcised Gentiles. A new movement needs time to get its roots growing and its foundation established. When Jesus was in Palestine, the apostles got answers to all questions from him. Now they had to depend on their own wisdom, or move as they were enlightened by the Holy Spirit and experience. On one occasion Jesus said, "He that believeth on me, the works that I do shall he do also; and greater works than these shall he do; because I go unto my Father" (John 14:12). The condition attached to this promise seemed predicated on their opportunities, since he would soon leave them. Their works were not to be greater in degree perhaps, but in expanse and length of service.

## BAPTISM OF GENTILES CALLED IN QUESTION

The word soon got back to "the apostles and brethren . . . in Judea" that the Gentiles "had also received the word of God" (v. 1). These Jewish Christians "contended with him" for entering the dwelling and eating with Gentiles (v. 2, 3). Peter related the circumstances in the order of their occurrence: the vision of the animals let down from heaven in the sheet, the command to slay and eat; his remonstrance against eating common or unclean [unlawful] meat. He told of being rebuked by the voice from heaven, "What God hath cleansed, that call not thou common." This was repeated the third time and then the vision disappeared. He related that three men had been sent for him from Caesarea and "the Spirit bade me go with them, nothing doubting." Peter, accompanied by six of the brethren from Joppa, went and they "entered in to the man's house" (v. 4-12).

He then related the experience Cornelius had had when an angel had told him to send for Peter "who shall tell thee words whereby thou and all thy house shall be saved. And as I began to speak, the Holy Ghost fell on them, as on us at the beginning" (v. 13-15). Peter recalled the promise of Jesus that while John baptized with water, they should "be baptized with the Holy Ghost." This very thing happened, after Cornelius and his household had been baptized in water. "For as much then as God gave them the like gift as he did unto us . . . what was I, that I could withstand God?" (v. 16, 17).

Hearing this testimony "they held their peace and glorified God" (v. 18). This feeling was not universal among the Christians, for the "circumcision party," sometimes referred to as "Judaizers," felt that the gospel was for the Jews only, and Gentiles should become Jews through obedience to the ceremonial laws before they might become Christians. They were not to be prohibited from membership in the church of Christ, but must first submit to circumcision and follow the meat laws also.

## Gospel Preached Abroad

Following the persecution in Jerusalem which culminated in the martyrdom of Stephen, the ministers for Christ went to such places as Phoenicia, a coastal country north of Palestine; Cyprus, an island in the eastern Mediterranean Sea; and

Antioch, the capital of Syria. Some of the disciples who had residence in Cyprus and Cyrene, a city on the northern coast of Africa across the Mediterranean from Greece, came to Antioch and preached Jesus to the Greek Gentiles. The Lord blessed their ministry and "a great number believed, and turned unto the Lord" (v. 19-21). Antioch became the capital of Gentile Christian work.[1]

When the leaders in Jerusalem heard of the success of the preaching in Antioch, they sent Barnabas to exhort them to "cleave unto the Lord." He was a Levite from Cyprus originally who "had seen the grace of God" and had become a pillar of the church in Jerusalem. Luke describes him as "a good man and full of the Holy Ghost and of faith." Many were added to the church (v. 22-24).

Saul was nearby in Tarsus where he had been sent to escape persecution from the Jews in Jerusalem who regarded him as a traitor (Acts 9:27-30). Barnabas went to Tarsus and persuaded Saul to come to Antioch to minister to the church at that place. They labored there a year "and taught much people. And the disciples were called Christians first in Antioch" (Acts 11:25, 26). This nickname was doubtless applied by the citizens of the city in derision. The church at Antioch was established about A.D. 42, or some nine years after Pentecost. The term did not gain popularity during the first century. Tacitus, writing about A.D. 115, spoke of those "whom the populace was want to style Christians."[2] The term is used only three times in the Bible. (See also Acts 26:28; I Peter 4:16.)

Certain men came to Antioch at this period who had the gift of prophecy. Agabus stood up and "signified by the Spirit that there should be great dearth throughout all the world; which came to pass in the days of Claudius" (v. 27, 28). "In these days" was A.D. 46. Claudius' reign was A.D. 41-54. Josephus (Ant. 20:5:2) puts the famine in the procuratorship of Alexander which was A.D. 46-48. In Galatians (2:1, 9, 10)

Paul said it was "fourteen years after [his conversion, A.D. 33] I went up again to Jerusalem with Barnabas."

"Throughout all the world" was used by the Greek writers to mean the Greek world as distinguished from the barbarian world. Later it came to mean the Roman Empire. See Acts 17:6; 19:27; 24:5.

"The disciples . . . determined to send relief unto the brethren which dwelt in Judea . . . and sent it unto the elders by the hands of Barnabas and Saul" (v. 29, 30). This is the first mention of Christian elders in the church, though they are mentioned frequently later as officers in Acts and the Epistles. They were ordained in every church or congregation (14:23), and had administrative duties (15:6; 20:17 ff.; I Tim. 5:17; Titus 1:5; Jas. 5:14).

## PERSECUTION UNDER HEROD
(Acts 12)

"Herod the King stretched forth his hands to vex certain of the church, and he killed James the brother of John with the sword" (v. 1, 2). This was Herod Agrippa I, the grandson of Herod the Great who caused the male children under two years to be slain in Jesus' infancy. Agrippa was educated in Rome and was a staunch friend of Emperors Gaius and Claudius. His zeal for the Jewish law made him popular with the Jews and he tried to increase this by a new orgy of persecution against the Christians. James was the son of Zebedee and Salome. When Herod saw that the killing of James "pleased the Jews, he proceeded further to take Peter also. (Then were the days of unleavened bread.)" (v. 3). Tyrants are not troubled with using councils or by written laws. They follow out measures which they think will make them more popular. The seven days which immediately follow the Passover (Nisan or Abib 15-21) the Jews were to eat unleavened bread (Exod. 23:15).

Peter was apprehended and put in prison with a guard of "four quaternions of soldiers." This consisted of four soldiers who had three-hour watches during the night. He was chained to two of them while the other two were posted at the door (v. 4-6). Such precautions seemed necessary after Peter's miraculous escape earlier (Acts 5:18, 19). Herod planned to bring Peter out "after Easter." This is a Christian term for the day following the close of Passover. "But prayer was made without ceasing of the church unto God for him" (v. 4, 5).

An angel of the Lord again interceded. He aroused Peter by striking his side, then raised him up. The chains fell from his hands. He was directed to "gird thyself, and bind on thy sandals. . . . Cast thy garment about thee, and follow me" (v. 7, 8). Peter did as commanded, but it seemed more like a vision than a reality. They passed the first and second wards, or guards, without incident. Then they came to the iron gate "which opened to them of his own accord." They passed through and after going a block the angel left him. The prison was probably part of the fortress of Antonio at the northwest corner of the temple (v. 9, 10).

By this time Peter was fully conscious that the Lord had delivered him from prison. Soon he came to the house of Mary, mother of John Mark. Many of the saints were still here praying for his release. Peter knocked at the door and it was opened by Rhoda, who was so shocked to see Peter that she left him standing here while she spread the news. The assembled saints thought this was incredible; "Thou art mad," they answered. To Peter's continued knocking they opened the door and looked on him in great astonishment. It seems that they did not have much faith in their prayers for his release, else they would have expected him to come to them. People act much the same today. They ask for direction, for healing, for rain, and other daily needs, but do not act as if they expected them. James wrote to such, "But let him ask in faith, nothing wavering; for he that wavereth is like a wave of the sea. . . . Let not that man think that he shall receive anything of the Lord" (James 1:6, 7).

Peter beckoned for the disciples to be quiet and told them "how the Lord had brought him out of the prison." He directed that they take word to "James, and to the brethren"; then he left them (v. 17).

---

1. A. S. Peake's *Commentary on the Bible*, p. 789.
2. E. E. Stringfellow, *op. cit.*, p. 69.

## QUESTIONS FOR DISCUSSION

1. How did the apostles do "greater works" than Jesus had done?
2. What objections were raised by some Christians to Peter's baptizing Cornelius and his household?
3. What was the center of the Gentile Christian work about A.D. 42 and how did it get started?
4. Who said, "What was I, that I could withstand God?" and why did he say that?
5. Who were the "Judaizers" or the "circumcision party"?
6. What did Agabus prophesy and how was it fulfilled?
7. What did Herod Agrippa do and why?
8. What precautions were taken to keep Peter in prison and what was planned for him?
9. How did he make his escape? Why?
10. Why does the astonishment with which Peter was received by the praying saints seem inconsistent?

# 10 HEROD DIES; BARNABAS AND PAUL GO ON A MISSION

(Acts 12:18 - 13:51)

Peter had been freed from prison by divine help for the second time. God had a work for him yet to do, and so interceded in such a way that Herod Agrippa could not carry out his designs on Peter's life. When the soldiers discovered the next morning that Peter was gone, they were greatly disturbed, fearing for their own lives. Herod had a search made for him without success, and commanded that the prison officials be put to death; then the king went to the military headquarters at Caesarea (v. 18-19).

## HEROD DIES ON HIS THRONE

The people of Sidon and Tyre, coastal cities to the north, caused Herod's displeasure evidently because of some preferred treatment which a chamberlain sought for them in the purchase of grain. The source of his anger could have been more the timing of the appeal, for it came during a celebration and feast for Emperor Claudius. Agrippa was sitting on his throne dressed in royal robes and "made an oration unto them" (v. 20, 21). Josephus said that the robe he wore was made entirely of silver (Ant. 19:8.2). As he spoke the people who idolized him shouted, "It is the voice of a god, and not of a man" (v. 22). The record then says he was smitten by the angel of death "because he gave not God the glory" (v. 23). Josephus says he was seized with sudden pains in his belly as he sat in his box at a theater and was carried to his palace where five days later he died a horrible death.

## The Calling of Barnabas and Saul
(Acts 13)

After carrying out their relief mission for the famine-stricken saints in Judea, Barnabas and Saul returned to Antioch (Acts 12:25; 13:1). Here were "certain prophets and teachers." Five are named, Barnabas heading the list. Simeon is another form of the spelling for Simon. That he was called "Niger" suggests that he was of African origin.[1] Nothing more is known of Lucius and Manaen. Saul completes the list. These were not itinerant prophets like Agabus. They were members of the local congregation.

"As they ministered to the Lord, and fasted" is rendered in the Revised Standard Version, "While they were worshiping the Lord and fasting" (v. 2). Under this favorable condition the Holy Spirit spoke saying, "Separate me Barnabas and Saul for the work whereunto I have called them." The carrying out of this charge was approached by more fasting and prayer. Then they were set apart by the laying on of hands (v. 2, 3).

If this was an ordination to the apostolic office, it is not mentioned. It could have been a consecration for their mission. That they were apostles is emphatically declared by Luke (Acts 14:14), but since there is no evidence of church action nor any apostle present to perform the sacrament, it is considered likely by some that this was not the ordination for apostolic succession.[2]

In writing the Galatian saints Paul declared that he was an apostle "Not of men, neither by man, but by Jesus Christ, and God the Father, who raised him from the dead." Some have interpreted this as referring to ordination. It seems more likely that it refers only to his calling which came directly by the voice of God (Acts 9:15; 13:2). His ordination could have been on the occasion of his visit to Jerusalem three years after his conversion (see Galatians 1:17, 18; 2:9), by those who "were apostles *before me.*" His reputation as a persecutor of the saints may have given reason for not publicizing the ordination at that time.

"When they had fasted and prayed, and laid their hands on them, they sent them away" (v. 3). This indicated their mission was not on individual initiative, but was by action of the body. "So they, being sent by the Holy Ghost, departed" (v. 4). This makes it clear that the body was not acting by human wisdom but after divine direction.

Seleucia is the seaport used by traffic to and from Antioch. From here Barnabas and Saul sailed to Salamis, a port on the island of Cyprus, the home of Barnabas. At Salamis they went to the synagogues and "preached the word of God . . . and they also had John to their minister [to assist them—R.S.V.]." This is John Mark, the author of the second Gospel (v. 5). Mark is his Grecian name (Acts 12:25). He was a cousin to Barnabas.

Next they went a hundred miles across the island to Paphos, a seaport on its west coast, where they found "a certain sorcerer, a false prophet, a Jew, whose name was Bar-Jesus," an associate of Sergius Paulus, the proconsul or deputy. "Bar" is Aramaic and used as a prefix to mean "son." "Jesus" is the Greco-Roman transliteration of the Hebrew common name, "Joshua." The deputy sent for Barnabas and Saul and "desired to hear the word of God" (v. 6, 7).

Elymas, the sorcerer, interfered in the meeting and tried to dissuade the deputy from the faith. "Elymas" is the Greek name for "Bar-Jesus." "Then Saul, (who is also called Paul,) filled with the Holy Ghost, set his eyes on him" and rebuked him (v. 9, 10). This is the first time Luke uses the Greek name "Paul" for the Hebrew "Saul." From this time on he gives Paul the dominant role, while heretofore Barnabas had the prominence.

"Thou child of the devil, thou enemy of all righteousness, wilt thou not cease to pervert the right ways of the Lord?" (v. 10). "Thou shalt be blind, not seeing the sun for a season." He needed someone to lead him from that moment on (v. 11). As a result of this miracle, the astonished deputy believed "the doctrine of the Lord" (v. 12).

The missionaries left the island and went north to Asia Minor. They landed at Perga in Pamphylia, a journey of 175 miles. It is low-lying malarial country, and Paul became ill. So they moved on to higher ground at Antioch of Pisidia. John Mark decided not to go farther with them and returned to Jerusalem (v. 13, 14).

At the invitation of the "rulers of the synagogue" in Antioch, Paul stood up and preached. In Palestine it was the custom for one to stand while reading the scriptures and sit down to speak (Luke 4:17-21). It seems that in the synagogues of the Gentile world the custom was different.

Paul reminded his hearers of God's deliverance of their fathers from Egypt, of their suffering in the wilderness for forty years, conquering "seven nations in the land of Chanaan," and dividing their lands to the tribes of Israel by lot (v. 15-19). He observed that they were ruled by judges for 450 years; and then desiring a king, God gave them Saul who reigned forty years, followed by David, "a man after mine own heart" (v. 20-22).

"Of this man's seed hath God, according to his promise, raised unto Israel a Savior, Jesus." Paul reminded them of John, who baptized for repentance in Jordan, and who said, "I am not he [the Messiah], but, behold, there cometh one after me, whose shoes of his feet I am not worthy to loose" (v. 23-25). He addressed the worshipers directly, "Children of the stock of Abraham, and whosoever among you feareth God, to you is the word of salvation sent" (v. 26).

68

This salvation through Jesus, Paul said, had been rejected in Jerusalem because they knew him not "nor yet the voices of the prophets which are read every Sabbath day." While they found no cause of death in him, they desired his death, and Pilate granted that he be slain. "But God raised him from the dead; and he was seen many days of them which came up with him from Galilee to Jerusalem . . . no more to return to corruption" (see Psalm 16:10). "But he, whom God raised again, saw no corruption" (v. 27-37).

Paul concludes his sermon by declaring, "Through this man is preached unto you the forgiveness of sins; and by him all that believe are justified from all things, from which ye could not be justified by the law of Moses" (v. 38, 39). He then quotes Habakkuk 1:5 concerning a marvelous work "in your days" which would be hard to believe (v. 40, 41).

When the Jews left the synagogue, the Gentiles lingered behind and urged Paul to preach to them the next Sabbath. Many of the Jews and proselytes followed Paul and Barnabas, as they walked away, for further teaching. The next Sabbath "came almost the whole city together to hear the word of God" (v. 44). But because the apostles attracted so many Gentiles to the meeting, the Jews became envious and contradicted Paul's teachings "and blaspheming." This meant speaking in a derogatory manner against Christ, the Son of God. Paul and Barnabas responded with boldness to the envious Jews, "It was necessary that the word of God should first have been spoken to you" (v. 46). Jesus said he was sent only "unto the lost sheep of the house of Israel" (Matt. 15:23). Paul declared that the gospel was "to the Jew first, and also to the Greek" (Rom. 1:16). Continuing their reproof, the apostles said, "Seeing ye put it [God's word] from you, and judge yourselves unworthy of everlasting [eternal—R.S.V.] life, lo, we turn to the Gentiles" (v. 46).

This caused rejoicing among the Gentiles and "the word of the Lord was published throughout all the region" (v. 48, 49). Among the Jews there was strong opposition. They

69

stirred up devout and honorable women and the chief men of the city who "expelled them out of their coasts" (v. 50). The women in Asia Minor had enough influence that they were considered worthy of mention, whereas in Palestine they were generally ignored. "They [the apostles] shook off the dust of their feet against them and came into Iconium" (v. 51). Shaking the dust from one's sandals was symbolic of judgment and leaving people to their own destiny (Matt. 10:12).

This chapter and some which follow reveal problems in the development of the early church which also attended the growth of the Reorganization. Some serious disagreements among our leaders came into the open regarding such things as the Sabbath day, the Communion, and music in the church (D. and C. 119:5-7). In fact, getting organized at all was considered by some of the leaders a hopeless task for two days at the April conference of 1853.[3]

---

1. *The Interpreter's Bible,* Acts, p. 164.
2. *Ibid.,* p. 165.
3. *Church History,* Vol. 3, pp. 219-221.

## QUESTIONS FOR DISCUSSION

1. What kind of man and king was Herod Agrippa?
2. Name three prophets and teachers who were in Antioch. What did they accomplish for the church?
3. Under what conditions did Barnabas and Saul start their mission to Asia Minor?
4. Why do you think the laying on of hands to send Barnabas and Saul out was or was not an ordination?
5. What was accomplished by the mission to Cyprus?
6. Who was Elymas and why did Paul rebuke him?
7. Tell of some happenings in Perga and Antioch of Pisidia.
8. What did Paul discuss in his first recorded sermon and what resulted?

9. The sermon at Antioch was directed to the Jews and recounts historic facts. How did it affect the Gentiles and why?
10. Who was said to be guilty of blaspheming and what was the basis of the charge?

# 11 THE SPREAD OF THE CHURCH IN GALATIA

(Acts 14:1-28)

The success of the apostles in winning the Gentiles to accept Christ in Antioch of Pisidia aroused the envy of the Jews. They interrupted Paul's preaching by contradicting his statements. The apostles rebuked them sharply, and this antagonism caused Paul and Barnabas to be expelled from the country. They moved eighty miles southeast to Iconium, the capital of Lyconia, a province of Galatia in Asia Minor.

## THE APOSTLES BOTH PERSECUTED AND IDOLIZED (Acts 14)

As was their custom Paul and Barnabas went first to the synagogue when they entered a city and here witnessed for Christ. In this respect they practiced the scriptural policy (Rom. 1:16), "To the Jew first, and also to the Greek," or to Gentiles. In Iconium there was "a great multitude both of the Jews and also of the Greeks who believed" (v. 1). This again stirred up the Judaizers[1] who turned the minds of the Gentiles "against the brethren" (v. 2).

Though they faced adverse conditions here, they continued their efforts for a "long time." This is one of Luke's indefinite phrases, but it is likely that the apostles' labors there extended over several months in giving their testimony of God's grace. Many "signs and wonders . . . [were] done by their hands" (v. 3). The division in the city became sharper with the continued success of the mission. Part of the people "held with the Jews, and part with the apostles" (v. 4). This is the first instance of Luke's applying the title "apostles" to Paul and Barnabas, though their work of opening up missions had been apostolic for at least two years. There was an assault ["attempt"—R.S.V.] to stone the missionaries, but they learned of the plan and "fled unto Lystra and Derbe," nearby cities in Lyconia (v. 5, 6).

## FAITH TO BE HEALED

Here they found an impotent (crippled) man who had never walked. Paul perceived that he had "faith to be healed" (v. 7-9). A modern prophet said, "He that has faith in me to be healed, and is not appointed unto death, shall be healed" (D. and C. 42:13 a). Provision is made for those who do not have such faith to "be nourished with all tenderness with herbs and mild food" (42:12 c).

In a commanding voice Paul said, "Stand upright on thy feet. And he leaped and walked." The people who saw this miracle said, "The gods are come down to us in the likeness of men. And they called Barnabas, Jupiter; and Paul, Mercurius, because he was the chief speaker" (v. 10-12). If these people had spoken the Greek language, they would have named the apostles Zeus and Hermes and Paul and Barnabas are called that in the Revised Standard Version. Zeus is the supreme god of the Greeks corresponding to Jupiter for the Romans. He presided over the other gods in Mount Olympus and at the Nemean games sat passively on the throne. This seemed to fit Barnabas, since Paul did the talking. Hermes was the messenger and herald of Greek gods.

"The priest of Jupiter . . . brought oxen and garlands unto the gates and would have done sacrifice," but the apostles would not accept their devotions. "They [Barnabas and Paul] rent their clothes [tore their garments—R.S.V.] and ran in among the people" (v. 13, 14). "We also are men of like passions with you, and preach unto you that ye should turn from these vanities unto the living God" (v. 15). Garlands are wreaths made of flowers and leaves. They are often put on the statue of the god before whom they offer sacrifice. In this instance they probably intended to put them around the necks of the apostles.

## Evidence of a Living God

Paul wanted to impress the Iconium people that this living God was creator of heaven and earth and needed no material offerings which they could give. While God had permitted "all nations to walk in their own ways," he had given evidence of his power and goodness by sending rain, fruits in season, "filling our hearts with food and gladness" (v. 16, 17). Hearing this, the people could hardly be restrained from making the sacrifice.

At this moment, however, the Jews from Antioch and those living in Iconium persuaded the people that these men were not what they supposed. Instead of garlands they stoned Paul, and thinking he was dead, dragged him out of the city. He regained consciousness and went back into the city with his friends for the night (v. 18-20).

The apostles thought it best to go away for a time, so they went to Derbe, a frontier city of Galatia fourteen miles southeast of Iconium. Here they started to retrace the ground which they had visited and where they had established the work (v. 6). After "they had preached the gospel . . . and had taught many, they returned again to Lystra, and to Iconium, and Antioch, confirming the souls of the disciples." Paul was aware that the way of Christ called for cross-bearing. Jesus had declared, "Whosoever doth not bear his cross, and come after me, cannot be my disciple" (Luke 14:27). So Paul told the Corinthian saints, "Christ sent me not to baptize, but to preach the gospel, not with wisdom of words, lest the cross of Christ should be made of none effect" (I Cor. 1:17).

## KEEP THE FAITH

In the light of this charge Paul and Barnabas exhorted the Galatian disciples "to continue in the faith, and that we must through much tribulation enter into the kingdom of God." Much strength would come from the fellowship of saints in their local congregations; yet these apostles were the spokesmen in winning them to Christ, and thus became their spiritual fathers. It seemed wise, therefore, to establish them in the work by a return visit before moving on to other fields. Hence, when they had "ordained them elders in every church, and had prayed with fasting, they commended them to the Lord" (v. 22, 23).

The Greek term translated "ordained" has been translated in verse 23 in the Revised Standard Version and some other modern versions as "appointed." However, the Greek term "means literally 'chose by a show of hands' and, strictly speaking, should imply some form of popular voting" (*The Interpreter's Bible,* Acts, p. 193). Thus the meaning for the word "appointed" in use today does not fit. When one is appointed to a committee, or to act as doorkeeper, no voting takes place. Jesus said, "Ye have not chosen me, but I have chosen you, and ordained you" (John 15:16). When Barnabas and Saul were called, they "laid their hands on them, . . . [and] sent them away" (Acts 13:3). This is also supported by the Classic Greek Dictionary which defines the Greek word here used as "to give one's vote, elect . . . ordain." It seems, therefore, that the word "ordained" best fits all these conditions.

The apostles visited in the provinces of Pisidia and Pamphylia. Antioch and Perga doubtless were ministered to again. Next "they went down into Attalia," the seaport, and took a ship to Antioch of Syria at which place they had received their calling (v. 24-26). Upon their arrival a meeting of the church was held and "they rehearsed all that God had done with them, and how he had opened the door of faith unto the Gentiles. And there they abode long time with the disciples" (v. 27, 28). Perhaps their stay was several months, probably from October A.D. 48 to the spring of 49.

It is worth noting that the apostles did not take credit for their successes.

They cleared away the clouds of ignorance and doubt, set forth the true as they had seen it in Jesus. . . . One serious obstacle that had to be removed [was] . . . the Jewish ceremonial law, and especially the requirement of circumcision for admission into the Christian fellowship.[2]

This might be compared to the problem confronting the early Restoration when converts from other denominations sought to impose doctrines of their former faith on this church. Section 49 given to Lemon Copley and others against celibacy and prohibiting the eating of meat is a case in point.

This chapter ends what is called "Paul's first missionary journey." One might wonder why they did not go to Jerusalem to report. However, they were missionaries to the Gentiles and not to the Jews. Paul, particularly, was under suspicion and attack by Judean Christians, so they established their headquarters in Antioch, capital of Syria.

---

1. "Judaizers" were Jewish Christians who believed that the Law of Moses and the Talmud (civil and canonical law) were fully binding on Christians and that Gentiles must be circumcised.
2. *The Interpreter's Bible*, Vol. 9, p. 193.

## QUESTIONS FOR DISCUSSION

1. Give reasons for Paul's going to synagogues to preach the Christian religion.
2. What is meant by "Judaizers"?

3. Relate the circumstances which caused the people of Iconium to move from worshiping Paul to stoning him.
4. Can "faith to be healed" be developed, and if so, how?
5. What was the significance of the oxen and garlands brought to the gathering in Iconium?
6. What argument was used to convince the people that there was "a living God"?
7. Why is it necessary to go through much tribulation to enter the kingdom of God?
8. Were the elders church officers or only venerated senior disciples?
9. Why did this first mission end where it started in Syria?
10. Discuss some problems encountered by Paul and Barnabas as they relate to the early Restoration.

# 12 THE EPISTLE TO THE GALATIANS

(Galatians 1:1 - 3:29)

The authorship and date of some of the epistles in the New Testament are not certain. None of them bear specific dates and only a few of them are signed. The writer of the Galatian epistle, Paul, seems to be positively identified by the opening statement as well as by the contents of the book. The date of its writing is generally given as the spring or summer of A.D. 49.

Galatians is Paul's declaration of religious independence from men and dependence on God. It is the Magna Charta of the Christian faith, repudiating all authorities, institutions, customs, and laws that interfere with the direct access of the individual to his God.[1]

It is quite probable that it was written in Antioch of Syria soon after his return from the first journey and before going to the Jerusalem conference (Acts 15). Messengers had brought word of some disturbing factors which had arisen in the churches after he left Galatia. Since "he could not go back immediately to straighten things out in person, because he saw that he would have to settle the matter first in Jerusalem, whence the troublemakers had come . . . he wrote a letter."[2]

78

Paul addressed his epistle "unto the churches of Galatia" (v. 2). The cities of Antioch, Iconium, Lystra, and Derbe in the southern part of the province were doubtless on his heart.

## Occasion for the Letter

The word brought to Paul in Antioch was that some of the Judaistic party had turned the Galatian saints from the gospel and implanted doubts in their minds as to his apostolic authority. He realized how disturbing this could be. "He wrote to get three matters in proper focus: experience, doctrine, and conduct (or life)." Indeed, "experience is the place where doctrine and conduct meet."[3]

"I marvel that ye are so soon removed from him that called you into the grace of Christ unto another gospel" (v. 6). The Revised Standard Version reads, "I am astonished that you are so quickly deserting him." "Some . . . would pervert the gospel of Christ, but though we, or an angel from heaven, preach any other gospel . . . let him be accursed" (v. 7-9). "But I certify you, brethren, that the gospel which was preached of me is not after man . . . but by [through—R.S.V.] the revelation of Jesus Christ" (v. 11, 12).

Paul was forthright and unequivocal.

He wrote to the Corinthians out of anguish of heart, through tears, for their failure in Christian living; he was even more severe in his letter to the Galatians, for the very core of the Christian message was at stake. Remembering that the letter to the Galatians has changed history, that all might have been different had Paul written differently, that its 149 verses altered the world, one is not surprised to find him using words that were like dynamite. They were God's words before they were Paul's.[4]

## Churches in Judea Rejoice

Paul admitted that he had, as a Jew, once "persecuted the church of God," and that he "profited [advanced—R.S.V.] in

the Jews' religion above many my equals [my own age—
R.S.V.]," but God had destined him before his birth to preach
Christ "among the heathen" (v. 13-16). He did not go to
Jerusalem after receiving the light (the Christ revealed to
him on the Damascus road) to confer with or learn from the
apostles (flesh and blood), but he went into Arabia. "What
Paul did there, and how long he stayed, no man really
knows."[5]

No doubt he felt directed by God to be alone and commune with the Lord as he adjusted his thinking to the new
way of life in Christ. His conversion was not easy, and he
could expect his former associates to be outraged by his acceptance of the gospel. He went back to Damascus and "after
three years I went up to Jerusalem to see Peter, and abode
with him fifteen days" (v. 17, 18). Paul did not say if the
three years were reckoned from his conversion A.D. 33 or from
his return to Damascus. The Hebrew custom was to speak
of a part of a day or year as one day or year, so it may have
been less than three full years.

The scripture, "Other of the apostles saw I none, save
James, the Lord's brother" (v. 19), tells us that Paul was there
for personal reasons and not for a council or conference. It
also tells us that one of Jesus' brothers had become an apostle
of rank, even though he did not accept Jesus as divine before
his resurrection and ascension (John 7:5; Matt. 12:40). Paul
said, "I . . . was unknown by face unto the churches of
Judea . . . and they glorified God on account of me" because
he was now preaching "the faith which once he destroyed"
(v. 21-24).

## PAUL CONDEMNS PETER AND BARNABAS
(Galatians 2)

"Fourteen years after, I went up again to Jerusalem with
Barnabas, and took Titus with me also" (v. 1). It is not certain when Paul started this reckoning, but it seems most likely

to be the time of his conversion, A.D. 33. This would bring the visit here mentioned to about A.D. 47, and refer to the visit made with famine relief in the days of Claudius Caesar (A.D. 46-48), mentioned in Acts 11:27-30. To the Galatians Paul had reason to relate an experience not revealed in Acts. Titus, a Greek Christian, was with him and was not compelled to be circumcised, though the Judaizers were spying on them to cause trouble. Paul paid no attention to them since "God accepteth no man's person [shows no partiality—R.S.V.]."

James, Cephas, and John, pillars in the church (leaders), "perceived the grace that was given unto me" and extended "the right hands of fellowship; that we should go unto the heathen, and they unto the circumcision" (v. 3-9).

Peter came to Antioch and because some of the Jewish Christians from Jerusalem (certain from James) were present he did not eat with the Gentiles (v. 12). Other Jewish Christians followed Peter's example, including Barnabas. Paul chastises them for what seemed to be insincerity, if not for hypocrisy. "We have believed in Jesus Christ, that we might be justified by the faith of Christ, and not by the works of the law; for by the works of the law shall no flesh be justified" (v. 16). Paul felt that the issue had to be made clear else he could not carry out his mission as apostle to the Gentiles. "For if I build again the things which I destroyed, I make myself a transgressor. . . . The life which I now live in the flesh I live by the faith of the Son of God, who loved me, and gave himself for me" (v. 18, 20).

## ANTIQUITY OF THE GOSPEL
(Galatians 3)

Paul then reproves the Galatians: "Who hath bewitched you, that ye should not obey the truth?" "Received ye the Spirit by the works of the law, or by the hearing of [with—R.S.V.] faith?" "Abraham believed God, and it was accounted to him for [as] righteousness. . . . They which are of faith, the same are the children of Abraham" (v. 1-7).

"And the Scripture, foreseeing that God would justify the heathen through faith, preached before the gospel unto Abraham, saying, In thee shall all nations be blessed" (v. 8). The word "gospel" used in this passage needs further study. A helpful statement is made in the commentary in *The Interpreter's Bible*:

So far from being an innovation and afterthought, the gospel of grace had been God's way of salvation from the beginning, revealed through faith and to faith. To prove this Paul personified scripture and represented it as having granted a preview of the gospel to Abraham two thousand years before the coming of Christ.[6]

The full significance of this statement is better seen when considered with Paul's prior declaration, "Though we, or an angel from heaven, preach any other gospel unto you than that which we have preached unto you, let him be accursed" (Gal. 1:8). Since the Lord is unchangeable (Mal. 3:6) the gospel he gave is the same from the beginning (John 12:48-50). We use the term "Old Jerusalem gospel" because it has clear significance to most Bible believers, yet there is but one gospel and it was preached to Adam "from the beginning" (Gen. 5:44, 45). We do better to emphasize, rather, "the everlasting gospel" (Rev. 14:6).

The last sentence in verse 8 is taken from Genesis 22:22 addressed to Abraham and reads, "In thy seed shall all the nations of the earth be blessed." Paul stresses this by declaring, "No man is justified by the law in the sight of God . . . for, The just shall live by faith. And the law is not of faith" (v. 11, 12). Faith in Christ is primary in the gospel. "Christ hath redeemed us from the curse of the law . . . that the blessing of Abraham might come on the Gentiles through Jesus Christ; that they might receive the promise of the Spirit through faith" (v. 13, 14).

Paul then strengthens his point by declaring, "He saith not, And to seeds, as of many; but as of one,[7] And to thy seed, which is Christ" (v. 16). He does not leave his argument there, but adds, "For if the inheritance is of the law, then it is no more of promise; but God gave it to Abraham by promise. Wherefore then, the law was added [to the gospel— D. and C. 83:4] because of transgressions, till the seed should come" (v. 18, 19). "The law was our schoolmaster until Christ. . . . Ye are all one in Christ Jesus" (v. 24, 28). The word translated "schoolmaster" is better translated "custodian" (R.S.V.), for the law was not a teacher, and the Greek word used really means a slave or worn-out soldier who accompanied the child to school. This fits Paul's argument quite well.

---

1. *The Interpreter's Bible,* Vol. 10, p. 429.
2. *Ibid.,* p. 438.
3. *Ibid.,* p. 445.
4. *Ibid.,* p. 450.
5. Prof. E. E. Stringfellow, *op. cit.,* p. 71.
6. *The Interpreter's Bible,* Vol. 10, p. 503.
7. Weymouth's New Testament reads, "but to your seed (Gen. 12:6) referring to one—and this is Christ."

## QUESTIONS FOR DISCUSSION

1. What have you learned about the writer, those addressed, the time and place of writing the Epistle to the Galatians?
2. Why did Paul write the letter instead of ministering in person?
3. What events did Paul include in his claim that he received the gospel through revelation?
4. When and why did he visit two of the apostles in Jerusalem?
5. When and for what purpose was Paul's next visit?
6. Who and what were the "pillars in the church"?

7. Why did Paul rebuke Peter in Antioch?
8. What promise was made to Abraham and when was it made? How and when was the promise fulfilled?
9. When and to whom was the gospel first preached? What teachings did the preaching include?
10. Discuss Paul's dictum, "The law is not of faith."

# 13

# THE TWO COVENANTS

(Galatians 4:1 - 6:18)

Paul was determined to set the churches in Galatia straight on the differences between the gospel of faith and the law of dead works (Heb. 6:1):

the law given to Moses, who was ordained by the hand of angels to be mediator [intermediary—R.S.V.] of this first covenant. . . . Now this mediator was not the mediator of the new covenant . . . who is Christ, as it is written in the law concerning the promises made to Abraham and his seed.—Galatians 3:19, 20.

## HEIRS OF GOD

Paul starts, in Chapter four, by discussing what was meant by saying that the Galatians were heirs according to the promise to Abraham's seed (3:29).

An heir "as long as he is a child, differeth nothing from a servant, though he be lord of all; but is under tutors and governors until the time appointed of the father" (v. 1, 2). So the Israelites, as children, were under bondage until "the fullness of the time was come, [and] God sent forth his Son . . . to redeem them that were under the law, that we might receive the adoption of sons. . . . Wherefore thou art no more a servant, but a son . . . an heir of God through

Christ" (v. 3-7). There was a time set, according to Paul, and the purposes of God are worked out. Then he makes a direct charge, "How turn ye again to the weak and beggarly elements, whereunto ye desire again to be in bondage? Ye observe days, and months, and times and years" (v. 9, 10). The fasts and celebrations under the law were observed by them. "I am afraid . . . I have bestowed upon you labor in vain" (v. 11). Paul was not afraid of them, but for them. This was the beginning of a retreat from the gospel to dead works. In verse twelve Paul is made to sound boastful—"be perfect as I am perfect."[1] The word "perfect" is not in other versions. In the Sermon on the Mount Jesus said, "Ye are therefore commanded to be perfect, even as your father who is in heaven is perfect" (Matt. 5:50). Paul told the Colossians that his preaching was "that we may present every man perfect in Christ Jesus" (Col. 1:28). Perhaps the word "perfect" did not have the offensive connotation we think of today when we believe all men are sinners and he is the worst who thinks himself guilty of none. To us Paul's attitude was better revealed when he said, "Be ye followers of me, even as I also am of Christ" (I Cor. 11:1).

## PAUL'S PHYSICAL INFIRMITY

Paul makes it clear that he had some physical ailment on his first missionary journey, but he only hints at the nature of it. The Jews and others of that period thought that sickness was a punishment for sin. Some even alleged that it was evidence that the sufferer was thus turned over to Satan. "And my temptation [affliction—Westcott and Hort; condition—R.S.V.] which was in my flesh ye despised not, nor rejected; but received me as an angel of God, even as Christ Jesus" (v. 13, 14). The last clause, doubtless, refers to the experience at Lystra when the people wanted to worship Paul and Barnabas (Acts 14:11-14).

"Ye despised not" might have referred to a superstition

that one could avoid a plague by spitting in the presence of one thought to be afflicted "as men were accustomed to do when they wanted to ward off an evil spirit. . . . What Paul actually says is, 'You did not scorn your temptation in my flesh, you did not spit.' "[2]

When Paul and Barnabas reached Perga on the first mission (Acts 13:13), instead of working for a time there and in the neighboring towns, they at once struck inland.

Sir William Ramsay's theory that Paul's original intention was to preach in the coastal districts of Pamphylia, but the enervating climate brought on malaria (Paul's "thorn in the flesh"?—II Cor. 12:7), and compelled him to seek the bracing air of Antioch [in Pisidia] which has an altitude of some four thousand feet.[3]

This may have been only one of his troubles, for Paul indicated he had eye trouble also. "I bear you record, that, if it had been possible, ye would have plucked out your own eyes, and have given them to me" (v. 15).

"My little children, of whom I travail in birth again until Christ be formed in you . . . for I stand in doubt of you" (v. 19, 20) is elegantly put. Paul had gone through great trial to bring them the gospel.

## AN ALLEGORY OF FREEDOM
(Galatians 4:21 - 5:17)

"Tell me, ye that desire to be under the law, do ye not hear the law?" Paul then tells of Abraham's two sons, "one by a bond-maid, the other by a free woman"; one after the flesh, the other by promise.

These are the two covenants; the one from the mount Sinai, which gendereth bondage, . . . but Jerusalem, which is above is free, which is the mother of us all. . . . Now we, brethren, as Isaac was, are the children of promise. . . . Nevertheless what saith the scripture? Cast out the bondwoman and her son; for the son of the bondwoman shall not be heir with the son of the free woman.—V. 21-31.

This is a cogent allegory and leads to Paul's exhortation,

Stand fast therefore in the liberty wherewith Christ hath made us free, and be not entangled again with the yoke of bondage. . . . If ye be circumcised, Christ shall profit you nothing . . . ye are fallen from grace. . . . For in Jesus Christ neither circumcision availeth anything, nor uncircumcision; but faith which worketh by love.—V. 1-6.

Then Paul gives a note of encouragement, "Ye did run well. . . . I have confidence in you through the Lord, that ye will be none otherwise minded" (v. 7-10).

## LOVE AS A SAFEGUARD TO FREEDOM

"Brethren, ye have been called unto liberty, only use not liberty for occasion to the flesh, but by love serve one another." Then follows one of Paul's finest pronouncements: "For all the law is fulfilled in one word, even in this; Thou shalt love thy neighbor as thyself" (v. 13, 14). Volumes have been written on this inexhaustible subject of Christian love. It is experienced consistently by so few; some believers have had one or two mountaintop experiences, but like Moses on Mount Nebo, are privileged "only to look over into the promised land."

"This I say then, Walk in the Spirit, and ye shall not fulfil the lust of the flesh . . . but if ye be led of the Spirit, ye are not under the law" (v. 16-18).

The works of the flesh and the fruit of the Spirit are then listed and contrasted. The fleshly manifestations are "adultery [immorality], fornication, uncleanness [impurity], lasciviousness [licentiousness], idolatry, witchcraft [sorcery], hatred [enmity], variance [strife], emulations [jealousy], wrath [anger], strife [selfishness], seditions [dissension], heresies [party spirit], envyings, murders, drunkenness, revellings [carousing], and the like . . . they which do such things shall not inherit the kingdom of God" (v. 19-21).

This last clause, doubtless, means that without repenting of these evil "works of the flesh" no one can enter into kingdom-of-God life, or dwell with the righteous in celestial glory. This is supported by the Emphatic Diaglott translation of the Greek word for "do" as "practice." The words in brackets are taken from the Revised Standard Version and help to broaden the terms used. Foreign words, as also our English, can have more than one correct translation; hence the danger of taking a given version too literally. If one who occasionally became angry, envious, or even drunk would be barred forever from the kingdom of God, many would be without hope today.

"The fruit of the Spirit is love [agape—godly devotion as contrasted with self-love which is eros], joy, peace [total well-being; the Hebrew "shalom"], long-suffering [patience], gentleness [kindness], goodness, faith [faithfulness], meekness [gentleness], temperance [self-control]; against such there is no law" (v. 22, 23).

## Do Good to All Men
(Galatians 6)

Paul continues by giving more excellent counsel on personal righteousness to the Galatian saints. "Brethren, if a man be overtaken in a fault, ye which are spiritual, restore such a one in the spirit of meekness; considering thyself, lest thou also be tempted" (v. 1). It is so much easier to see another's faults and offer reform measures than to see our own and make the necessary corrections. To restore the erring is not work for the casual friend. One must be convinced that the reformer is a spiritual brother acting in the spirit of love to accept his ministry, and even then he will need God's grace to profit by his criticism.

"Overtaken seems to suggest that temptation comes upon us unawares. Most sin is committed not by deliberate intention or planning but in weakness and surprise, in the passion of a rash moment."[4]

"Bear ye one another's burdens, and so fulfil the law of Christ" (v. 2). This is the service attitude of a true Christian who follows the love ethic. The other half is not a paradox, but the complementary principle of loving one's neighbor. "Every man shall bear his own burden [load—R.S.V.]" (v. 5). One has no right to take advantage of one's love and enslave him for a selfish purpose. "Let every man prove his own work, and then shall he have rejoicing [inner satisfaction] in himself alone, and not in another" (v. 4).

One of the apostle Paul's most quoted aphorisms is, "Be not deceived, God is not mocked; for whatsoever a man soweth, that shall he also reap" (v. 7). This is true of kindness or of anger; of things of the flesh or things of the Spirit. It is true socially and individually. "And let us not be weary in well doing; for in due season we shall reap, if we faint not. As we have therefore opportunity, let us do good to all men, especially unto them who are of the household of faith" (v. 9, 10). The kingdom of God is a fellowship; we are special friends and should cultivate this friendship into ripened, brotherly love.

In concluding the epistle Paul said, "See how large a letter I have written unto you with mine own hand" (v. 11). The Revised Standard Version reads, "What large letters . . ." There is uncertainty whether he meant the length of his epistle or the size of his handwriting. The *Emphatic Diaglott* favors the first rendering, the New English Bible the latter version.

---

1. Young's Concordance renders the word "perfect" in Galatians 3:3 as meaning complete.
2. *The Interpreter's Bible,* Vol. 10, p. 534.
3. *Ibid.,* Vol. 9, p. 175.
4. *Ibid.,* Vol. 10, p. 573.

## QUESTIONS FOR DISCUSSION

1. What was Paul's purpose in contrasting an heir and a servant?
2. Was Paul demanding the Galatian saints to be perfect?

3. What was surprising about the attitude of the Galatians regarding Paul's afflictions?
4. Discuss Paul's allegory of freedom and the application he made of it.
5. What was meant by saying that all the law was fulfilled in the word "love"?
6. Discuss the works of the flesh.
7. Discuss the fruits of the Spirit.
8. Can a murderer or a drunk enter the kingdom?
9. Why is it difficult to help one who is overtaken in a fault?
10. How far-reaching is Paul's aphorism of reaping what we sow?

# 14

# THE CONFERENCE
# IN JERUSALEM

(Acts 15:1-41)

Luke's record of Acts of the Apostles has taken us through the early stages of church growth in Jerusalem and then its spread to the rest of Judea and Samaria. The spreading of the church throughout the Gentile world has entered its initial phase in the first missionary journey of Paul and Barnabas. Mark went with them through Cyprus, but turned back at Perga soon after reaching Asia Minor. The apostles raised up several congregations in the provinces of Pamphylia, Pisidia, Lyconia, and Galatia. The journey started in the spring of A.D. 47 and this chapter relates the conference at Jerusalem in late spring of A.D. 49.

## MEN FROM JUDEA CAUSE DISSENSION

"Certain men which came down from Judea taught the brethren" (v. 1). These men were converts from the Pharisees who had come to Antioch. They became known as "Judaizers" for they boldly advocated that without circumcision "after the manner of Moses" the Gentiles could not be saved. Paul and Barnabas joined in making an issue of this. But the dispute could not be settled by reasoning. It caused only dissension, so an appeal had to be made to higher authorities. It was agreed that Paul and Barnabas and certain others of them

92

should go up to Jerusalem "unto the apostles and elders" for a decision. "They determined" reads "were appointed" in the Revised Standard Version. This indicates that the branch in Antioch took some action (v. 2).

This issue was no small difference over semantics, nor much adieu about inconsequentials. Peter had faced the problem of bringing God-fearing Gentiles into the church in Caesarea (Acts 11). The major question was whether Christianity was a national religion or was a universal church. The decision in Caesarea was based on God's acceptance of Gentiles by sending the Holy Spirit to the uncircumcised. The Judaistic party knew that if the door was opened by omitting circumcision, the keystone of Mosaic religion, the whole system of Jewish law would go.

As the Antioch delegation "passed through both Phoenicia and Samaria, reporting the conversion of the Gentiles" (R.S.V., v. 3) it gave great joy to the brethren there. After reaching Jerusalem "they were received of the church, and of the apostles and elders, and they declared all things that God had done with them" (v. 3, 4). Then the proselytes from the sect of Pharisees had opportunity to present their case. After hearing both sides, "the apostles and elders came together for to consider this matter" (v. 6). While the church as well as the officials received them (v. 4), it is possible that only the latter were to make the final decision.

## A Decree Is Issued

At this conclave Peter, Paul, and Barnabas all presented arguments for a universal church and against the Judaistic viewpoint. Peter based his reasoning on his experience in Caesarea:

Ye know how that a good while ago [about A.D. 40] God made choice among us, that the Gentiles by my mouth should hear the word of the gospel, and believe . . . giving them the Holy Ghost, even as he did unto us; and put no difference between us and them.—V. 7-9.

In the light of this history, Peter asks, "Now, therefore, why tempt ye God, to put a yoke upon the neck of the disciples, which neither our fathers nor we were able to bear?" He concluded his appeal by affirming that both Jew and Gentile will be saved through "the grace of the Lord Jesus" (v. 10, 11).

"Then all the multitude kept silence" seems to indicate that a larger body of the church was present at the conference. Then "Barnabas and Paul" told of the "miracles and wonders God had wrought among the Gentiles by them" (v. 12). No rebuttal speeches are mentioned; the issue was clear, and the judgment was prompt. James, the Lord's brother, gave the decision: "Men and brethren, hearken unto me; Simeon [the Jewish spelling for Simon, meaning Peter] hath declared how God at the first did visit the Gentiles, to take out of them a people for his name" (v. 13, 14).

James then declared that this agrees with "the [twelve minor] prophets." He quoted Amos (9:11, 12), and though the wording is not exact, it says that the blessing of God should come to the Gentiles. The division of the kingdom after David's reign was regarded as ruinous. It should be set up again in all its glory in a Messianic reign, as was planned by God from the beginning, or from the creation of the world (v. 15-18). "Wherefore my sentence is, that we trouble not them, which from among the Gentiles are turned to God; but that we write unto them that they abstain from pollutions of idols, and from fornication, and from things strangled and from blood" (v. 19, 20).

The wording of this decree indicates that James presided over the conference and council. He must have been the leading official of the church. A problem arises regarding the conditions of the decree. The first two mentioned are ethical and Christian—abstain from idolatry and fornication. The last two are ceremonial under Jewish law—refrain from eating the meat of strangled animals and from drinking blood.

Various Western authorities (Codex Bezer, Latin versions, and such fathers as Irenaeus, Cyprian, and Tertullian) omit "what is strangled," so that we have a three-clause decree which can be interpreted as a prohibition against three typical sins—idolatry, fornication, and murder ("blood").[1]

This interpretation seems more in harmony with the views of the three debaters mentioned by name.

## A DELEGATION TAKES THE LETTER TO ANTIOCH

Then it pleased "the apostles and elders, with the whole church to send chosen men" with Paul and Barnabas and with the letters explaining the decree. Judas called Barsabas[2] and Silas from "their own company" in Jerusalem were selected to go to Antioch and present the letters to those who had been disturbed previously. "We have heard, that certain men which went out from us have troubled you . . . saying, Ye must be circumcised, and keep the law; to whom we gave no such commandment" (v. 22-24). The letter continued, naming their representatives "Judas and Silas, who shall also tell you the same things by mouth. For it seemed good to the Holy Ghost, and to us, to lay upon you no greater burden than these necessary things" (v. 25-28).

It is significant that the letter states specifically that the decision or sentence of James, the president of the conference, makes clear that the Lord did not leave such an important matter solely to the wisdom of a man or a set of men. It was the Holy Ghost and "us" who arrived at this judgment and, therefore, it carries divine approval. Likewise the Lord has directed that "all things shall be done by common consent in the church, by much prayer and faith" (D. and C. 25:1 b). The only purpose of much prayer and faith would be to obtain the direction of the Holy Spirit which would give God's seal of approval.

When the company reached Antioch, a call went out and the multitude (church) came together. The epistle (report) was read to them and "they rejoiced for the consolation" (v. 30, 31). That last word might be rendered better as "encouragement" or "relief" as from concern. Judas and Silas stayed "there a space," then Judas returned to Jerusalem. Paul and Barnabas remained in Antioch, "with many others," "preaching the word of the Lord" (v. 32-35).

## START OF PAUL'S SECOND MISSIONARY JOURNEY

After some days, "Paul said unto Barnabas, Let us go again and visit our brethren in every city where we have preached . . . and see how they do" (v. 36). This was the summer of A.D. 49, and the initiation of the second missionary journey. However, Barnabas wished to take Mark with them, while Paul thought this was unwise. Doubtless Paul felt that Mark was unstable because he had returned to Jerusalem from Perga soon after the start of their first mission (Acts 13:13). The contention was so sharp between the apostles that they decided to separate. Barnabas took Mark and sailed to Cyprus, and Paul chose Silas for his traveling companion, "and he went through Syria and Cilicia, confirming the churches" (v. 39-41).

Much has been written about this rift between these apostles. The Greek interpreted here as a sharp contention is rendered "violent passion" by Westcott and Hort. Our word "paroxysm" is a transliteration. Moffatt's Bible renders it "irritation." While it must have been very disappointing to each man, the evidence shows that it was not a personal conflict. Luke's record does not mention Barnabas again, but Paul speaks of him in a favorable light in I Corinthians 9:6 and Colossians 4:10. The latter reference shows that Mark had regained Paul's favor, as also does Philemon 1:24. There is no evidence that Paul and Barnabas ever met again.

The place filled by Barnabas in the apostolic circle caused him to be "credited (by Tertullian and others in the Western Church) with the authorship of the anonymous 'Epistle to the

Hebrews' and with the Alexandrian *Epistle of Barnabas* (Codex Sinaiticus)."[3]

---

1. *The Interpreter's Bible*, Vol. 9, p. 203.
2. The name is spelled Barsabbas in the Revised Standard Version and he is probably the brother of Joseph called Barsabas mentioned in Acts 1:23.
3. *New Standard Bible Dictionary*, Funk and Wagnalls, p. 96.

## QUESTIONS FOR DISCUSSION

1. Tell what disrupted the work in Antioch soon after the apostles returned from their mission.
2. What was the proposal made to settle the dissension?
3. What did the delegation report to the church and officials at Jerusalem?
4. Who presented counter arguments?
5. What is the significance of James's statement, "My sentence is"?
6. Discuss the differences between the four-point decree and the three-typical-sins decree.
7. What did the Jerusalem conference do to quiet the dissension in Antioch?
8. What is given in the letter to indicate that there was divine inspiration in the decree?
9. What was the issue which separated Paul and Barnabas on their next mission?
10. Does the evidence indicate that the quarrel was personal and final?

# 15

# PAUL AND SILAS GO TO GALATIA

(A.D. 49—Acts 16:1-40)

Our last chapter ended on a sour note. When Paul had proposed to Barnabas, "Let us go again to visit our brethren," there was a sharp contention between them over whether they should take John Mark. It was decided that they separate. Barnabas would take Mark and Paul chose Silas as his traveling companion. The latter went through Syria and Cilicia over the Taurus mountain pass into Galatia. Derbe, the easternmost city where the gospel had been preached, was visited first, then Lystra.

## TIMOTHY JOINS THE MISSIONARY TEAM

"A certain disciple was there, named Timotheus, the son of a certain woman [Eunice—II Tim. 1:5], which was a Jewess, and believed; but his father was a Greek; which was well reported of by the brethren that were at Lystra and Iconium" (v. 1, 2). Paul later wrote that Timothy was pointed out by prophecy (I Tim. 1:18). He was probably baptized by Paul on the first journey, A.D. 47. Both Timothy's mother and grandmother had accepted the gospel, but the inference is that his father was an unbeliever.

Under divine direction, Paul asked Timothy to accompany Silas and him on the mission. Timothy was agreeable and even willing to have Paul circumcise him, which was done "because of the Jews which were in those quarters; for they knew all that his father was a Greek" (v. 3).

This raises some questions since Paul had rebuked Peter and Barnabas for inconsistency and compromising by refusing to eat with Gentiles when some brethren from Jerusalem were present (Gal. 2:11-14). It also may be hard to understand why Paul would not circumcise Silas in Jerusalem (Gal. 2:3), but felt it necessary to do so with Timothy. While Luke's account in Acts is quite brief, from the facts available the best explanation seems to be that the two geographical situations made a real difference. Here in Galatia Paul was engaged in trying to win the Gentiles to Christ. To have yielded in Jerusalem would have resulted in defeating the very purpose for which the conference was called (Acts 15).

Paul's attitude is understood better in the light of his statement in his Corinthian epistle:

Unto the Jews I became as a Jew, that I might gain the Jews; to them that are under the law, as under the law, that I might gain them that are under the law. . . . I am made all things to all men, that I might by all means save some.—I Corinthians 9:20, 22.

This is also consistent with his teaching, "In Christ Jesus neither circumcision availeth anything, nor uncircumcision" (Gal. 6:15). If he could disarm the hostile Judaizers who were constantly interfering with his missionary work by performing this ceremonial act of the law, he would do it, for "neither circumcision availeth anything, nor uncircumcision." His objective was to save souls. He was forthright in the matter and doubtless considered it consistent to perform this nonessential rite for the good which it might do.

## MANY UNITE WITH THE CHURCH

"As they went through the cities, they delivered them the decrees for to keep" which came from the Jerusalem conference (Acts 16:4 ff.). "And so were the churches established in the faith, and increased in number daily" (v. 5). Here is real evidence that Paul's sensitivity to the feelings of the people among whom he labored was paying off. A stubborn resistance to any accommodation would have embroiled him in controversy which would surely have stopped this daily increase in new members.

"Now when they had gone throughout Phrygia and the region of Galatia," the Holy Ghost forbade them to preach any more in Asia, Mysia, and Bithynia, and they "came down to Troas" (v. 6-8). This city was on the northwestern coast of Asia Minor. Thus Luke made it clear that the missionaries were not passing up the churches in Antioch and Perga, nor did they overlook the evangelistic possibilities in such cities as Miletus, Ephesus, Samos, and Thyatira deliberately, but by direction of the Holy Spirit.

While at Troas, Paul was given a night vision in which a man of Macedonia stood beseeching him, "Come over into Macedonia and help us." Paul interpreted this "that the Lord had called us for to preach the gospel unto them" (v. 9, 10). "W. M. Ramsay . . . attractively conjectures that the man of the vision was Luke himself. He thinks that Luke may have been a native of Philippi."[1]

## MOVE INTO EUROPE

In response to this call, the missionaries "came with a straight course to Samothracia, and the next day to Neapolis; and from thence to Philippi, which is the chief city of that part of Macedonia" (v. 11, 12). It is important to note that beginning with Acts 16:10, Luke frequently includes himself in the narrative: "We endeavored to go"; "We were in that city."

100

Samothracia was an island in the Aegean Sea, halfway between Neapolis and Troas. Neapolis was a seaport for the province of Thracia. Macedonia was a Roman province north of Achaia (Greece) with Thrace on the east and Illyricum on the west. Thessalonica was the official capital of the province as a whole.

"Came with a straight course" means the boat had a tail wind and did not have to tack. Philippi was "a [Roman— R.S.V.] colony." It enjoyed "self-government, immunity from imperial tribute and the same rights as Italian citizens."[2] Hence it was the "chief" or "leading" (R.S.V.) city.

"On the Sabbath we went out of the city by a river side, where the people resorted for prayer . . . and spake unto the women which resorted thither. . . . Lydia, a seller of purple [goods—R.S.V.], of the city of Thyatira . . . heard us" (v. 13). Philippi had no synagogue. "The riverside seems to have been a customary place for a Jewish place of prayer. The word is commonly used by Philo, Josephus, and in inscriptions as a synonym for 'synagogue.' "[3] Lydia is the name of a province in Asia Minor where Thyatira is located. The woman named Lydia seems to have been a God-fearer of some means. She may have had the distinction of being the first convert to Christianity in Europe. "When she was baptized, and her household, she besought us, saying, If ye have judged me to be faithful to the Lord, come into my house, and abide there" (v. 14, 15).

## Ministers Beaten and Imprisoned

One day as the group was going to the place of prayer, a girl with "a spirit of divination . . . which brought her masters much gain by soothsaying" followed "Paul and us" saying, "These men are servants of the most high God, which show unto us the way of salvation." She continued this for several days till Paul rebuked the spirit. "I command thee in the name of Jesus Christ to come out of her" (v. 16-18).

"Her masters saw that the hope of their gains was gone" so they brought Paul and Silas into the marketplace (also translated "courthouse") to the rulers. They made a complaint against them as troublesome Jews who "teach customs, which are not lawful for us to receive, neither to observe, being Romans" (v. 19-21). "Active proselytizing was frowned upon as a menace to the national cult of the emperor."[4]

The magistrates tore the clothes from Paul and Silas, commanded them to be beaten, and cast them into prison where their feet were put in stocks. The "inner prison" was likely underground. At midnight Paul and Silas prayed and sang praises to God, and the prisoners heard them. "And suddenly there was a great earthquake, so that the foundations of the prison were shaken; and immediately all the doors were opened, and everyone's bands were loosed" (v. 22-26). The walls and ground where their chains were attached were broken so as to release them. The prison keeper, seeing the doors open, drew his sword to kill himself, but Paul said, "Do thyself no harm; for we are all here." The keeper called for a light, came in, and fell before Paul and Silas. He led them from the prison darkness and asked, "What must I do to be saved?" They answered, "Believe on the Lord Jesus Christ, and thou shalt be saved and thy house." Then they taught "the word of the Lord, and to all that were in his house" (v. 27-32).

## KEEPER OF THE PRISON CONVERTED

The jailer washed the the prisoners' stripes which likely had dried blood on them; then "he and all his" were baptized. Next he fed the missionaries and all rejoiced. Word came from the magistrates to liberate the prisoners. Paul protested this action. "They have beaten us openly uncondemned, being [men who are—R.S.V.] Roman [citizens], . . . now do they thrust us out privily? nay verily; but let

them come themselves and fetch [take—R.S.V.] us out."
This was done [with apologies—R.S.V.] and the officials
asked them to leave their city. After a brief visit to comfort
the saints who gathered at Lydia's house, they departed
(v. 33-40).

No doubt these magistrates could have suffered severe
penalties for their high-handed and illegal way of treating
Roman citizens. It doubtless was fear of losing their office
and also fear of the mob which brought about such prompt
reversal of judgment and the missionaries' departure. "Roman
citizenship in the first century conferred exemption from de-
grading punishment such as flogging and crucifixion, the right
to appeal to the emperor, freedom from direct taxation, and
the right to hold office."[5]

1. *The Interpreter's Bible*, Vol. 9, p. 215.
2. *Ibid.*, Vol. 9, p. 218.
3. *Ibid.*, Vol. 9, p. 219.
4. *Ibid.*, Vol. 9, p. 221.
5. Prof. E. E. Stringfellow, *op. cit.*, p. 109.

## QUESTIONS FOR DISCUSSION

1. What have you learned about Timothy?
2. Was Paul's practice in Timothy's case consistent with his teaching regarding circumcising a Gentile?
3. What were the decrees the missionaries delivered as they visited the churches?
4. Which churches in Asia Minor were visited, and why were not the other churches given ministry?
5. Where was the first labor in Europe performed, and who was the first convert?
6. What is known about this convert?
7. Why were Paul and Silas beaten and imprisoned?
8. What brought about the conversion of the jailer?
9. Why did Paul refuse to leave the prison secretly?
10. What caused the magistrates to fear?

# THE GOSPEL PLANTED
# IN EUROPE

(Acts 17:1-18:18)

Paul and his party were victims of severe persecution in Philippi and were asked to leave the city. Had they not been Roman citizens they would have been kept in prison stocks for a long time. They had not revealed this relationship at the time of being given stripes and committed to jail. The magistrates had classed them as troublesome Jews on the word of the mob which brought them into court.

"Now when they had passed through Amphipolis and Apollonia, they came to Thessalonica, where there was a synagogue of the Jews" (v. 1). This is the site of the modern city of Salonika with a population of 150,000. Silas and Timothy accompanied Paul, but Luke evidently did not leave Philippi, which may have been his home, for he drops the "we" in his writing at this point.

For three Sabbaths, Paul and company went to the synagogue and "reasoned with them out of the Scriptures, opening and alleging [explaining and proving—R.S.V.] that Christ must needs have suffered, and risen again from the dead" (v. 2, 3). The idea of a Messiah (Christ) as a suffering servant (Isaiah 53:3 ff.) was alien to the Jews. Their hope was in a mighty king who, by power, could liberate them from the Roman yoke. The glory of the cross (Gal. 6:14) was also a difficult concept, for to be hanged on a cross was an ignominious death reserved for base criminals and not for a Messiah. We would not think that one who had been sent to the electric chair today would be worthy of much honor. Paul was bold in his assurance, "This Jesus, whom I preach unto you, is Christ" (v. 3).

Some of the Jews, many of the devout Greeks, "and of the chief women not a few" believed and fellowshiped with Paul and Silas. But the unbelieving Jews were jealous and gathered a rabble crowd to set up an uproar in the city and attack the home of Jason where the missionaries were guests. Not finding them, the mob took Jason and others to the rulers where they accused them: "These that have turned the world upside down are come hither also; whom Jason hath received" (v. 6, 7).

There is no evidence that Jason was a Christian, though it is probable that he was won to the church at the synagogue. He was deemed guilty of crime by association. "And these all do contrary to the decrees of Caesar, saying that there is another king, one Jesus" (v. 7). This disturbed the rulers, so they put Jason and his company under bond which would be forfeited in case there was further trouble. "And the brethren immediately sent away Paul and Silas by night unto Berea" (v. 8-10).

Here they went to the synagogue of the Jews. The Jews in Berea were found "more noble [liberal] than those in Thessalonica, in that they received the word with all readiness of mind, and searched the Scriptures daily, whether those things were so" (v. 11). Many believed, including honorable [high standing—R.S.V.] Greek women "and of men, not a few" (v. 12).

When the troublemakers in Thessalonica learned of the success of the preaching in Berea "they came thither also, and stirred up the people. . . . Immediately the brethren sent away

Paul . . . but Silas and Timotheus abode there still" (v. 13, 14). Paul took ship to Athens and sent word for his companions "to come to him with all speed" (v. 15). As he looked around, Paul observed a "city wholly given to idolatry" and "his spirit was stirred." He disputed with the Jews and devout persons in the synagogue, and in the marketplace[1] "daily" (v. 15-17). Here he had encounters with "certain philosophers of the Epicureans and Stoics." These two were the most influential schools of philosophy at that time. The former had "happiness" as its main theme; pleasure was the supreme good. The Stoics, founded by Zeno, 300 B.C., "advocated conduct according to nature, but 'happiness' and 'nature' were so interpreted that the practical ethics were virtually identical." They taught that virtue was the highest good, and that man should master his feelings and actions. Tarsus, Paul's birthplace, was a great center of Stoic teaching.[2]

As these men came near Paul, he would hear them ask each other, "What will this babbler say?" Others said, "He seemeth to be a setter forth of strange gods; because he preached unto them Jesus, and the resurrection" (v. 18). They brought him to Mars' Hill and asked him to explain this new doctrine. The Athenians and visitors of that time spent much time in telling or listening to some new thing (v. 19-21).

Paul was glad to respond to the invitation, and began by addressing them, "Ye men of Athens, I perceive that in all things ye are too superstitious" (v. 22). A better version might be, "You are very religious" (R.S.V.), for to accuse one of being "too superstitious" is to antagonize him. Paul supported this observation by referring to an altar inscription, "To the unknown God." He continued, "Whom therefore ye ignorantly worship [you worship as unknown—R.S.V.] him declare I unto you" (v. 23). He then affirmed that this was the Creator of heaven and earth and

dwelleth not in temples made with hands; neither is worshipped with men's hands, as though he needed any thing . . . and hath made of one blood[3] all nations of men for to dwell on all the face of the earth, and hath determined the times before appointed, and the bounds of their habitation; . . . he is not far from every one of us; for in him we live, and move, and have our being. . . . For we are also his offspring.—V. 24-28.

The last part of the quotation was taken from the book, *Phaenomena,* by the Stoic poet Aratus.

Paul then began his argument for Christianity. Since we are God's offspring, we should not think of the Godhead as material, graven images.

The times of this ignorance God winked at; but now commandeth all men everywhere to repent; because he hath appointed a day, in the which he will judge the world in righteousness by him whom he hath ordained; and . . . hath raised him from the dead.—V. 29-31.

At the mention of the Resurrection "some mocked, and others said, We will hear thee again of this matter." So Paul took his leave, but some believed including Dionysius and a woman named Damaris (v. 32-34). Athens is the only place of record where Paul's preaching did not result in persecution. It is not that the Athenians were better, but they did not get excited about teachers of strange doctrines. It is probable that Paul never returned to Athens.

## PAUL LABORS AT CORINTH
(Acts 18)

Leaving Athens the missionaries went to Corinth, the commercial and political capital of Achaia, situated on the isthmus which connected the Peloponnesos with the mainland. At its zenith it had 750,000 population, two-thirds of whom were slaves. Strabo said

the city was rich and opulent at all times. . . . Their chief devotion was to Aphrodite, the goddess of lust, whose thousand priestesses were prostitutes. . . . To live like a Corinthian was a synonym for gross immorality.[4]

At Corinth Paul "found a certain Jew named Aquila," a recent arrival from Italy because Emperor Claudius had decreed that all Jews leave Rome. He and his wife, Priscilla, were tentmakers. Since Paul was of the same craft, he found hospitality in their home. On the Sabbath he went to the synagogue and reasoned "with the Jews and the Greeks" (v. 2-4). Silas and Timothy joined him here. "Paul was pressed in the spirit, and testified to the Jews that Jesus was Christ" (v. 5). This brought opposition and blasphemy from the Jews, so Paul "shook his raiment,[5] and said unto them, Your blood be upon your own heads; I am clean [innocent—R.S.V.]; from henceforth I will go unto the Gentiles" (v. 6).

In the house next door to the synagogue lived Justus, a convert. Paul was given hospitality here. What must have been even more galling to the Jews was to lose the chief ruler of the synagogue, Crispus, who with his family "believed on the Lord . . . and were baptized" (v. 7, 8).

That night Paul was told by the Lord in a vision, "Be not afraid, but speak, and hold not thy peace; for I am with thee, and no man shall set on thee to hurt thee; for I have much people in this city" (v. 9, 10). This must have been most comforting to Paul who faced a hard task in a licentious city, and had Jewish opposition. The prophecy was fulfilled in his establishing "the most vigorous and perhaps the largest of all Paul's churches."[6] He continued laboring here "a year and six months."

"When Gallio was the deputy of Achaia, the Jews made insurrection with one accord against Paul and brought him to the judgment seat." They accused him of persuading men to worship God "contrary to the law" (v. 11-13). Paul was about to speak in defense when "Gallio said unto the Jews, If it were a matter of wrong or wicked lewdness, . . . I should bear with you; but if it be a question of words and names, and of your law, look ye to it." He then drove them out of his court (v. 14-16). The Greeks took out their resentment

108

on "Sosthenes, the chief ruler of the synagogue, and beat him before the judgment-seat," but Gallio paid no attention to this. He could see no difference between Judaism and Christianity. This was not a judicial matter of his concern.

Paul remained in Corinth "yet a good while." Then accompanied by Aquila and Priscilla, he sailed for Ephesus. Before leaving the port city of Cenchrea, he took a vow and had his head shorn[7] (v. 18).

---

1. This was really the center of the business and intellectual life of Athens as the Forum was in Rome. "It was a square surrounded by porticos embellished by sculptures and by some of the famous buildings . . . the Acropolis, . . . the Areopagus, or Mars' Hill." See Stringfellow, *op. cit.*, p. 115.
2. See Stringfellow, *op. cit.*, p. 115, and *The Interpreter's Bible*, Vol. 9, p. 233.
3. "The older and better manuscripts have only the word 'one.' Some later manuscripts have 'one blood.' Ramsay supplies 'nature.' Rendall supplies 'father.' "—Prof. Stringfellow, *op. cit.*, p. 116. Westcott and Hort Bible uses "parentage"; however, all mean the same thing. Some segregationists try to make a point of this variation.
4. Prof. Stringfellow, *op. cit.*, p. 119.
5. This Jewish formula is reflected in II Samuel 1:16 and Matthew 27:26.
6. *The Interpreter's Bible*, Vol. 9, p. 243.
7. The Nazarite vow (Num. 6:1-21) is here referred to. The Jews sometimes took a modified form of this vow when they were afflicted with disease or other distress. Josephus wrote that it is usual for such "to make vows and for thirty days before they are to offer their sacrifices, to abstain from wine and to shave the hair from their head" (B.J. 2:15, 1). See Stringfellow, *op. cit.*, pp. 131, 132.

## Questions for Discussion

1. What evidence is there that Luke stayed at Philippi when the missionaries left?

2. Which conflicting ideas of a Messiah made it hard for the Jews to accept Christ?
3. What caused the Jews to attack the home of Jason?
4. Why were the Jews in Berea said to be "more noble" than those in Thessalonica?
5. Whom did Paul encounter at Mars' Hill and what were their main doctrines?
6. What were the words of the poet on which Paul based his argument for Christianity?
7. In what ways did Athens differ from Corinth in Paul's day?
8. What did it mean then "to live like a Corinthian"?
9. Why did Aquila and Priscilla come to Corinth?
10. What reasons can you give for Paul's long stay in Corinth?

# 17

# PAUL'S FIRST LETTER TO
# THE THESSALONIANS

(December A.D. 50—I Thess. 1:1-5:28)

While Paul, Silas, and Timothy were together in Corinth they decided to write to those of the church in Thessalonica who were still suffering persecution. Timothy had remained in Thessalonica after Paul and Silas were driven out. They longed to return, but the pledge and bond exacted from Jason (Acts 17:9, 10) made this impractical. Paul went alone to Athens. Silas stayed in Berea and after Paul's departure was joined by Timothy (Acts 17:14). The younger men were too late to meet with Paul at Athens, but found him in Corinth. Timothy was sent back to Thessalonica to establish and comfort the saints in the faith (I Thess. 3:1-6). Based on the report which he brought back to Corinth it was decided that this epistle should be written.

The message to the church at Thessalonica starts on a note of thanksgiving for their "work of faith, and labor of love, and patience of hope in our Lord." They were reminded that "our gospel came not unto you in word only, but also in power, and in the Holy Ghost, and in much assurance" (v. 1-5). This has long been a popular theme of Restoration preachers. While Paul was considered an educated man, he had no conceit and did not feel that man's learning was of chief importance. "God hath chosen the foolish things of the world to confound the wise" (I Cor. 1:27). "To be learned is good," said Nephi, "if they hearken to the counsels of God" (II Nephi 6:61).

"Ye became followers [imitators—R.S.V.] of us, and of the Lord . . . so that ye were ensamples to all that believe in Macedonia and Achaia" (v. 6, 7). "Your faith toward God is spread abroad; so that we need not to speak any thing. . . . Ye turned to God from idols to serve the living and true God, and to wait for his Son from heaven, whom he raised from the dead, even Jesus" (v. 8-10).

It is characteristic of those who have a newfound faith to want to spread the word "in every place." It is also noted that when our initial efforts are rebuffed, or bring small returns, we often get "weary in well doing" (Gal. 6:9).

## CONCERNING THE COMING OF CHRIST
(I Thess. 2)

The church was reminded that God's servants had suffered indignities to bring the gospel to Macedonia. "We were bold in our God to speak unto you the gospel." "In the face of much opposition" is added in the Revised Standard Version. "We speak; not as pleasing men, but God" (v. 2-4).

The letter continues to remind the church that the missionaries had not used flattering words, nor sought the glory of men "when we might have been burdensome, as the apostles of Christ." That is, they might have made demands on the saints there, but instead "we were gentle among you, even as a nurse cherisheth her children" (v. 5-7). "Remember, brethren, our labor and travail . . . night and day, because we would not be chargeable unto any of you" while preaching the gospel (v. 9). Paul was a tentmaker (Acts 18:3), and indicates that he was "working with our own hands" (I Cor. 4:12).

112

"We exhorted . . . every one of you, as a father . . . that you would walk worthy of God." Paul thanked God that when they received the word it worked effectually. He reminded them that the Jews "both killed the Lord Jesus, and their own prophets, and have persecuted us . . . forbidding us to speak to the Gentiles that they might be saved" (v. 11-16).

"We would have come unto you, even I Paul, once and again, but Satan hindered us." He said his hope and "crown of rejoicing" was that the Thessalonians would be "in the presence of our Lord Jesus Christ at his coming" (v. 17-20).

## TIMOTHY SENT TO THEM; PAUL'S PRAYER
(I Thess. 3)

While Paul was working in Athens alone, he was so concerned that he directed Timothy to return to them to give ministry so that they would not be overcome in the afflictions which he had warned them would surely come. Paul sent Timothy to them so that he might know their faith, "lest by some means the tempter have tempted you, and our labor be in vain" (v. 1-5). When Timothy came back with a good report Paul was comforted and thanked God for them (v. 6-9).

As a good pastor and administrator, Paul revealed his love and concern for the lambs of his fold, and he prayed that he might see them personally and "perfect that which is lacking in your faith." Those who are newborn in God's kingdom have to endure some growing pains and learn by the things which they suffer. He closed his prayer with the plea that

the Lord make you to increase and abound in love one toward another, and toward all men, even as we do toward you; to the end he may establish your hearts unblamable in holiness . . . at the coming of our Lord Jesus Christ with all his saints.—V. 10-13.

113

## HOLINESS ENJOINED — CHRIST'S RETURN
(I Thess. 4)

The remainder of this epistle deals with personal and social conduct; "how ye ought to walk and to please God" and for their sanctification. Each

should abstain from fornication . . . and to possess his vessel in sanctification and honor, not in the lust of concupiscence [passion—R.S.V.], even as the Gentiles who know not God. . . . God hath not called us unto uncleanness, but unto holiness.—V. 1-7.

He is saying that any sin against another person is to despise God who by his Holy Spirit has taught us to love our neighbor as ourselves.

"Study to be quiet, and to do your own business, and to work with your own hands . . . that ye may walk honestly . . . and lack nothing" (v. 11-12). This is surely an expression of brotherly love (v. 9). No one should claim the right to do anything which disturbs others and limits their liberty to carry on their own work. "The idler shall not have place in the church" (D. and C. 75:5 b). Those who do not work are often tempted to lay their hands on other men's goods.

The epistle then turns to the discussion of the resurrection of the dead, "them which are asleep." We should not sorrow for our departed "as others which have no hope. . . . For if we believe that Jesus died and rose again, even so them also which sleep in Jesus will God bring with him" (v. 13, 14). The word "asleep" emphasizes the temporary nature of the grave. God will cause the righteous who have passed on to be changed to immortality and come with Christ at his—the second—coming. And further, speaking by the Spirit, "they who are alive at the coming of the Lord, shall not prevent them who remain unto the coming of the Lord, who are asleep" (v. 15).

The Revised Standard Version makes this more clear by saying, "We who are alive, who are left until the coming of

the Lord, shall not precede those who have fallen asleep."
In fact, the epistle goes on to declare that the "dead in Christ
shall rise first" and come with the Lord and then "they who
are alive, shall be caught up together into the clouds with
them" (v. 17).

## CONCERNING THE TIME OF HIS COMING
(I Thess. 5)

"The day of the Lord so cometh as a thief in the night."
Paul must have talked to them when he was there about the
uselessness of speculating on the "times and seasons" of the
Lord's return.   When a nation talks of peace and safety
"then sudden destruction cometh upon them, as travail upon
a woman with child" (v. 1-3).   This last simile is a favorite
of Jeremiah (6:24; 13:21; 22:23).   An expectant mother
does not know the hour of her delivery, but lives in expectancy
and readiness.   There is ultimately no "escape," so also God's
promises shall all be fulfilled.

"Ye are all the children of light, and . . . of the day. . . .
Therefore let us not sleep, as do others; but let us watch
and . . . be sober, putting on the breastplate of faith and love;
and for a helmet, the hope of salvation" (v. 6-8).

Sexual excesses and drunken debaucheries are often associated
by Paul with the coming of the night (Rom. 13:12, 13; Gal. 5:19,
20 . . .).   Rejecting both sleep and emotional "escapes," the Thessalonian disciples, as sons of the day, are to remain sober and alert.[1]

## EXHORTATION TO GOOD WORKS

"We beseech you, brethren, to know them which labor
among you, and are over you in the Lord" (v. 12).   The last
phrase makes clear that Paul is talking of ministerial labors
rather than their daily vocations.

Esteem them very highly in love for their work's sake. And be at peace among yourselves. . . . Warn them that are unruly, comfort the feeble-minded, support the weak, be patient toward all men. See that none render evil for evil . . . follow that which is good, both among yourselves, and to all men.—V. 13-15.

The tone of the exhortation now changes from the ethical to the religious. "Rejoice evermore. Pray without ceasing. In everything give thanks. . . . Quench not the Spirit. Despise not prophesyings" (v. 16-20). The word "quench" is often associated with fire and seems quite appropriate here. Baptism of the Holy Spirit and the gift of the Spirit is often associated with fire (Matt. 3:38; Acts 2:3; II Tim. 1:6). It is a little more difficult to see the reason for men to despise the exercise of the gift of prophecy. Perhaps experience had taught Paul that one who speaks in the name of the Lord sets himself apart from the rest in a conspicuous way. Satan fills the hearts of those who are out of tune with spiritual things to question and doubt the sincerity of the gift (see Moroni 10:7-19).

"Prove all things; hold fast that which is good. Abstain from all appearance of evil. And the very God of peace sanctify you wholly. . . . Brethren, pray for us" (v. 21-25). He closes by asking them to read this epistle to all the brethren.

---

1. *The Interpreter's Bible*, Vol. 11, p. 310.

## Questions for Discussion

1. What was the particular situation in Thessalonica which kept Paul from returning?
2. What did Paul mean by "a gospel in word only"?
3. Explain Paul's statement, "We might have been burdensome as apostles of Christ."
4. How had those from Judea prevented "us to speak to the Gentiles"?

5. What was Timothy's report on the disciples after his return visit to Thessalonica?
6. In what connection did he say one would be guilty of despising God?
7. What counsel was given regarding idleness and work?
8. Tell what was meant by "asleep in Christ" and the concern of "those who remain."
9. What was said about "times and seasons" with respect to Christ's second coming?
10. Tell what was said about prophesying and why.

# 18 PAUL'S SECOND LETTER TO THE THESSALONIANS

(Early A.D. 51—II Thess. 1:1-3:18)

While still in Corinth and shortly after sending the first epistle to the church in Thessalonica, Paul found it necessary to write another letter. It was occasioned by a rumor, or a teaching "that the day of the Lord, for which they had been instructed to be in readiness, had arrived."[1] This had a widespread effect on the members of the young church. Paul and his colaborers saw the need of correcting the error promptly before more serious damage was done, as they were greatly excited and troubled in Thessalonica.

## "THEM THAT TROUBLE YOU"
(II Thess. 1)

This epistle has the same greeting as was used in the first letter. Silas and Timothy join in greetings to the church. This is followed by citing reasons for thanking God, "because that your faith groweth exceedingly, and the charity of every one of you all toward each other aboundeth" (v. 1-3). He then comes to the subject of his deep concern, "seeing it is a righteous thing with God to recompense tribulation to them that trouble you; and to you who are troubled rest with us,

118

when the Lord Jesus shall be revealed from heaven with his mighty angels" (v. 6, 7). The tribulation or punishment is to be revealed at the time of Christ's return to earth "taking vengeance on them that know not God, and that obey not the gospel." It will consist of "destruction [exclusion— R.S.V.] from the presence of the Lord . . . when he shall come to be glorified in his saints" (v. 8-10).

Paul then reflects his concern for them in relating, "We pray always for you, that our God would count [make— R.S.V.] you worthy of this calling . . . that the name of our Lord Jesus Christ may be glorified in you" (v. 11, 12).

Many of the ideas of this first chapter repeat those in the opening of the first letter, but in a more restrained mood. The reason for this less exuberant tone will be made more clear in his next chapter.

## THE APOSTASY — THE MAN OF SIN
(II Thess. 2)

We should remember that the church in Thessalonica was made up largely of Gentile converts to whom most of the gospel teachings were new. Since their spiritual fathers had been forced to leave them by decrees of local officials and by violence, it was easy for false leaders to arise and, either ignorantly or willfully, lead the church there astray. In the early days of the Restoration we find some parallels. The prophet and apostles spent much time in trying to straighten out the troubles brought in by unwise and unauthorized teachers whose ideas on food, marriage, economics, and society led the Saints away from the way of truth and the Zionic law. (See Doctrine and Covenants 49; *Church History*, Vol. 2, p. 732.)

"Now concerning the coming of our Lord Jesus Christ and our assembling to meet him, we beg you, brethren, not to be quickly shaken in mind or excited" (R.S.V., v. 1, 2) . . . "that the day of Christ is at hand" (I.V., 2:2). Whether the proclamation of the return of Christ to reign on earth comes by some spirit, or by word, "or by letter purporting to be from us" (v. 2, R.S.V.). This is intended to cover all the sources from which the rumor may have started.

It will be noted that in his first epistle, each chapter has some mention of Christ's return (the Parousia), but in none of them is there justification for believing that the event was imminent (1:10; 2:19; 3:13; 4:16, 17; 5:23). The clause used in II Thessalonians 2:2, "or by letter purporting to be from us," suggests to some scholars that a letter had circulated among them to which Paul's name had been forged. Some had even assembled on a hill awaiting Christ's coming.

"Let no man deceive you by any means; for there shall come a falling away first" (v. 3). This is emphatic and prophetic. The Greek word, *apostasia*, from which we get the word "apostasy," is here translated "falling away"—a departure from "the way" of truth as revealed through Christ. Not only would there be an apostasy, but

that man of sin [will] be revealed, the son of perdition; who opposeth and exalteth himself above all that is called God [every so-called god or object of worship—R.S.V.] . . . so that he as God sitteth in the temple of God showing himself that he is God.—V. 3, 4.

"The son of perdition" is Hebrew idiom for the ultimate doom of the lawless one. It is applied to Judas Iscariot (John 17:12). Satan has always insisted that man set aside all other gods or objects of worship and worship him only. Thus he does intend to set himself on the throne in the temple of God.

The last of the three temptations offered to Jesus was when he was shown

all the kingdoms of the world and the glory of them. And the devil came unto him again, and said, All these things will I give unto thee, if thou wilt fall down and worship me. . . . Get thee hence, Satan; for it is written, Thou shalt worship the Lord thy God.—Matthew 4:9, 10.

120

Paul reminded the Thessalonian saints that he had told them these things when he was with them; "And now ye know what withholdeth [is restraining Him—R.S.V.] that he might be revealed in his time" (v. 5, 6).

## CHRIST GIVEN ALL POWER — EVENTUALLY

Continuing his explanation regarding this man of sin, Paul said, "Christ suffereth him to work, until the time is fulfilled that he shall be taken out of the way" (v. 7). In what sense did Christ suffer him to continue his work? Does he have the power to remove Satan and evil from the world or from his children? Just before he gave the "great commission" to the eleven, Jesus said, "All power is given unto me in heaven and on earth" (Matt. 28:17). This would indicate that Jesus had the power by the sufferance of the Father, yet he must operate within the framework of the divine plan whereby men became "agents unto themselves" (D. and C. 58:6 d). Nephi wrote, "It must needs be, that there is an opposition in all things" (II Nephi 1:81). In Jesus' valedictory prayer he said, "I pray not that thou shouldest take them [the believers—saints] out of the world, but that thou shouldest keep them from the evil" (John 17:15).

Paul then repeats his prophecy and warning that Christ's coming will not be "until after there cometh a falling away, by the working of Satan with all power, and signs and lying wonders, and with all deceivableness of unrighteousness in them that perish; because they received not [refused—R.S.V.] the love of the truth, that they might be saved. And for this cause God shall send them strong delusion, that they should believe a lie [what is false—R.S.V.]" (v. 9-11). This is a typical way of Jewish thinking. "Persistent refusal to hear the truth and pleasure in evil bring the inevitable result—a natural outcome, but only because God has placed us in a world of moral meaning and order."[2] "Whatsoever a man soweth, that shall he also reap" (Gal. 6:7). Man cannot have freedom of

121

choice (agency), without responsibility for consequences. Our damnation comes because of our not accepting truth, but have "pleasure in unrighteousness" (v. 12).

Paul then reminds the saints that "God hath from the beginning chosen you to salvation through sanctification of the Spirit and belief of the truth" (v. 13). This passage might be used to support the doctrine of election or predestination, but that does violence to all of Paul's teachings and the gospel of universal salvation through sincere obedience to Christian principles. "From the beginning" probably refers to their first hearing the gospel. Some ancient manuscripts add, "as the first converts."[3] Sanctification comes only through "belief of the truth."

## WARNING AGAINST IDLENESS
(II Thess. 3)

Paul then encourages them to "stand fast" and hold the traditions which ye have been taught, whether by word, or our epistle" (v. 15).

The closing chapter of this epistle begins with a request, "Brethren, pray for us, that the word of the Lord may have free course . . . and that we may be delivered from unreasonable and wicked men" (v. 1, 2). With the exception of Athens, in every place their missionary work had been cut short by persecution. "Withdraw yourselves from every brother that walketh disorderly." The Revised Standard Version reads "who is living in idleness" (v. 6). This agrees with verses 10 and 11. It seems that some of the brethren who believed so strongly in the immediacy of Christ's return to earth had quit work and were waiting only for this climactic event.

"Neither did we eat any man's bread for naught; but wrought with labor and travail night and day, that we might not be chargeable to any of you" (v. 8). He adds that they had the right to expect support in the gospel work, but wanted to set a good example. The apostles also had commanded

122

"that if any would not work, neither should he eat" (v. 10). Word had reached Corinth that some were "working not at all, but are busy bodies. . . . We command and exhort by our Lord Jesus Christ, that with quietness they work, and eat their own bread. But ye, brethren, be not weary in well doing" (v. 11-13).

The instruction was given to the Saints in latter days that every man "is obliged to provide for his own family. The idler shall not have place in the church" (D. and C. 75:5 a, b). Alma counseled, "See that ye refrain from idleness" (Alma 18:15). Nephi pronounced "Wo be unto him that is at ease in Zion" (II Nephi 12:30).

---

1. *The Interpreter's Bible*, Vol. 11, p. 251.
2. *Ibid.*, Vol. 11, p. 330.
3. See marginal note in Revised Standard Version.

## QUESTIONS FOR DISCUSSION

1. Why was the second epistle written to the Thessalonians so soon after the first epistle was sent?
2. What reasons can be given that explain why some were so soon "shaken in mind"?
3. Was the apostasy to come in the latter days only, or had it begun in Paul's day?
4. From what source is it likely that the idea of Christ's immediate coming was received?
5. What part does the son of perdition have in the "falling away"?
6. Since "all power" was given to Christ, why did he suffer (permit) Satan to deceive men?
7. In what way were the Thessalonians "chosen to salvation"?
8. What command had been given the saints at Thessalonica about working?
9. What had influenced them to quit work?
10. Why do you think Paul emphasized that he wrote every epistle with his own hand?

# 19 PAUL RETURNS TO ANTIOCH IN SYRIA

(Spring of A.D. 52—Acts 18:19-19:41)

Paul's labors in Corinth came to an end in the usual way of conflict. This came near the close of the longest stay in any city of his mission so far—eighteen months. The Jews accused Paul before Gallio, the deputy [proconsul] of Achaia, of worshiping God contrary to the law. Gallio's real name was Marcus Annaeus Novatus, the elder brother of the well-known Stoic philosopher, Seneca.[1] He told the Jews, "If it be a question of words and names, and of your law, look ye to it." Paul stayed in Corinth a while longer, took a Nazarite[2] vow, and then sailed for Ephesus in Asia Minor with Aquila and Priscilla.

## PAUL MAKES SOME SIDE TRIPS
(Acts 18)

The record mentions that Paul visited the synagogue in Ephesus where he "reasoned with the Jews." He expressed his desire to attend the feast of the Passover in Jerusalem. The Jews in Ephesus urged him to tarry longer, but the time element and transportation opportunities forbade this. So he bade them farewell with a promise to return "if God will" (v. 19-21).

124

Luke gives no details of Paul's visit to Jerusalem; perhaps he was unable to get them since he was doubtless still in Philippi. We are told only that Paul landed at Caesarea, the seaport for Jerusalem of that day, and when he had "gone up, and saluted the church, he went down to Antioch" (v. 22). This was in Syria, his missionary headquarters. He spent some time there; then, in the spring of A.D. 53, he started his third missionary journey which lasted four years.

"He departed, and went over all the country of Galatia and Phrygia in order, strengthening all the disciples" (v. 23).

## APOLLOS CAME TO EPHESUS
(Acts 18:24)

Some time before Paul's return, a Jew from Alexandria, Egypt, "an eloquent man and mighty in the Scriptures, came to Ephesus." Because he was an educated man in "the way of the Lord; and being fervent in spirit" he was able to exercise a great influence over the people. His handicap was that he knew "only the baptism of John" (v. 24, 25).

When Aquila and Priscilla heard him "speak boldly in the synagogue"[3] they took him into their home (Rom. 16:3-5) "and expounded unto him the way of God more perfectly" (v. 26). The statement, "This man was instructed in the way of the Lord," has led some to say he was a Christian, but this does not prove it. "Lord" is used to refer to either God the Father or Christ the Son. Since he knew "only the baptism of John" we infer that he knew little or nothing about Jesus the Christ.

Apollos planned to go over to Achaia; the brethren gave him letters of introduction to the disciples in Corinth, and he proved helpful there in proselyting among the Jews (v. 27, 28).

## Receiving the Holy Spirit
(Acts 19)

After the departure of Apollos, Paul arrived in Ephesus, "and finding certain disciples" asked, "Have ye received the Holy Ghost since ye believed?" They answered, "We have not so much as heard whether there be any Holy Ghost."[4] Like Apollos, these knew only "John's baptism" and were not in any full sense Christians (v. 1-3).

Paul did not tell them that they were in the wrong church, but that they had not gone far enough. "John verily baptized with the baptism of repentance, saying to the people, that they should believe on him which should come after him, that is, on Christ Jesus" (v. 4).

As a result of Paul's ministry, these twelve disciples were rebaptized, but this time "in the name of the Lord Jesus." After he had performed that ordinance and "had laid his hands upon them, the Holy Ghost came on them; and they spake with tongues and prophesied" (v. 5, 6). One of the evidences of receiving the Holy Spirit is manifested in the exercise of these two outward gifts. It should not be assumed that unless baptized believers receive these particular gifts they have not received the Spirit. As Paul later explained to the Corinthian saints, "The manifestation of the Spirit is given to every man to profit withal." Then he enumerates nine gifts of the Spirit which God is "dividing to every man severally [individually—R.S.V.] as he will" (I Cor. 12:4-11).

## The Word Confirmed by Miracles
(Acts 19:8)

For three months things went well in Ephesus as Paul "spake boldly . . . disputing and persuading the things concerning the kingdom of God" (v. 8). As usually happened sooner or later, the unbelievers made trouble for him and "spake evil of that way before the multitude." So Paul found

126

it necessary to withdraw and form his own church assembly. He rented "the hall of Tyrannus" (R.S.V., v. 9) and lectured or argued daily. "This continued by the space of two years" (v. 9, 10). As a result of this ministry by Paul and his companions, "all . . . Asia heard the word of the Lord Jesus, both Jews and Greeks" (v. 10).

Probably [this] means that from his base at Ephesus Paul endeavored to conduct a more extensive mission. It may, for example, have been at this time that the Christian communities were formed at Colossae, Laodicea, and Hierapolis (Col. 2:1; 4:13) and perhaps in the remainder of the "seven churches" of the Apocalypse."—Revelation 1:20.[5]

"And God wrought special miracles by the hands of Paul." Even the handkerchiefs and aprons which he blessed were brought to the sick, and they were healed, "and the evil spirits went out of them [the people]" (v. 11, 12). This may seem to some like magic rather than the gospel of Christ as taught elsewhere in the New Testament. It was not practiced nor taught as a part of Christian ministry. Jesus did say to two blind men, "According to your faith, be it unto you" (Matt. 9:35), and they could see. One woman touched Jesus' garment and was healed of a chronic ailment (Matt. 9:26-28). These two were "special miracles" in that they were not in accordance with the regular pattern as given in Mark 6:7 and James 5:14, 15.

## PAUL FORCED TO LEAVE EPHESUS
(Acts 19:13)

Certain of the vagabond [itinerant—R.S.V.] Jews, exorcists, took upon them to call over them which had evil spirits the name of the Lord Jesus, saying, We adjure you by Jesus whom Paul preacheth. . . . And the evil spirit answered and said, Jesus I know, and Paul I know; but who are ye?—V. 13, 15.

In Paris there is an ancient manuscript, "Magical Papyrus," which reads: "I adjure thee by Jesus the God of the Hebrews."

This indicates that exorcists of that day were convinced that there was power in the name "Jesus."

The man possessed by the evil spirit "leaped on them, . . . and prevailed against them, so that they fled out of that house naked and wounded" (v. 16). This experience is remarkable in that one demented person could overcome and unclothe several normal men. That superhuman strength is given men under some such conditions is well known. Likely the element of surprise and fear helped him in this unequal struggle. As the news of this event circulated in Ephesus,

fear fell on them all, and the name of the Lord Jesus was magnified. And many that believed came, and confessed, and showed their deeds [divulging their practices—R.S.V.]. Many of them also which used curious arts [practiced magic—R.S.V.] brought their books together, and burned them.—V. 17-19.

## UPRISING OF THE SILVERSMITHS
(Acts 19:21)

Moved by the Spirit, Paul resolved to go to Jerusalem after he had moved through Macedonia and Achaia, and then go to Rome. But instead of going to Europe himself, he sent Timothy and Erastus, his helpers (v. 21, 22). Where Silas was at this time is not known. Some think that he accompanied Paul to Jerusalem (Acts 18:22) and remained there.[6] Peter revealed (I Peter 5:12) that he became his collaborator, and he may have joined him at this place and time.

The success of the missionaries in Ephesus is attested by the uproar of men whose crafts were endangered by obedience to the gospel. The world-famous temple of Diana, goddess of fertility, one of the seven wonders of the world, was located here. The opposition, however, was not religious but economic. A great many men made their living by making silver images of Artemis (Latin is Diana), and since Christianity taught faith only in the living God and against idols, the

128

preaching of this threatened to take the bread out of the mouths of the silversmiths' families.

Demetrius called his fellow craftsmen together and said, "Sirs, ye know that by this craft we have our wealth. . . . Throughout all Asia, this Paul hath persuaded and turned away much people, saying that they be no gods, which are made with hands" (v. 23-26).

Demetrius argues that not only would their craft suffer, but their great temple would be despised which "all Asia and the world worshipeth." At this the anger of the assembly flared and soon "the whole city was filled with confusion." The people (Greek—*demos*) rushed into the theater dragging Paul's companions, Gaius and Aristarchus, with them. Paul wanted to enter, but his disciples restrained him. There was so much confusion inside that the incoming crowd could not tell what was happening.

The Jews, whose religion forbade idol worship, put forth Alexander to speak. But as soon as the crowd saw that he was a Jew, they began to chant, "Great is Diana of the Ephesians," and kept this up for two hours. The town clerk [7] finally quieted the crowd and reminded them that since Ephesus worshiped Diana and "the image [sacred stone—R.S.V.] which fell down from Jupiter," and

*meteor*

since these things cannot be spoken against [contradicted—R.S.V.], ye ought to be quiet, and to do nothing rashly. . . . The law is open, and there are deputies; let them implead [bring charges—R.S.V.]. . . . For we are in danger to be called in question for this day's uproar.— V. 35-40.

Rome would hold them for consequences.

1. Prof. Stringfellow, *op. cit.*, p. 130.
2. See Chapter 16, page 109.
3. "His teaching was probably some type of 'Gnostic' philosophy based on an allegorical interpretation of scripture. Possibly it would resemble the kind of teaching we have in Hebrews, which

indeed has been ascribed to Apollos—a pure conjecture."—*The Interpreter's Bible*, Vol. 9, pp. 247, 248.

4. "The Western text reads, 'whether any are receiving the Holy Spirit.' "—*The Interpreter's Bible*, Vol. 9, p. 252.

5. *The Interpreter's Bible*, Vol. 9, p. 254.

6. *Ibid.*, p. 247.

7. "He was also known as the secretary of the city and was the most important native official of Ephesus, who was liaison officer between the municipal government and the proconsul representing the imperial government."—Stringfellow, *op. cit.*, p. 159.

## Questions for Discussion

1. Where did Paul go soon after leaving Corinth and for what purpose?

2. Where was the start of Paul's third missionary journey, and where did his labors take him during the next two years?

3. Who was Apollos and what did he do in Ephesus?

4. Why did Paul rebaptize twelve disciples in Ephesus?

5. What kind of evidence can be expected to indicate that a believer has been born of the Holy Spirit?

6. What kind of trouble did the seven sons of Sceva get in and what was the result?

7. What were the special miracles performed through Paul?

8. Who was Demetrius and what did he tell the silversmiths?

9. What indicates that the mission in Ephesus was very successful?

10. Why was the town clerk able to quiet the mob and what arguments did he use?

# 20 PAUL WRITES TO THE SAINTS AT CORINTH

(Spring A.D. 55 — I Cor. 1:1 - 6:20)

While Paul was still at Ephesus (see I Corinthians 16:8) he wrote an epistle to "the church of God which is at Corinth, . . . called to be saints" (v. 1, 2). Apollos had returned (16:12) after a successful period of evangelism. Three of the Corinthian church leaders had come to Ephesus with a report on certain problems. "Chloe's people" (probably slaves)[1] had informed Paul about party divisions (v. 11). Because Paul could not personally attend to the matter, he wrote this letter to help them adjust as true Christians should live.

Sosthenes, who joined Paul in the salutation, may have been the successor of Crispus, chief ruler of the synagogue in Corinth (Acts 18:8, 17). After a gracious introduction, the letter admonishes that "Ye all speak the same thing, and that there be no divisions among you" (v. 10). He gives as witness of this "the house of Chloe." There was human loyalty, many saying "I am of Paul; and I of Apollos; and I of Cephas; and I of Christ. Is Christ divided? Was Paul crucified for you? or were ye baptized in the name of Paul?" (v. 12, 13). Paul mentioned that he had baptized only two and the household of Stephanus, for "Christ sent me not to baptize, but to preach the gospel" (v. 14-17).

Despite the fact that I Corinthians does not contain a systematic presentation of the gospel, every part of the letter deals with some aspect of it [the gospel]. Though Christ is the center of the message, its beginning and end are found in God our Father.[2]

From Paul's statement on baptism "some commentators have drawn the false conclusion that Paul was depreciating baptism. This was farthest from his intention. Faith and baptism brought the believer into union with Christ."[3]

## The Gospel vs. Human Wisdom
(I Cor. 1:18 - 2:16)

Paul then reasons that preaching the cross is foolishness to the heathen, but the power of God to us. For "it pleased God by the foolishness of preaching to save them that believe" (18-21). Preaching about the crucifixion of Christ is a stumbling block to the Jews and to the Greeks foolishness but to the believing "both Jews and Greeks, Christ [is] the power of God, and the wisdom of God. . . . For God hath chosen the foolish things of the world to confound the wise . . . that no flesh should glory in his presence" (v. 23-31).

Paul reminds the Corinthian saints that when he came among them with the testimony of God, he did not try to impress them "with excellency of speech or of wisdom . . . but in demonstration of the Spirit and of power" (2:1-4).

But we speak the wisdom of God in a mystery, even the hidden wisdom [a secret and hidden wisdom—R.S.V.], which God ordained before the world [ages—R.S.V.] unto our glory. . . . But God hath revealed them unto us by his Spirit . . . for what man knoweth the things of a man, save [by] the spirit of man which is in him? Even so the things of God knoweth no man, except he has the Spirit of God.—V. 7, 10, 11.

Every trade and profession has its particular terminology and symbolism. No one can understand, much less explain, these fields of skill and knowledge properly until he has mastered the language and made some progress in its techniques. Paul has used this approach to convince the Corinthians that his ministry was "not in the words which man's wisdom teacheth, but which the Holy Ghost teacheth . . . for who hath known the mind of the Lord, that he may instruct him? But we have the mind of Christ" (v. 13-16).

## LABORERS TOGETHER — THE BODY A TEMPLE (I Cor. 3)

As "babes in Christ . . . I have fed you with milk, and not with meat . . . for ye are yet carnal . . . whereas there is among you envying, and strife, and divisions, are ye not carnal, and walk as men?" (v. 1-3). Those who claimed loyalty to Paul strove with those who were followers of Apollos, yet both were ministers of Christ. "I have planted, Apollos watered; but God gave the increase" (v. 4-7). Therefore, such strife is carnal "for we are laborers together with God. . . . I have laid the foundation, and another buildeth thereon, . . . but let every man take heed how he buildeth thereupon" (v. 9, 10).

It is rather unusual that any person is converted to Christ by the sole effort of one person. The groundwork is laid by parents, neighbors, and special friends; yet the final decision is usually obtained by one minister aided by the drawing power of the Spirit. Paul's chief concern was that their faith be based on the gospel. "For other foundation can no man lay than that is laid, which is Jesus Christ" (v. 11). He then emphasized the duty of personal purity.

Know ye not that ye are the temple of God, and that the Spirit of God dwelleth in you? If any man defile the temple of God, him shall God destroy. . . . The wisdom of this world is foolishness with God. . . . Therefore let no man glory in men.—V. 17-23.

133

## Humble Fellow Laborers
### (I Cor. 4)

As ministers of Christ, Paul had a stewardship over the mysteries of the kingdom of God. All stewards are required to be faithful in duty. He was not worried over man's judgment of him, "for though I know nothing against myself; yet I am not hereby justified; but he who judgeth me is the Lord" (v. 1-4). While he had written much about himself and Apollos, it was only to illustrate

that ye might learn in us not to think of men above that which is written. . . . For I think that God hath set forth us the apostles last [of all], as it were appointed to death [like men sentenced to death— R.S.V.] . . . a spectacle unto the world, and to angels, and to men. . . . Even unto this present hour we both hunger, and thirst, and are naked, and are buffeted, and have no certain dwelling- place.—V. 6-13.

"I write not these things to shame you, but as my beloved sons I warn you . . . I have begotten you through the gospel, wherefore I beseech you, be ye followers of me" (v. 14-16). While Paul could not come to them then, he promised he would "come to you shortly, if the Lord will," but I have sent Timothy, "who shall bring you into remembrance of my ways which be in Christ" (v. 17, 19). The tense used indicated that the epistle was not complete when Timothy left.

## Moral Standards of Christian Life
### (I Cor. 5:1-13)

The epistle becomes more specific at this point. A report had come to Paul of a case of incest. A prominent member of the church had married his stepmother, presumably after his father's death. This was forbidden by Roman and Jewish law (Lev. 18:8). Paul was also concerned about the community's attitude regarding this sin. "And ye are puffed up [arro- gant—R.S.V.] and have not [ought ye not—R.S.V.] rather mourned" (v. 2). While he had not been there personally, he was present in spirit and had passed judgment. Such a man should be delivered "unto Satan for the destruction of the flesh, that the spirit may be saved in the day of Lord Jesus" (v. 5). The realm of the flesh can be touched by Satan, "and thus his sins will lead to his death . . . but Satan was powerless in relation to the higher faculty of man."[4] While it is not easy to harmonize the possibility of ultimate salvation with other New Testament teachings, it may mean that after the resurrection with a new body, a new spiritual life might begin.

"Your glorying is not good . . . a little leaven leaveneth the whole lump" (v. 6). He continues in this general vein: "I wrote unto you in an epistle not to company with fornicators" and the covetous, extortioners, or idolaters. This holds equally as well of those in the church as those of the world. "Therefore put away from among yourselves that wicked person" (v. 9-13). No other record of this writing can be found.

## UNRIGHTEOUS WILL NOT INHERIT THE KINGDOM
(I Cor. 6:1-20)

Paul rebukes those who go to law against a brother before the courts of the land rather than the church courts. The saints shall judge the world, and even angels. How much more should they be able to judge between brethren? (v. 1-5). It would be better to endure wrong and "suffer yourselves to be defrauded" than to take our wrongs for adjudication before the unrighteous. "Be not deceived; the unrighteous shall not inherit the kingdom of God." He then repeats and lists many of those who are in this class, "and such were some of you; but ye are washed . . . sanctified . . . justified in the name of the Lord Jesus, and by the Spirit of our God" (v. 1-11).

"Know ye not that your bodies are the members of Christ?" . . . and "that he which is joined to a harlot is one body? for two, saith he, shall be one flesh." He again refers to the body as "the temple of the Holy Ghost which is in you, which ye have of God, and ye are not your own" (v. 15-19). No man has a right to desecrate his own or another's body. Our friends, kinsfolk, and God have an interest in our person. We do not live or die to ourselves alone. In the United States and other countries the act of attempting suicide is a crime against society. Likewise, "Every sin that a man committeth is against the body of Christ . . . for ye are bought with a price; therefore glorify God in your body, and in your spirit, which are God's" (v. 20).

The apostle to the Gentiles makes use of this simile frequently because it is easily understood by even the weakest of saints. All of us together form one body in Christ. Each member of that body is essential to its functioning and should be respected in its place. Yet when we follow the wrong crowd, and yield our bodies to the devices of Satan, the whole body suffers and is held up to open shame.

It seems quite likely that the "wicked person" which called forth such strong denunciation from the apostle was a man of influence, perhaps a potential leader in the church at Corinth. Satan strikes where it will reward him most, as the Lord through Zechariah said, "Smite the Shepherd and the sheep shall be scattered" (Zech. 13:7). Well did Jesus tell us to pray daily, "Suffer us not to be led into temptation."

---

1. *The Interpreter's Bible,* Vol. 10, p. 20.
2. *Ibid.,* Vol. 10, p. 9.
3. *Ibid.,* Vol. 10, p. 24.
4. *Ibid.,* Vol. 10, p. 62.

## QUESTIONS FOR DISCUSSION

1. What was the nature of the disunity in the church in Corinth? Has that ever happened in the Restoration movement?

2. Do you think that Paul meant he was not anxious to baptize people, or just that he preferred his helpers to go into the water? Why?

3. Why is "preaching of the cross foolishness" to some? Why a stumbling block to the Jews?

4. What were Paul's strong points as a preacher? In what ways was he weak?

5. In what ways is the calling of a minister similar to that of the professions and skilled trades?

6. What reasons had Paul to write that the Corinthian saints were "babes," and were "yet carnal"?

7. How many and who have parts to play in the usual winning of one soul to the kingdom of God?

8. What were some of the trials the early-day apostles had to endure?

9. What was the sin of "that wicked person" mentioned in 5:13, and why did Paul devote so much attention to him?

10. What reasons can you give why we should not use our courts of law against a member who had wronged us?

# 21 PROBLEMS OF MARRIAGE AND CELIBACY

(I Corinthians 7:1 - 8:13)

Paul had written about moral standards for Christians, and now turns to answer some questions put by the Corinthian members in a letter to him. He had made it clear that saints are to live differently than Gentiles (pagans—R.S.V.), for to follow after them destroys the church body and causes all such persons to forfeit the kingdom of heaven (6:9, 10). He had especially condemned immorality between the sexes and also homosexuality. He stressed the fact that the body of man is the temple of the Holy Spirit "which ye have from God, and you are not your own" (6:19).

## VIRGINITY AND MARRIAGE
(I Cor. 7:1-6)

"It is good for a man not to touch a woman" wrote Paul in answer to their letter. This does not refer to the married state. God said to his Only Begotten in the morning of creation "that it was not good that the man should be alone"; so he made woman for his helpmeet (Gen. 2:33). Likewise, Paul follows his opening statement by adding, "Because of the temptation to immorality, each man should have his own

138

wife and each woman her own husband" (v. 2—R.S.V.). Each should respect the other in the conjugal privileges. One should not disregard the feelings of the other in selfish demands, but prefer the other in "due benevolence." ✗

The apostle recognized that there are times when the husband and wife will need to be apart. He especially mentioned for purposes of worship or evangelism. Today he might also include for business reasons. However, he says this should be by mutual consent, "that Satan tempt you not for your incontinency [lack of self-control—R.S.V.]" (v. 3-5).

Here Paul injects a very significant statement: "And now what I speak is by permission, and not by commandment" (v. 6). He is not trying to pose as the oracle, or voice of God, in this matter, but gives that which he sincerely believes is sound advice. He closes this chapter by the humble admission, "And I think also that I have the Spirit of God" (v. 40).

## VIEWS ON CELIBACY
(I Cor. 7:7-11)

"I say . . . to the unmarried and widows, It is good for them if they abide even as I[1] [remain single as I do. But if they cannot exercise self-control, they should marry —R.S.V.] . . for it is better to marry than that any should ✗ commit sin" (v. 8, 9). "Than to burn" (K.J.) and "to be aflame with passion" (R.S.V.) make clear that the burning does not refer to hell fire.

Speaking by command of the Lord, Paul said, "Let not the wife depart [separate—R.S.V.] from her husband . . . and let not the husband put away his wife" (v. 10, 11). Knowing that some will disregard this injunction, Paul adds that if they separate they should "remain unmarried, or be reconciled." Catholic .

## ON MARRIAGE TO AN UNBELIEVER
(I Cor. 7:12-16)

Paul strongly advises his Corinthian brethren against divorce, called "putting away" (Mal. 2:16; Matt. 5:35, 36; 19:9, 10). However, he expresses his judgment that in a mixed marriage, if the unbelieving spouse desires separation, "let him depart." The believer "is not under bondage in such cases; but God hath called us to peace." The idea of enduring indignities in the hope that the unbeliever will change and be saved is quite uncertain. "Marriage is not a sphere for missionary work."[2]

The time to help our youth avoid unwise marriages is before they "fall in love." The parents are given about a dozen years to mold the ideals and thought processes of their children. But it is easy to put off the idea that they need instruction in these formative years and to ignore the need to act now; many parents wait until it is too late and love "blindness" has stolen away their opportunity.

## VIEWS ON CELIBACY
(I Cor. 7:25-35)

Speaking for himself and not by way of the Lord's commandment, Paul advised the brethren in Corinth against taking a wife. It was not that he felt marriage was sin or displeasing to God, but the times of "the present distress" made it inadvisable; considering the need for taking the gospel into all the world, and also the few who were available to do it, Paul held that those who remained single "may do greater good" (v. 26).

When Jesus was asked, "What is the sign of thy coming, and of the end of the world" (Mark 13:9), he indicated it would come in a time of "great tribulation." Following this, "the powers of the heavens shall be shaken, then shall appear the Son of Man in heaven; . . . coming in the clouds of heaven, with power and great glory" (Mark 13:41-44).

"But if thou marry, thou hast not sinned, and if a virgin marry, she hath not sinned. Nevertheless, such shall have trouble in the flesh" (v. 28). Speaking directly Paul reveals his concern, "Brethren, the time that remaineth is but short," and even those who "have wives . . . are called . . . to do the Lord's work" (v. 29). They were admonished to magnify their calling as ministers. He realized that he who was married sought "how he may please his wife" and therefore "is hindered." He was anxious for God's servants to "attend upon the Lord without distraction" (v. 32-35).

"If any one thinks that he is not behaving properly toward his betrothed" (v. 36, R.S.V.) may mean an engaged couple, who had resolved to accept Paul's advice and refrain from marriage. If, then, because of close association and strong passions they find that they are tempted, it is better to reject the vow of celibacy and get married. Once they have married, they are bound to each other for life. Should the husband die, she is at liberty to remarry, but "only in the Lord." Paul is strongly against mixed marriages where one party is an unbeliever. He encouraged the older widows to remain single, and adds the significant line, "I think also that I have the Spirit of God" (v. 36-40). In his letter to Timothy, Paul urged that widows be not accepted in the group "under three-score years old" (I Tim. 5:9).

## FOOD OFFERED TO IDOLS
(I Cor. 8:1-13)

A philosophic sect of Paul's day called gnostics[3] caused considerable schism in the church. "If any man think that he knoweth anything, he knoweth nothing yet as he ought to know" (v. 2). God alone knows man's ways and the intents of the heart. Then Paul comes directly to the subject of eating meat "offered in scarifice unto idols." Idols of wood and stone know nothing, so why try to placate them. There are many that are called gods, "but to us there is but one God, the Father, of whom are all things, . . . and one Lord Jesus Christ. . . . Howbeit there is not in every man that knowledge" (v. 1-7).

The eating of meat or abstaining does not make one better or worse, and is not a matter of worship.[4] But by eating that offered in idol worship one might become a stumbling block to a weaker brother who followed the example set, and thus "through thy knowledge shall the weak brother perish, for whom Christ died?" Paul closes his exhortation on this subject with a noble vow, "If meat maketh my brother to offend [fall—R.S.V.], I will eat no flesh while the world standeth." The Revised Standard Version adds, "lest I cause my brother to fall" (v. 13).

---

1. Many scholars believe that Paul never married. One thinks he may once have married. "He may have married [when] about twenty [years old]. This is inferred from his voting against the Christians in the Sanhedrin probably (Acts 26:10), for membership in which marriage was required according to Jewish tradition."—Prof. Stringfellow, op. cit., p. 44.
2. The Interpreter's Bible, Vol. 10, p. 80.
3. The term "Gnostic" comes from the Greek gnosis which means "knowledge." We frequently hear the term "agnostic" applied to one who does not deny God's existence (an atheist does), but says, "I do not know whether God exists."
   "The gnostic claimed special esoteric or secret knowledge. It could be possessed only by that section of humanity which was 'pneumatic,' or spiritual. They alone led back to the realm of light of the Supreme God.
   "There was a second class of men, those who were only 'psychic' and could not get beyond faith. The prophets and other good Hebrews belonged to this class but they must be eternally in a sphere much inferior to that occupied by the 'gnosis.'
   "There was a third class represented by the overwhelming mass of human kind. They were merely 'hylic' (i.e., subject to matter) and their case was utterly hopeless for they were in endless bondage to Satan and their own lusts, and their end was to be completely destroyed. . . . Matter was utterly and irretrievably

evil. . . . The historical Christ was a mere man, but he was taken possession of by the heavenly Christ who was the brightest of all aeons. This heavenly Christ acted in the man Jesus but was never incarnate."—*Baker's Dictionary of Theology*, pp. 237, 238.

4. See Matthew 15:10.

## QUESTIONS FOR DISCUSSION

1. Have Christians the promise that they shall be spiritually mature so as to be above sexual temptations?
2. What proof does the Corinthian letter give that the scriptures are not all inspired by God?
3. What was Paul's view of the married state?
4. What did he teach concerning divorce? Did he make an exception of mixed marriage divorces?
5. When is the best time for parents to discuss sex with daughters and sons?
6. How much truth is there in the aphorism, "Love is blind"?
7. What did Christ's expected early return from heaven have to do with Paul's counsel on marriage?
8. Under what conditions were widows encouraged to re-marry?
9. Who were the gnostics and in what ways did they oppose Christianity?
10. To what extent was Paul opposed to eating meat?

# 22 THE STATUS OF AN APOSTLE

(I Corinthians 9:1 - 11:1)

Apparently the Judaizers who had been to Corinth had planted doubts in the minds of the saints that Paul was a bona fide apostle. So he turned abruptly from the discussion in our last chapter on the impropriety of eating meats offered in the worship of idols to assure the Corinthians that he was a genuine apostle.

## QUALIFICATIONS FOR APOSTLESHIP

"Have I not seen Jesus Christ our Lord?" (v. 2), he asked. Luke revealed that there was in the church the tradition that only those "who from the beginning were eye-witnesses and ministers of the word" (Luke 1:2; Acts 1:21) were eligible to be apostles. Not only did he ask the question but Paul had an answer, "And last of all he [Jesus] was seen of me also, as one born out of due time" (I Cor. 15:8). This doubtless refers to the vision on the road to Damascus, for there is no evidence that he ever saw Christ while our Savior was on earth, though they were born about the same year.

"Are not ye my work in the Lord? If I be not an apostle unto others, yet doubtless I am to you, for the seal of mine apostleship are ye in the Lord" (v. 2). It seems that some

144

criticism had been raised also because Paul and his companions had not accepted food and money from those among whom they had labored as had other apostles. Likewise, if he were a real apostle, why would he not take a sister or a wife as did the brothers of Jesus and Peter? Paul's answer was that he was free to live on their food, and also to marry, but preferred not to do so. The law and customs gave him the right to receive his needs as would a soldier, a vineyard keeper, or a shepherd (v. 4-10).

It may seem strange today that Paul would prefer to mend or make tents for a living instead of using that time in evangelism. But since we do not know all the conditions and psychology of the times in which Paul labored, we cannot rightly appraise his judgment.

If we have sown unto you spiritual things, is it a great thing if we shall reap your carnal things? . . . Nevertheless we have not used this power; but suffer [endure—R.S.V.] all things, lest we should hinder the gospel of Christ.—V. 12.

Attention was called to those who served the temple altar and received meat not consumed by the altar fire. "Even so hath the Lord ordained that they which preach the gospel shall live of the gospel" (v. 14).

## RENUNCIATION AND SELF-DISCIPLINE
(9:15-27)

While Paul acknowledged the right, he did not think it necessary nor wise to have done these things. "For it were better for me to die, than that any man should make my glorying void." The charge of exploitation had been leveled at traveling evangelists from that day to our own period, and Paul did not want even the suspicion of such a charge to be brought against his work.

"For though I preach the gospel, I have nothing to glory of; for necessity is laid upon me; woe is unto me, if I preach not the gospel" (v. 16). He was only doing his job. His reward was in the blessings which came to others who heard the preaching of the gospel without charge, and that he "abuse not my power in the gospel. . . . Yet have I made myself servant unto all, that I might gain the more." He adapted his ministry to the Jews—to those under the law—and to those without the law (v. 18-21). Paul was not a compromiser, but he had respect for the conscientious scruples of others. "To the weak became I as weak. . . . I am made [have become— R.S.V.] all things to all men, that I might by all means save some" (v. 22, 23).

Paul closes this part of his epistle by an admonition on self-discipline. Several runners enter a race for a prize, but only the swiftest one gets the reward.

And every man that striveth for the mastery is temperate in all things. Now they do it for a corruptible crown [perishable wreath—R.S.V.], but we an incorruptible. . . . I keep under my body, and bring it into subjection, lest that by any means, when [after—R.S.V.] I have preached to others, I myself should be a castaway [disqualified— R.S.V.].—V. 24-27.

## LESSONS FROM THE WILDERNESS OF SINAI (10:1-15)

When Moses led the Israelites out of Egypt, they underwent severe trials before reaching the land of Canaan. They passed through the sea and were guided by the cloud. They ate and drank of spiritual meat (manna and quail) and that spiritual rock that was Christ. Both were supernaturally supplied. "But with many of them God was not well pleased. . . . The people sat down to eat and drink, and rose up to play." He could have added that only two of those who left Egypt got into Canaan. Because of immorality, twenty-three thousand of them fell in a day [likely those mentioned in Numbers 25:1-9] (v. 1-7).

The blessings of deliverance, food, and drink were received by all, but not all profited by them. Here was a lesson ("ensample") for the Corinthians. The reception of sacraments alone will not save anyone.

Let him that thinketh he standeth take heed lest he fall. There hath no temptation taken you but such as is common to man; but God is faithful, who will not suffer you to be tempted above that ye are able [beyond your strength—R.S.V.]; but will with the temptation also make a way to escape, that ye may be able to bear it.—V. 8-13.

## COMMUNION OF CHRIST AND OF DEVILS
(10:16-23)

The sacrament of the Lord's Supper is next discussed by Paul, and the unity and welfare of the body of saints emphasized. The word "communion" here used has given us a shorter term for the Lord's Supper. Some prefer the term "Eucharist."[1] Sacrament is used many times for it in the Doctrine and Covenants, but since there are really eight sacraments in the church, that term is inadequate or needs modification.

The bread and wine placed on the Communion table typify the body and blood of Christ. By participation in this sacrament of the Lord's Supper, "We being many are one bread, and one body" (v. 17). (See Doctrine and Covenants 17:22, 23). But by eating the meat offered in idol sacrifice there is no unity. "The Gentiles sacrifice . . . to devils, and not to God" (v. 20). Do we provoke the Lord to jealousy?

Doubtless Paul is here alluding to the gnostic[2] claim that because their superior powers brought to them revelations, they were not bound by Christian and ethical laws. "All things are lawful for me, but all things are not expedient: [helpful—R.S.V.] . . . but all things edifieth not" (v. 23, K.J.). "Let not man seek therefore his own, but every man another's good" (v. 24).[3]

## FOR CONSCIENCE'S SAKE
(10:25-33)

Paul now returns to the discussion of general principles and to the answering of the slogans of his gnostic opponents. He is advising them not to be scrupulous about the foods they buy in the marketplace [meat market—R.S.V.], "for the earth is the Lord's, and the fulness thereof." The era for kosher meat was past. God created all things and called his work "good." Therefore if you are invited to feast in the home of an unbeliever in Christ, eat what is set before you, "asking no questions for conscience's sake" (v. 25-27). However, if the host shall say, "This is offered in sacrifice unto idols," do not eat it lest you offend the conscience of others. "Whether therefore ye eat, or drink, or whatsoever ye do, do all to the glory of God" (v. 28-31).

In Christ's church the scruples of the Law of Moses can be a stumbling block to those who have not been traditioned in that law. However, with the Jews, disrespect for their conscientious scruples might blind their eyes to the truth in the gospel. So Paul said, "Give none offence, neither to the Jews, nor to the Gentiles, nor to the church of God" (v. 32). This is a difficult policy. One trying to please everybody is apt to please nobody in the end. Nevertheless Paul was striving to subordinate himself that others might be saved.

His concluding admonition is in 11:1, "Be ye followers of me, even as I also am of Christ." Most people find it easier to be loyal to a person than to a principle. Hence great causes have always been associated with great leaders. The unfortunate part of this is that unscrupulous leaders often deceive the people and capitalize on their loyalty. For this reason Mosiah counseled his people against having a king (Mosiah 13:21-30). Thus Paul wisely modifies his plea for loyalty by asking for the Corinthians to follow him only as far as he is a follower of Christ.

1. The original meaning of "Eucharist" is, "a giving of thanks, to show favor or grace."—Webster's Dictionary.

2. Gnosticism—"Among the majority of followers of the movement, 'Gnosis' was understood not as meaning 'knowledge' or 'understanding' in our sense of the word but as 'revelation.' It was a mystic religion.

   "In spite of the fact that in a few of its later representatives Gnosticism assumed a more refined and spiritual aspect, and even produced blossoms of a true and beautiful piety, it is fundamentally and essentially an unstable religious syncretism, a religion in which the determining forces were a fantastic oriental imagination and a sacramentalism which degenerated into the wildest superstitions, a weak dualism fluctuating between asceticism and libertinism."—*Encyclopaedia Britannica,* 1961, pp. 452-454.

3. The King James Version reads, "another's wealth." The Revised Standard Version supports the Inspired Version. Undoubtedly Paul is urging that love does not insist on having its own way. One needs to seek those things which will promote his own welfare, but it is unchristian to strive for that when it is at another's expense.

## QUESTIONS FOR DISCUSSION

1. What qualifications are given in the Bible for those selected to the Council of Twelve?

2. Why did Paul prefer to work at his trade when he might have been cared for by the saints?

3. In what ways did he make himself a servant of all?

4. What did Paul say which indicates he did not feel sure of his own salvation?

5. Why does the term "the sacrament" prove inadequate?

6. Relate some ways in which the doctrines of the gnostic were in conflict with the gospel.

7. Was Paul's counsel on eating meats sacrificed to idols always consistent? (See 8:13 and 10:27.)

8. Is it always right to seek another's welfare and not your own? Explain your answer.

9. What is the danger in the principle, "Let conscience be your guide"?
10. To what extent should one try to please all men?
11. Why must one be careful in following a leader?

# 23  WOMEN'S PLACE, THE LORD'S SUPPER, AND SPIRITUAL GIFTS

(I Corinthians 11:2-12:31)

Paul turns from his discussion of questions for conscience's sake and from presenting his criteria of sainthood involving the loyalty of the Corinthians to his leadership, and takes up a domestic problem. It is neither doctrinal nor moral, but it does have great significance in the worship life of the church. Here in Corinth the Judaistic and rabbinical interpretations on the status of women needed clarification.

It has been said that Christ was the first great religious leader to discover and admit that women had souls. Before his time they carried their religion in their husbands' or their fathers' names. Even among the Jews whose scriptures revealed that man and woman were created equal (Gen. 1:28-30), the woman was really treated as man's property (Gen. 3:22; 31:14, 15; Deut. 24:1). Among the Greeks, woman's status was markedly worse than among the Hebrews. Knowing these things will help one to see some of Paul's reasoning and objections more clearly.

## To Glorify Man
(11:2-17)

The men of Corinth were praised for keeping in mind the gospel teaching and for observing the ordinances Paul had taught them. "But I would have you know, that the head of every man is Christ; and the head of the woman is the man [her husband—R.S.V.]." When a man prays or prophesies with his head covered he dishonors his head, who is Christ (v. 1-3). Even today when a man wishes to be courteous to a lady, he removes his hat. When a woman worships with uncovered head, she reflects on her husband and "the angels" who minister in the worship service. It is the same as if she were shorn—"if it be a shame for a woman to be shorn or shaven, let her be covered [wear a veil—R.S.V.]".

In the orthodox synagogues today the women worshipers regularly do not wear hats, and neither do they sit with the men who always wear hats or caps. However, they pray or read with uncovered heads.

Paul then intensifies his argument by referring to the creation. "For the man is not of the woman; but the woman of the man" (v. 8). (See Genesis 2:28.) The one is not independent of the other. She is his helpmate. "If a man have long hair, it is a shame unto him; [Ezekiel 44:20; though many Greek men wore long hair] but if a woman have long hair, it is a glory to her, for her hair is given her for a covering" (v. 4-15). Shaving the head was a sign of mourning (Amos 8:10), and baldness was a disgrace (II Kings 2:23).

"But if any man seem to be contentious, we have no such custom, neither the churches of God" (v. 16). The Revised Standard Version reverses this interpretation, making Paul to say, "We recognize no other practice, nor do the churches of God." It is apparent that Paul was not wanting to bind the liberty found in the gospel by imposing the traditions of the rabbinical covenant, but neither did he wish to discard autocratically those which might needlessly alienate the Jews who were interested in the gospel.

152

# THE SIGNIFICANCE OF THE LORD'S SUPPER
(11:17-34)

> I hear that there be divisions [factions—R.S.V.] among you. . . .
> When ye come together into one place, is it not to eat the Lord's
> supper? But in eating every one taketh before his own supper; and
> one is hungry, and another is drunken.—V. 18-21.

In this infant church they misconstrued the purpose and nature
of the Lord's Supper and were having "a love feast" called
*agape*. It might have been a "covered dish" meal in which
the first got the most.[1] It provided an occasion for gluttony
and even for drunkenness. Then Paul reminds them that this
was not in harmony with his instructions nor the example
given by the Lord.

> The Lord Jesus, the same night in which he was betrayed, took bread;
> and when he had given thanks, he brake it, and said, Take, eat; this
> is my body, which is broken for you; this do in remembrance of me.
> After the same manner also he took the cup, when he had supped, say-
> ing, This cup is the new testament in my blood; this do ye, as oft as ye
> drink it, in remembrance of me. For as often as ye eat this bread,
> and drink this cup, ye do show the Lord's death till he come.—V.
> 22-26.

This is the clearest picture of the serving of the Communion emblems in the scriptures. It reveals that Jesus set the
example by partaking first (v. 25), and then invited his
disciples to do likewise. This is the custom we follow and
shows the worthiness of those who handle the vessels of the
Lord. Another aspect of the Communion is that Jesus never
used the term "wine" so far as the New Testament reveals.
However, it is used in the Book of Mormon (III Nephi 8:28
ff., Moroni 5:1) and in the Doctrine and Covenants (17:8 a,
23 a; 119:5 c-f; 26:1 d, "Made new among you").

Paul warns against partaking unworthily. "Let a man
examine himself . . . for he that eateth and drinketh unworthily, eateth and drinketh condemnation to himself, not

discerning the Lord's body." Much has been written about the meaning of this passage. With the light given in our Three Standard Books it seems quite obvious that worthiness consists of genuine repentance and sincere resolve to keep all of the commandments of God. Those who hold some favorite sins in reserve may fool men, but the Lord looketh on the heart (I Sam. 16:7; Ps. 44:21). Only if a member is known to the officers to be in sin should he be refused the emblems (III Nephi 8:60-62).

"Discerning the Lord's body" does not refer to the crucified body, nor the resurrected body of Christ, but to the church which Paul has likened to the Lord's body (10:16; 12:27). Failure of the Gentiles or proselytes to recognize the living church for which Christ died (Eph. 5:25) has brought on spiritual weakness, also sickness and death (v. 27-30).

Paul closes his exegesis on the Communion by advising the church at Corinth to desist from having communal meals in connection with the Lord's Supper. "If any man hunger, let him eat at home. . . . The rest will I set in order when I come" (v. 31-34).

## The Functioning of Spiritual Gifts (12:1-31)

The outward manifestation of spiritual gifts, except prophecy, were not evident among the Jews. Neither did the Greeks have experience with them, since they worshiped "dumb idols." Therefore Paul felt it wise to discuss all the gifts of the Spirit. "No man can say that Jesus is the Lord, but by the Holy Ghost" (v. 3). Faith in Jesus' divinity rests upon the light and power of the Holy Spirit which confirms one in his worship. Jesus told his disciples that he would "go unto my Father" . . . and I will pray the Father, and he shall give you another Comforter . . . and I will love him [the disciple], and will manifest myself to him" (John 14:12, 16, 21).

154

"There are diversities of operations, but it is the same God which worketh all in all. But the manifestation of the Spirit is given to every man to profit withal" (v. 6, 7). Paul then names these "diversities of gifts":

To one is given by the Spirit the word of wisdom.
To another the word of knowledge.
To another faith (see D. and C. 42:13).
To another the gifts of healing.
To another the working of miracles.
To another prophecy.
To another discerning of spirits.
To another divers kinds of tongues.
To another the interpretation of tongues (v. 6-11).

He then compares these to the members of the physical body of man. It has "many members, and all the members . . . are one body; so also is Christ."

Paul shifts to another type of metaphor. The church is made up of many persons, Jews and Gentiles, bond and free, yet all drink of the one Spirit. The foot cannot say, "Because I am not the hand, I am not of the body," nor the ear, "Because I am not the eye, I am not of the body," for if "they were all one member, where were the body?" (v. 12-19). "But now hath God set the members every one of them in the body, as it hath pleased him." They are all equally important to sustaining the life of the body whether it be the human or church body.

"There should be no schism in the body; but that the members should have the same care one for another" (v. 25). Then Paul goes a step further by applying this analogy to church organization. "And God hath set some in the church, first apostles, secondarily prophets, thirdly teachers, after that miracles, then gifts of healings, helps, governments, diversities of tongues" (v. 28). This is a mixed metaphor, for apostles are not analogous to a spiritual gift. Neither is the apostle cataloging the officers of the church, placing first the apostolic

155

office and third the teachers. He is continuing his analogy of showing the many members and functions in the church and that each is needed in its place.

Paul ends his dissertation on the gifts by suggesting to the Corinthian saints that all are not apostles, nor do all speak with tongues, or interpret, "for I have shown unto you a more excellent way, therefore covet earnestly the best gifts" (v. 29-31). It may seem strange that the saints need encouragement to seek these gifts; however, they are not just for the asking. The word "covet" is a strong action term. Then to it is added the adverb "earnestly." Those who have been moved upon by the Spirit to voice the mind of God in prophecy or tongues say it carries a weight of responsibility which weaker persons wish to avoid. But for the good of the church body, some need to exercise these "outward gifts" so that Christ may commune with and direct his church.

---

1. *The Interpreter's Bible,* Vol. 10, p. 131.

## QUESTIONS FOR DISCUSSION
1. What was the status of women in home and church when Jesus was born?
2. What did the hair and hats of worshipers have to do with the early Christian religion?
3. What caused the schism in the church at Corinth regarding the Lord's Supper?
4. What purpose does partaking of the Communion emblems have in the church?
5. Should any member be refused the emblems? Defend your answer.
6. What is meant by "discerning the Lord's body"?
7. Which gifts of the Spirit did Paul name?
8. Which are "the best gifts" we are to covet?
9. In what sense did Paul mean, "God hath set in the church, *first* apostles"?
10. Why should one covet the best spiritual gift? What is that gift?

# 24

# MORE ON THE GIFTS, AND WOMEN'S STATUS

(I Corinthians 13:1-14:32)

Paul continues his discussion of the nature of spiritual gifts and gives his answer to the question of which gifts should be most desired. "Though I speak with the tongues of men and of angels, and have not charity [love—R.S.V.], I am become as sounding brass, or a tinkling cymbal." Thus Paul starts one of his best literary efforts on the subject of love. A cymbal is a noisy percussion instrument which is without melody. Speaking in tongues, also called "glossolalia," is likewise without meaning. Similarly prophecy, understanding the mysteries, knowledge,[1] and faith to remove mountains, without charity, is of little value.

"Though I bestow [give away—R.S.V.] all my goods to feed the poor, and give my body to be burned, and have not charity, it profiteth me nothing" (v. 1-3). Giving generously to the poor is not charity unless it is also a manifestation of love.

## CHARITY IS THE GREATEST GIFT
(13:4-13)

Paul wrote the Galatian saints, "All the law is fulfilled in one word, even in this; Thou shalt love thy neighbor as

157

thyself" (5:14). To the Roman saints he wrote, "Love is the fulfilling of the law" (13:10). Mormon admonished the people to "cleave unto charity, which is the greatest [gift] of all. . . . Charity is the pure love of Christ" (Moroni 7:52).

In discussing the nature of charity Paul says: It suffereth long (patient), is kind, envieth not (is not jealous), vaunteth not itself (is not boastful), is not puffed up (arrogant). It is not rude, selfish, irritable, or resentful. Charity does not rejoice in wrong, but appreciates the right. It bears, believes, hopes, and endures all things. It never fails and never ends; but prophecies, tongues, and knowledge shall cease, "for we know in part, and we prophesy in part, but when that which is perfect is come, then that which is in part shall be done away" (v. 4-10).

These statements by Paul have been interpreted differently by various scholars. Perhaps the majority, guided by history, hold that as the church grew and became stable, the need for and function of prophecy and tongues ceased.[2] This was not what Paul was saying. He and the whole church were looking forward to the return of Christ to earth as the Redeemer and perfect Son of God. Only then should our partial knowledge and imperfect spiritual gifts "be done away." Then we shall see "face to face." Paul adds, "Now I know in part; but then shall I know even as also I am known. And now abideth faith, hope, charity, these three; but the greatest of these is charity" (v. 11-13).

## The Wise Use of the Gifts
(14:1-40)

Paul dispelled the notion that charity had or would make the exercise of the gifts of the Spirit unnecessary by writing, "Follow after charity and desire spiritual gifts, but rather that ye may prophesy" (v. 1). Then he reasons that speaking in another tongue only edifies the speaker and God, but prophecy edifies the church. However, if he interpret the tongue so the church receives edification, one gift is as important as the other (v. 2-6).

"If the trumpet [bugle—R.S.V.] give an uncertain sound, who shall prepare himself to the battle?" Paul used different illustrations, but all were designed to help the saints to understand that they should not speak in tongues by which the hearers would not be edified. "Wherefore let him that speaketh in another tongue pray that he may interpret." Paul had the gift of tongues "more than ye all" and knew what he was saying (v. 7-18).

It may seem paradoxical that such advice is necessary, since no one should presume to project "a tongue" as though it were a gift of the Spirit, except God had moved him to speak. And this being the case, why should he be discouraged by questions of doubt and heresy? Two things need to be recalled: "The spirits of the prophets are subject to the prophets" (v. 32), and it is Satan's business to throw confusion in the gatherings and to deceive the saints wherever possible. Jesus said that in our times "false Christs, and false prophets" should "deceive the very elect" (Matt. 24:23).

"Tongues are for a sign, not to them that believe, but to them that believe not; but prophesying serveth not for them that believe not, but for them which believe" (v. 22-25). Why the gift of tongues should be a better sign of divine recognition than prophecy may not be readily apparent to us, since both must be accompanied by spiritual power to be valid. However, to those who might not recognize God's confirming Spirit, not having any experience with it, the speaking in tongues, especially if the unbeliever was acquainted with the person through whom the gift came and knew he had no knowledge of the language used, would be more spectacular than prophecy.

"Let your women keep silence in the churches; for it is not permitted unto them to rule [to speak—R.S.V.]; but to be under obedience [subordinate—R.S.V.] as also saith the law" (v. 34; see also Col. 3:18; I Tim. 2:11, 12). This reflects the Old Testament attitude toward women, as well as the Christian view of priesthood specialization. Homelife with children is not fostered by women who carry many outside responsibilities. While they may be just as capable and just as spiritual as the men, the Lord has not seen fit to invite them to preside over congregations or to administer the sacraments.

"Covet to prophesy, and forbid not to speak with tongues. Let all things be done decently and in order" (v. 39, 40). This is Paul's concluding admonition concerning the spiritual gifts. This is valuable counsel. These two gifts are valuable to the guidance and uplift of the church, but the danger of counterfeiting must be recognized, for manifestations of false gifts can work havoc in a branch. "Let the prophets speak two or three, and let the other judge [weigh what is said—R.S.V.]. . . . For ye may all prophesy one by one, that all may learn, and all may be comforted" (v. 29, 31). Each may speak in turn, or "in order." God has seen fit for one to interpret a tongue given by another. But should the interpretation not be forthcoming, the congregation should pray for it to be given; otherwise it brings rank confusion and has no value. "God is not the author of confusion" (v. 33).

## THE RESURRECTION OF JESUS
(I Cor. 15:1-32)

"Keep in memory what I preached unto you . . . how that Christ died for our sins according to the Scriptures [Deut. 21:23; Isa. 53:5] . . . was buried, and that he rose again the third day" [Hosea 6:2] (v. 1-4). Then Paul arrays a battery of witnesses who saw Christ moving about following his resurrection. He was seen of Cephas (Peter), then of the twelve [eleven in many early manuscripts], over five hundred brethren at once, then by James, again by all the apostles, "and last of all he was seen by me also" (v. 5-8). Other writers mention also his appearance to the women at the tomb on Easter morning and to the two disciples on the road to Emmaus. In a reflective mood Paul says, "I am the least of the apostles, . . . because I persecuted the church of God . . . and his grace which was bestowed upon me was not in vain; for I labored more abundantly than they all" (v. 9, 10).

"How say some among you that there is no resurrection of the dead?" The Sadducees did not believe in a resurrection (Matt. 22:23). But if there is no resurrection, "If Christ be not risen, then is our preaching vain, and your faith is also vain. Yea, and we are found false witnesses" (v. 12-15). The consequences do not stop there: "Ye are yet in your sins" and those who sleep in Christ are perished. So Paul concludes, "If in this life only we have hope in Christ, we are of all men most miserable" (v. 16-19).

## What Are the Facts?

At this point Paul quits his philosophic discussion and quotes what he knows to be true.

But now is Christ risen from the dead, and become the first fruits of them that slept. . . . For as in Adam all die, even so in Christ shall all be made alive. But every man in his own order; Christ the first fruits; afterward they that are Christ's at his coming.—V. 20-23.

Following these events and Christ's having put down all earthly rule, authority, and power, Christ shall deliver up "the kingdom of God" (v. 24). But "he must reign, till he hath put all enemies under his feet. The last enemy, death, shall be destroyed; . . . then shall the Son also himself be subject unto him [God], that put all things under him, that God may be all in all" (25-28). The relating of these events by Paul was prophetic. But all of them support his argument for a general resurrection.

It seems that some in Corinth had been practicing baptism for ["on behalf of"—R.S.V.] the dead. So Paul turns this to his purpose by asking, "Else what shall they do [what do people mean—R.S.V.] who are baptized for the dead, if the dead rise not at all?" (v. 29). It must be noted that Paul is not endorsing nor acknowledging baptism for the dead as a gospel ordinance but using a reference to the practice of some in Corinth in a hypothetical question.

"I protest unto you the resurrection of the dead." Paul starts to affirm his faith once more in life after death. "Protest" has for its primary meaning "to witness before" an event, to "affirm." Thus the leaders of the Protestant movement in the sixteenth century were not *against,* but were making affirmation of their particular principles of faith and doctrine.

---

1. As the Gnostics claim for themselves.
2. "Paul looks forward with hope, and he bids the church in Corinth to do the same, to a day when like Moses—this would seem to be the thought in the background of his mind—we shall see God and speak with him face to face. . . . In the fullness of that vision and intercourse, perfection of knowledge will come and prophecy will cease."—*The Interpreter's Bible,* Vol. 10, p. 190.

## QUESTIONS FOR DISCUSSION

1. In what way does charity outrank all other gifts?
2. Explain the scripture which declares, "Love is the fulfilling of the Law."
3. Name six or more characteristics of charity.
4. When are prophecies and the gift of tongues to cease?
5. What is the primary purpose of speaking in tongues?
6. Would Paul be against women teaching classes and conducting worship services today? Defend your answer.
7. What reasons can you give for Paul's counsel, "Let all things be done decently and in order"?

8. Give reasons for the skepticism of many concerning Jesus' resurrection when they seemingly did not question the raising of Jairus' daughter, Dorcas, and Lazarus from the dead.

9. Name all the post-resurrection appearances of Jesus you can recall.

10. Discuss Paul's reference to baptism of the dead by proxy in Corinth. Is its practice today commanded?

# 25

# THE ORDER OF RESURRECTION; SOME PERSONAL MATTERS

(I Corinthians 15:35-16:24; Acts 20:1, 2;
II Corinthians 1:1-24)

The apostle Paul continued his "protest" or affirmation on the resurrection by saying that though he was willing to die by fighting beasts in the arena, he would not risk this "if the dead rise not" (v. 31, 32).

## NATURE OF THE RESURRECTED BODY

"But some man will say, How are the dead raised up? and with what body do they come?" He illustrates the answer by recalling the planting of a kernel of grain. It is not the same kernel which is reproduced, but one like it, "to every seed his own body." As there are different kinds of flesh, so also in the resurrection there will be different bodies: celestial, terrestrial, and telestial.

He shifts his illustration again by comparing the dwelling places of resurrected persons to the glory or brightness of the stars and planets, the sun, moon, and stars. "For one star differeth from another star in glory; so also is the resurrection of the dead. . . . It is sown a natural body, it is raised a spiritual body" (v. 35-44). Then he refers to the written word. The first man Adam was made a living soul (Gen. 2:8, 9); the last Adam was a quickening spirit (Eccles. 12:7; Heb. 1:14). To the Greek word for "man," *anthropos,* is added the Hebrew word "Adam." The historian, Philo, a contemporary of Paul,

drew the conclusion that in Genesis 1:26 we have the account of the creation of ideal man [spiritual], the Platonic archetype. This man was made in the image of God. When Genesis 2:7 tells of the forming of man out of the dust of the earth, it describes the creation of the empirical man, the one who sins.[1]

References here are to the Revised Standard Version. This is supported by the Inspired Version also. However, most scholars now say it is the fusing of the one creative act in two ancient accounts.

"As we have borne the image of the earthy, we shall also bear the image of the heavenly . . . [but] flesh and blood cannot inherit the kingdom of God" since these are corruptible (v. 45-50). Then Paul unveils a mystery of infinite dimensions:

We shall not all sleep [die], but we shall all be changed, in a moment . . . at the sound of the last trump; . . . and the dead shall be raised incorruptible. . . . Then shall be brought to pass the saying . . . , Death is swallowed up in victory. . . . The sting of death is sin; and the strength of sin is the law.—V. 51-56.

By reversing the poetic order of this last verse, we learn that sin imparts the poisonous sting of death. The extension of the code of law is the measure of the strength of the "sin which doth so easily beset us." Paul then gives the exultant cry of the conqueror, "But thanks be to God, which giveth us the victory through our Lord Jesus Christ." The enemy, death, has lost its power and the graves will be emptied by Him who first broke the bands of death. This being true, the apostle admonishes his brethren to be "steadfast, unmovable, always abounding in the work of the Lord . . . your labor is not in vain in the Lord" (v. 57, 58).

It is to be noted that Paul does not introduce any discussion here of the nature of the judgment. He sets forth the concept of eternal life in different degrees of glory or "dwelling places" (John 14:2, New English Bible). He makes it clear that the life beyond the grave is not a simple "go to heaven or failing that descend to hell."

## OFFERINGS FOR THE SAINTS AND TRAVEL PLANS (16:1-13)

The church in Jerusalem was going through some adverse times in A.D. 53-56. Paul believed that the church should practice the doctrine of loving its neighbor and set up a system for the churches which he had established in Galatia which he hoped the saints of Corinth would follow. "Upon the first day of the week let every one of you lay by him in store, as God hath prospered him, that there be no gatherings when I come" (v. 1, 2). This is the first mention by Luke or Paul of any meetings on Sunday, "the first day of the week." This gathering of funds was not the tithe or a fixed amount from each family. Each was asked to lay aside such amounts as he wished to contribute according as he had prospered.

"When I come, whomsoever ye shall approve by your letters" shall I send with the funds to Jerusalem. If it seemed expedient he would accompany them (v. 3, 4). He still planned to visit Corinth after a trip through Macedonia. He was considering spending the winter there. However, he expected to stay "at Ephesus until Pentecost. For a great door and effectual is opened unto me, but there are many adversaries" (v. 5-9). This trip corresponds with that mentioned in Acts 19:21 and 20:16. The work of the adversaries is also vividly described in Acts 19:23-41.

## SENDS OTHERS TO CORINTH
(I Cor. 16:8-18)

Paul wished to assure the Corinthian church of his concern by sending Timothy (Acts 19:22) to them, but since Timothy was to travel by land through Macedonia, Paul's letter would reach them first. He also recognized the uncertainties of the times as he said, "Now *if* Timotheus come, see that he may be with you without fear [put him at ease among you—R.S.V.]; for he worketh the work of the Lord, as I also do. Let no man . . . despise him" (v. 10, 11). The reason for uneasiness that Paul felt about Timothy's reception was not disclosed; however, Titus seems to have taken first place in subsequent events.

"As touching our brother Apollos, I greatly desired him to come unto you"; but he thought best to wait for a more convenient time. This cordial reference to Apollos shows that there was no schismatic discord between these men over leadership or doctrines.

"Watch ye, stand fast in the faith" (v. 13). This probably has the return of Christ in view. Paul solicits their goodwill for Stephanas and his family, and for others laboring in "ministry of the saints." The letter carries greetings for Aquila and Priscilla who labored effectually in Corinth before coming to Ephesus (Acts 18:18, 26). His greetings also include "the church that is in their house," showing that their home was open for worship services. In closing Paul mentions his writing a salutation "with mine own hand" as he did in his second Thessalonian letter (3:17). Doubtless he dictated the main part to others who wrote for him.

## PAUL GOES TO MACEDONIA
(Acts 20:1; II Cor. 1:1-29)

The history and chronology at this point are not clear. It seems that while Paul only intended to stay in Ephesus till

Pentecost, his plans were changed and his labors there extended. During this time Timothy is thought to have returned from Corinth with disappointing news about an open rebellion against the gospel and Paul's leadership, doubtless caused by Judaistic emissaries who came to Corinth (II Cor. 11:4). Profesor E. E. Stringfellow held that "Paul made a hurried and sorrowful trip to Corinth to win back the defectors without success."[2]

"After the uproar was ceased, Paul called unto him the disciples, and embraced them, and departed for . . . Macedonia" (Acts 20:1). The uproar in Ephesus was agitated by the silversmiths. Obviously Luke did not know much of this history or else wished to make his account brief so as to present other matters of more concern to him. All he records is that when Paul "had gone over those parts, and had given much exhortation, he came into Greece" (v. 2). It is certain that Paul wrote and sent his second Corinthian epistle before him. It is probable that it was written and sent in two parts: "The Thankful Letter," chapters 1-9; and the "Stern Letter," chapters 10-13.

There is no evidence of persistent rebellion and unrepentant immorality in chapters 1-9. Neither is there the slightest hint in chapters 10-13 that Paul is addressing only a minority; he speaks to the church of Corinth as a whole, and envisions a situation different from that described in chapters 1-9.[3]

## Greetings and Relations with the Church at Corinth
(II Cor. 1:1-24)

Paul's salutation carries greetings from Timothy also. He stresses their tribulations, but also acknowledges their comforts. He is conscious that the Corinthian saints have experienced these same conditions, "And our hope of you is steadfast, knowing, that as ye are partakers of the sufferings, so shall ye be also of the consolation." Paul then becomes more specific by saying that in Asia "We despaired even of life," but our trust was not in ourselves, "but in God which raiseth the dead" (v. 1-9). This reference is probably to that mentioned in I Corinthians 15:32, "I have fought with beasts at Ephesus."

Paul acknowledges the help of their prayers and the rejoicing of many at their delivery. Because of this protection and blessing, Paul reminds them, they could go into Macedonia, and on to Corinth, and eventually reach Judea (v. 10-16).

It seems that Paul's traducers had charged him with vacillating, that he was not reliable in his plans and statements. "But as God is true, our word toward you was not yea and nay . . . but . . . was yea. For all the promises of God in him are yea, and in him Amen" (v. 17-20). A promise is both serious and sacred to Paul. "Amen" has the significance of our phrase, "so let it be." "Moreover I call God for a record [to witness against me—R.S.V.] upon my soul, that to spare you I came not as yet unto Corinth."

Paul wanted to prepare them and himself for this visit, as he knew he might have to deal harshly with some who had continued in sin. "Not . . . that we have dominion over your faith, but are helpers of your joy; for by faith ye stand" (v. 23, 24). Christian faith cannot be forced, but is a free trust. Man's agency is God-given and must be respected.

---

1. *The Interpreter's Bible*, Vol. 10, page 247.
2. Stringfellow, *op. cit.*, p. 154; *The Interpreter's Bible*, Vol. 10, page 267.
3. *The Interpreter's Bible*, Vol. 10, p. 270.

## QUESTIONS FOR DISCUSSION

1. What kind of a material body do you believe will come forth from the grave in the resurrection?

2. When and how will the assignment of the immortal soul be made to one of the glories?

3. What do you understand is meant by "death shall be destroyed"? (I Cor. 15:26)

4. Explain this: "The sting of death is sin."

5. What significance do you see to the time that Paul set for putting their offerings in store?

6. What condition prevailed in Corinth which called for the sending of Timothy and for Paul's concern that he arrive and be received as a minister of Christ?

7. What special reason can you give for Paul's mention of Apollos in his letter?

8. Why did Paul say, "We even despaired of life"?

9. Why was the second Corinthian letter written so soon after the first one?

10. Why did the charge that Paul vacillated seem to need a defense?

# 26 PAUL'S DEFENSE AGAINST ENEMY CHARGES

## (II Corinthians 10:1 - 13:14)

While Paul was still in Ephesus he received some very disturbing reports from Corinth. (The Judaizers had not only won some converts to their idea that the Gentiles should obey the Mosaic law as a first step toward becoming Christians but had also attacked Paul personally and officially) The apostle's defense was prompt and vigorous. It is thought that he wrote his "stern letter" at this time in the summer of A.D. 55 or 56.[1] Much of this is contained in the last four chapters of Second Corinthians. As time passed it was added to the "thankful letter," but perhaps in a modified form.

We need not assume that the two letters were joined by accident; rather, it would seem that when the two letters were first prepared for use in the church at large, the section we call II Corinthians 10-13 was taken from the "stern letter" and added to the "thankful letter," in order to preserve its picture of Paul's apostolic ministry and leadership. Other parts, of more painful nature to the Corinthians, were omitted as of no direct value for other churches.[2]

Since this "stern letter" was written first and sent before his departure for Macedonia, it will be discussed first.

## Paul's Qualifications as a Minister
(II Cor. 10:1-18)

"Now I Paul myself beseech you by the meekness and gentleness of Christ, who in presence am base [humble— R.S.V.] among you, but being absent am bold toward you"; then he expresses the hope that he will not have to use boldness when he comes to them. He desires to use patience and moral appeal rather than harsh measures.

Paul warns them not to let any other person's claim to recognition obscure the real authority he had as the apostle to the Gentiles. "For though I should boast somewhat more of our authority, which the Lord hath given us for edification, and not for your destruction, I should not be ashamed" (v. 7, 8). He did not intend to be boastful as some may have accused him, but if it seemed that way his defense was that he had used his authority to edify and build, and not to destroy as his opponents had done.

They had said, "His letters . . . are weighty and powerful; but his bodily presence is weak, and his speech contemptible." Paul's answer was that he was consistent in his doctrine whether absent or present. Then he warned against those who "compare ourselves with some that commend themselves; but . . . [by] comparing [and measuring] themselves among themselves, are not wise." Paul assured them that he had stayed in his own field and not stretched "ourselves beyond our measure . . . for we are come as far as to you also in preaching the gospel of Christ." He had intentions of moving on beyond Greece, perhaps as far as Spain (Romans 15:23-26). "But he that glorieth, let him glory in the Lord" (v. 10-17).

## Beware of False Leaders
(11:1-33)

Paul begs the Corinthians to indulge him in what may seem folly. "I am jealous over you, with godly jealousy." I

172

have betrothed you to Christ and want to present you as a pure bride to her one husband. But he recalls that Eve was beguiled by the serpent through subtilty and feared lest "your minds should be corrupted from the simplicity that is in Christ." For you might be led to accept another Christ and another gospel than I presented. "I was not a whit behind the very chiefest apostles." He admitted that he might be rude in speech, but was not lacking in knowledge. He preached to them without charge, not wishing to be a burden to them, so he asks, "Have I committed an offence in abasing myself?" (v. 1-9).

## Love Calls for Sacrifices
(11:10-33)

If this be boasting, he would not stop, for it was because of his love for them. He intended to continue to support himself "that I may cut off occasion for them which desire" to be found just like us. "They boast of being apostles who are entitled to support; they demand and receive it. They want Paul to accept support too."[3] "For such are false apostles, deceitful workers, transforming themselves into the apostles of Christ" (v. 10-13). Don't marvel at this, for even Satan disguises himself as an angel of light.

"Let no man think me a fool," said Paul in apology for making this defense, but accept me for what I am. "I speak it not after the Lord," but in personal confidence, "seeing ye yourselves are wise." But you will suffer if any man enslaves you, or preys upon you, or takes advantage of you, puts on airs, or smites you on the face (v. 14-20). Then he refers to his traducers, "Are they Hebrews [Jews who spoke Aramaic]? so am I. Are they Israelites [covenant people]? so am I. Are they the seed of Abraham [heirs of the promise]? so am I. Are they ministers of Christ?" Here he indulges in foolish boasting to make his point. "So am I; in labors more abundant, in stripes above measure, in prisons more frequent, in deaths [near death—R.S.V.] oft." Then Paul becomes more specific by enumerating the times he was in peril. "Besides those things that are without, that which cometh upon me daily, the care of all the churches" (v. 21-28).

"Who is weak, and I am not weak? who is offended, and I anger not?" Paul is saying that he feels for and suffers with his people. As Jesus warned, "Whoso shall offend one of these little ones which believe in me, it were better for him that a millstone were hanged about his neck and he were drowned in the depth of the sea" (Matt. 18:5). His boasting is in the things which show what he endured. He concludes this part of his narrative by referring to his escape from the garrison in Damascus through a window in the wall, being lowered in a basket (v. 29-33).

## A THORN TO CHECK HIS PRIDE
(12:1 - 13:10)

Paul's "boasting" now turns from his sacrifices in giving ministry to his spiritual gifts, the visions and revelations of the Lord he had received. He modestly tells of some of his experiences indirectly: "I know a man in Christ who fourteen years ago was caught up to the third heaven" (v. 2—R.S.V.). There in paradise he heard words which were too sacred to utter. "Of such a one will I glory," yet since they were undeserved gifts and did not happen because of any human worth, it would be foolish for him to boast.

And lest I should be exalted above measure through the abundance of the revelations, there was given to me a thorn in the flesh, the messenger of Satan to buffet me. . . . For this thing I besought the Lord thrice, that it might depart from me. And he said unto me, My grace is sufficient for thee; for my strength is made perfect in weakness.—V. 4-9.

174

This is not only good scripture but it shows the humility and clear understanding of this great apostle. One may wonder why this apostle to whom Christianity owes so much for this detailed presentation of the gospel would have to bear such a cross of physical affliction. Many in our day who have done little in comparison to prove their loyalty and devotion to the gospel have been quick to question God's power and love when they have had to face physical and social adversities. Some scholars hold that Paul's "thorn in the flesh" was malaria; others that it was eye trouble. There is evidence of both. It is well for us to remember that the narrow road to heaven was a thorny way even for God's Son. There is redemptive power in patient suffering. (See Hebrews 12:11.)

Hence Paul could say, "I take pleasure in infirmities, in reproaches, in necessities, in persecutions, . . . for Christ's sake." He assured the Corinthians that he compared well with the chiefest apostles and said the true sign of an apostle was manifest in signs, wonders, and mighty deeds. "Behold, the third time I am ready to come to you; and I will not be burdensome to you; for I seek not yours, [material things] but you" (v. 11-14). His stern epistle closes by asking if Titus and "a brother" whom he sent did not follow his example.

I write to them which heretofore have sinned, and to all other, that if I come again, I will not spare; since ye seek a proof of Christ speaking in me . . . though he was crucified through weakness, yet he lived by the power of God. For we also are weak in him, but we shall live with him by the power of God toward you. Examine yourselves, whether ye be in the faith; prove your own selves.—13:1-5.

He prays that they be honest though we be as reprobates. For we can do nothing against the truth. He again reminds them of his purpose of presenting these things in writing that perchance he might not need to "use sharpness, according to the

175

power which the Lord hath given me to edification, and not to destruction" (v. 7-10).

1. Stringfellow, *op. cit.*, p. 154; *The Interpreter's Bible.* Vol. 10, p. 390.
2. *The Interpreter's Bible*, Vol. 10, p. 271.
3. *Ibid.*, Vol. 10, p. 397.

## QUESTIONS FOR DISCUSSION

1. What was the "stern letter" and why was it sent to Corinth before the "thankful letter"?
2. How did Paul's "boasting" differ from that of a modern braggart?
3. Why was Paul concerned about his standing as an apostle?
4. What is the significance of the comment, "His letters are weighty but his bodily presence is weak and his speech contemptible"?
5. How can we apply the counsel about comparing and measuring ourselves with others?
6. Why did Paul say so much about his policy of being a self-supporting minister?
7. What was the nature of Paul's perils and persecutions?
8. Why did Paul seek the Lord three times to remove "the thorn in the flesh" if it were given to keep from exultation?
9. Why do the righteous have to suffer while the wicked often prosper?
10. What did Paul say were "truly the signs of an apostle"?

# 27 PAUL'S RELATIONS WITH THE CHURCH IN CORINTH

(II Corinthians 1:1-5:21)

Paul started the "thankful letter" as usual by identifying himself as an apostle of Jesus Christ. He is joined in his salutation by "Timothy our brother." The letter is to be read aloud to the church at Corinth.[1] Paul expressed his gratefulness for God's deliverance, for while still in Asia (Ephesus may have been the locale, I Cor. 15:32), he was under "sentence of death." His purpose in writing this was not to arouse sympathy but to remind them that all Christians must bear some crosses and "the disciple is not above his master; nor the servant above his lord" (Matt. 10:21).

And our hope of you is steadfast, knowing, that as ye are partakers of the sufferings, so shall ye be also of the consolation . . . but we had the sentence of death in ourselves, that we should not trust in ourselves, but in God which raiseth the dead.—V. 7, 9.

Paul thanked the Corinthians for the help of their prayers.

## REASON FOR CHANGE IN TRAVEL PLANS
(II Cor. 1:12)

Paul assured the church at Corinth that his actions and letters were in good conscience, simplicity, and godly sincerity,

177

not of fleshly wisdom but by the grace of God (v. 12). "And in this confidence I was minded to come unto you before, that ye might have a second benefit" (a double pleasure—R.S.V.), that is, he would see them both on his way to Macedonia and on his way back from there toward Judea (v. 15, 16). "The shift of plans led to two charges: (a) he was vacillating; he was not serious and responsible in statements and plans. (b) He planned according to the flesh."[2] "But as God is true, our word toward you was not yea and nay . . . but in him was yea" (v. 18, 19). He explains his change was to spare them: "I would not come again to you in heaviness" (v. 23:2:1).[3] So he wrote to them his "stern letter" instead (v. 3, 4).

Paul mentioned the offender who had been chastened and he freely forgave him. This ringleader had in some measure brought pain and damage to the church and thus was "inflicted of many. . . . I beseech you that ye would confirm your love toward him" (v. 6, 8).

While the decision concerning the offender was for the church at Corinth to make, Paul urged that he be forgiven, "lest Satan should get an advantage of us" by capturing the erring brother's loyalty by his crafty devices (v. 11).

## APOSTOLIC MINISTRY AND THE NEW COVENANT (II Cor. 2:12-3:6)

At this point in his writing, Paul had left Ephesus and had come to Troas on his way north to Macedonia. This was according to his original travel plans. Titus was to travel north from Corinth, east through Macedonia, and then south to Troas which was on the tip of Asia where he was to meet Paul.[4] Titus failed to arrive. This worried Paul, but he found "a door opened unto me of the Lord" in Troas, which made his waiting there profitable. Thus he moved on to Macedonia.

"Now thanks be unto God, which always causeth us to triumph in Christ" (v. 14). This rejoicing is due to his meeting with Titus and to receiving some good news (mentioned in 7:5-13). "For we are unto God a sweet savor of Christ, in them that are saved, and in them that perish" (v. 15). The gospel brings a sweet fragrance even to those who are dying. The love and justice of God will reach all and give comfort even to the perishing.

"For we are not as many, which corrupt [peddlers of— R.S.V.] the word of God" (v. 17). Paul is telling the Corinthians that true apostles are sufficient because of God's favor and the words of Christ. However, the false apostles who have sought personal advantage and profit are only hucksters who adulterate God's word.

"Ye are our epistle written in our hearts, known and read of all men" (3:2). There is a suggestion in verse one that "the false apostles" had brought with them "epistles of commendation." Paul's epistles are "written not with ink, but with the Spirit of the living God . . . in fleshly tables of the heart" (v. 3). Lest they think he is boasting, Paul adds, "Not that we are sufficient of ourselves . . . but . . . of God; who also hath made us able ministers of the new testament [covenant—R.S.V.]; . . . for the letter killeth, but the Spirit giveth life" (v. 5, 6).

## Gospel's Superiority to the Mosaic Law (3:7-18)

Paul reverts to his old theme at this point: "the law . . . made nothing perfect." He refers to the Ten Commandments as "the ministration of death . . . engraven in stones." While the glory of that dispensation was such that the children of Israel could not look steadfastly upon the face of Moses after he had been with God on Mount Sinai, "much more that which remaineth [in the gospel] is glorious" (v. 7, 12).

It was necessary for Moses to put a veil over his face because "their minds were blinded" and are still the same, in the reading of the Old Testament, "which veil is done away in Christ . . . when their heart shall turn to the Lord" (v. 13-16).

"Now the Lord is that Spirit; and where the Spirit of the Lord is, there is liberty [freedom—R.S.V.]" (v. 17). The "Lord" here refers to the risen Christ "who now has a 'spiritual body' and has become 'a life-giving spirit' (I Cor. 15:44-45), he and the Spirit are one in nature and share in the active guidance of the Church."[5]

Paul now returns to his illustration taken from Exodus 34:29-35 of the glory on Moses' face as he came from Mount Sinai. The people were afraid to come near him till he covered his face with a veil. "But we all, with open face beholding as in a glass [mirror] the glory of the Lord, are changed into the same image" (v. 18). The Spirit of the Lord works on his children to transform them from glory to glory.

## GOSPEL EXPERIENCES RECOUNTED
(4:1)

A minister for Christ must carry his own cross, but by God's mercy he will not faint. In listing the trials one must face, Paul mentioned the renouncing of the hidden things of dishonesty and craftiness in "handling the word of God deceitfully." "But if our gospel be hid [veiled—R.S.V.], it is hid to them that are lost," who have let the god of worldliness blind their minds to "the glorious gospel of Christ" (v. 1-4).

"We preach not ourselves but Christ Jesus the Lord; and ourselves your servants" because of "the light of the knowledge" given us. "But we have this treasure in earthen vessels that the excellency of the power may be of God, and not of us" (v. 5-7). Paul here suggests human frailty and man's origin from "dust of the ground" (Gen. 2:8). He then cites

180

four contrasts: troubled, yet not distressed; perplexed, but not in despair; persecuted, but not forsaken; cast down, but not destroyed. This is "for Jesus' sake that the life also of Jesus might be made manifest in our mortal flesh" (v. 8-11).

All these things can be endured because

He which raised up the Lord Jesus shall raise up us also by Jesus, and shall present us with you. . . . But though our outward man perish, yet the inward man is renewed day by day. . . . The things which are seen are temporal; but the things which are not seen are eternal.—V. 12-18.

## AN ETERNAL HOME WITH THE LORD (5:1-21)

Without a shadow of doubt, Paul assured the Corinthian saints, "We know that, if our earthly house . . . were dissolved, we have a building of God, a house not made with hands, eternal in the heavens. . . . For we that are in this tabernacle do groan, being burdened" (v. 1-4). Yet this serves a good purpose, "knowing that, whilst we are at home in the body, we are absent from the Lord," and will in the end work out a greater glory. This is guaranteed by the fact that God "hath given unto us the earnest[6] of the Spirit" (v. 5-6).

## A MINISTRY OF RECONCILIATION

Paul concludes his affirmation:

Wherefore we labor, that, whether present or absent, we may be accepted of him . . . [at] the judgment-seat of Christ, that every one may receive a reward of the deeds done in the body . . . whether good or bad. Knowing the terror [fear—R.S.V.] of the Lord, we persuade men . . . and I trust also are made manifest in your consciences.—V. 9-11.

"We commend not ourselves again unto you." The "again" perhaps refers to some previous experiences, such as his conversion (Acts 9:3-9), his "visions and revelations"

(II Cor. 12:1-4), and his speaking in tongues (I Cor. 14:18). But he went on to explain that "whether we glory, it is to God, or whether we be sober [serious or sad], it is for your sakes."

Then under constraint of the Spirit, Paul assures the saints that if Christ "died for all, then are all dead. . . . Wherefore, henceforth live we no more after the flesh . . . but unto him which died . . . and rose again" (v. 12-16).

"If any man live in Christ, he is a new creature; old things are passed away; behold, all things are become new." Such new creatures identify themselves with Christ, for "God is in Christ, reconciling the world unto himself, not imputing their trespasses unto them; and hath committed unto us the word of reconciliation" (v. 17-19). This indicates that men are not held accountable for Adam's sin, and all who come to him are accepted on the same terms (Matt. 11:29; Acts 17:29). As ambassadors for Christ, "we pray you in Christ's stead, be ye reconciled to God" (v. 20, 21).

---

1. *The Interpreter's Bible,* Vol. 10, page 277.
2. *Ibid.,* Vol. 10, p. 287.
3. *Ibid.,* Vol. 10, p. 293.
4. *Ibid.,* p. 297.
5. *Ibid.,* p. 311.
6. Earnest is "money paid in advance to bind a bargain."—*Standard Universal Dictionary.*

## QUESTIONS FOR DISCUSSION

1. What was the "thankful letter" mentioned in the opening of this chapter?
2. In what way was Paul under a "sentence of death"?
3. What was the basis of the charge that Paul was vacillating and irresponsible?
4. What reason did Paul give for the saints to forgive the troublemaker, and what did he mean?
5. Tell about Titus' movements and what he reported.

6. Who were the false apostles and with what evil in Corinth were they charged?
7. In what ways did Paul refer to the Ten Commandments or to the old law?
8. How did Paul use the illustration of the veil over Moses' face? What comparison can be made with our relation to Christ today?
9. What was Paul's purpose in recounting his trials? What significance has this testimony for us?
10. What made Paul so sure of a resurrected life with Christ? Is his assurance sufficient for you?

# 28 PAUL TRIES TO RESTORE CONFIDENCE

(II Corinthians 6:1 - 9:15)

The last chapter closed with a discussion of the ministry of reconciliation and of the hope of immortality. Because Christ took upon him our sins and died for us, we should endeavor to attain the "righteousness of God in him."

## WORKERS WITH CHRIST
(6:1-13)

Now Paul exhorts his brethren in Greece to a faithful ministry "as workers together with Chirst . . . that ye receive not the grace of God in vain" (v. 1). In the language of Isaiah (49:8), he stressed that there was an acceptable time for each to work "in a day of salvation." For them that time was now, "in all things approving ourselves as the ministers of God, in much patience, in afflictions, in necessities." To this counsel he adds a list of things from his own experiences of ministry (v. 2-4).

It may seem that there are some contradictions when he says to work "by honor and dishonor; by evil report and good report, as deceivers, and yet true; as unknown, and yet well known; as dying, and, behold, we live" (v. 8, 9). In these paradoxes Paul tells us that regardless of the conditions under

184

which one labors, good or adverse, we can win by patience, faith, and diligence.

Then in a direct appeal, Paul said, "O ye Corinthians, our mouth is open unto you, our heart is enlarged" (v. 11). Perhaps this expression came from the fact that he was dictating the epistle, and he wanted them to know of his affection for them regardless of past misunderstandings. He declared in archaic language, "Ye are not straitened in us, but ye are straitened in your own bowels" (v. 12). Perhaps by reading the Revised Standard Version you may catch his thought better, "You are not restricted by us, but you are restricted in your own affections." Whatever of cramping coldness there might be between them, he said, was not due to his attitude. On another occasion Paul asked the brethren to "put on . . . bowels of mercies" (Col. 3:12).

## Avoid Worldly Alliances
(6:14 - 7:10)

"Be ye not unequally yoked together with unbelievers" is counsel against mismated marriages, but also against any corrupting associations with the world. "What concord hath Christ with Belial, or what part hath he that believeth with an infidel?" (v. 14, 15). "Belial" is a synonym for Satan. "Wherefore come out from among them, and be ye the separate, saith the Lord, and touch not the unclean thing; and I will receive you, and will be a Father unto you" (v. 14-18).

In Chapter 16 mention was made of the phrase "Live like a Corinthian." As it was used in Paul's day, immorality was rampant and the apostle warned against the danger of the saints there being infected. "Let us cleanse ourselves from all filthiness of the flesh and spirit" (7:1). Then reverting to personal relations, he pled, "Receive us [open your hearts to us—R.S.V.]; we have wronged no man. . . . I speak not this to condemn you; for . . . ye are in our hearts to die and live with you" (7:2, 3).

# Rejoice over the Changes in Corinth
(7:4-16)

Paul then referred to the comfort he received through the report that Titus brought from them. His troubles and fears which had robbed his flesh of rest as he came into Macedonia were now gone and the views of their deep concern for him had replaced them with consolation. He was no longer worried or sorry for sending his "stern letter," even though it may have made them sorry "for a season." "Now I rejoice . . . for godly sorrow worketh repentance to salvation" (v. 5-10).

The apostle lists the conditions and changes which had been made as a result of their godly sorrow: carefulness, eagerness to clear yourselves, indignation, alarm, zeal, revenge ["punishment"—R.S.V.]. Thus they stood approved in the matter. But his main purpose was not to redeem the evildoer but to show his love and concern for the saints there (v. 11, 12). "Therefore we were comforted, . . . and exceedingly the more . . . for the joy of Titus" (v. 13). His confidence in Titus might have appeared to be boasting, but the results confirmed the truth of all he had said. "He remembereth the obedience of you all, how with fear and trembling ye received him."

# Help for Needy Saints in Jerusalem
(8:1 - 9:15)

Paul next turns to the fund-gathering for the poor in Jerusalem. He mentioned first the poverty and afflictions of the churches in Macedonia, yet they had done well and he rejoiced in their expression of liberality. "Beyond their power they were willing of themselves" to give of their means. "This they did, not as we required, but first gave their own selves to the Lord" (v. 1-5).

The narration of Macedonian generosity was a challenge

to Corinth. Now he proposed to send Titus back to them to complete this work of grace which had begun about a year before. "I speak not by commandment," but to test the "sincerity of your love." Paul then reminded them of the love and sacrifice of Christ, who, "though he was rich, yet for your sakes he became poor." He urged them to complete the collection as a demonstration of their willingness and love. The amount given is second in importance to their manifest devotion. They are asked to give "according to that a man hath." The principle is that of faithful stewardship: "From each according to his ability." It is not a gospel principle that one should be burdened so that another be eased. Stewardship seeks an equality by the consecration of one's abundance to supply another's want. There is no hint of an "all things in common" in Paul's teachings, though it is permissible for this communal arrangement in a group stewardship to be voluntarily carried out (v. 6-15).

## Trusted Leaders Will Come to Corinth
### (8:16 - 9:15)

Paul thanked God that Titus shared his concern for them and shared his views. While Titus accepted Paul's exhortation, he came to them of his own accord. Now he wanted to return in that spirit and he comes with the goodwill of the churches, having been appointed by them. With him Paul is sending two brethren[1] "whom we have proved diligent in many things." Paul is doubtless sending the epistle by them and asks the Corinthian saints to receive them. Titus was given the chief position among the three, as Paul referred to him as "my partner and fellow-laborer" (v. 16-24).

The generosity and willingness of the saints in Achaia (Greece) and in Macedonia have been evidenced, but the fact that Paul labored the point showed that he still is not sure. He is taking nothing for granted even though his letter expressed confidence in the church at Corinth. "I have sent the brethren" is said in anticipation. The Revised Standard Version reads "I am sending" (9:1-5). Paul is to follow soon, and if he finds them unprepared, his boasting to the Macedonians of their readiness to give will be embarrassing. So he reminds them that "he which soweth sparingly shall reap also sparingly. . . . Every man according as he purposeth in his heart, so let him give; not grudgingly, or of necessity; for God loveth a cheerful giver" (v. 6, 7). Lest their fear of coming to want later by giving now hold back their generosity, Paul assures them that "God is able to make all grace abound toward you; that ye, always having all sufficiency in all things, may abound to every good work." He supports this with a quotation from Psalm 112:9, which in effect says, "As a man soweth, so also shall he reap" (v. 8-11).

His "thankful letter" is drawn to a close by affirming that their giving will serve a dual purpose: (1) It will help to supply the necessities of the destitute saints in Jerusalem, and also (2) their generous giving will overflow in thanksgivings offered to God. Giving of our tithes and offerings is love in action. Christianity does not come naturally, nor by one or two emotional experiences. It is a way of living and needs to be built into our daily thoughts and deeds. The younger one begins, the easier it becomes to build a stable Zionic character. Paul is therefore moved to pray for the "exceeding grace of God in you." Then he closes by thanking God for "his unspeakable gift" (v. 12-15). The gift he had in mind could have been the bringing together of diverse groups and nations through love and goodwill in Christ Jesus. He might well have had in mind all the rich benefits God bestows in the gospel of the kingdom. Perhaps it is much of both.

Weaker men despair of the perverseness of human nature and its constant resistance to the demands of righteousness. Paul would never quit. He had seen the vision of a redeemed man. He bore the marks of opposition in his flesh as a badge of honor that he could suffer gracefully even as his Lord. "I know whom I have believed, and am persuaded that he is able

188

to keep that which I have committed unto him" (II Tim. 1:12). To commit ourselves, our wealth, our destiny to Him in such confidence is a satisfaction which comes at a price. Each one must decide whether he wants to buy it, or risk eternal life without it.

---

1. *The Interpreter's Bible*, Vol. 10, p. 371.

## QUESTIONS FOR DISCUSSION

1. In what sense is there "an acceptable time" for man's salvation?
2. What is meant by "Be ye not unequally yoked together with unbelievers"? How many ways can this be done?
3. Discuss the phrase, "Live like a Corinthian."
4. What is "godly sorrow" and what does it do?
5. In what way did Paul mean that in his letter his purpose was not to redeem the evildoer?
6. Why did Paul compare the fund-raising zeal of the Macedonian churches with that at Corinth?
7. How can the publication of the rating of stakes and districts in their contributions in the *Herald* be justified?
8. Why did Paul stress the fund-raising in Corinth so much if he felt sure of their generosity?
9. What inferences can be drawn from this epistle about having "all things common"? (See Acts 2, 44; III Nephi 12:11.)
10. What reason can be given for Paul's sending Titus and the brethren ahead of him to collect the offerings of the saints in Corinth?

# 29 PAUL PREPARES TO GO TO JERUSALEM

(Winter, A.D. 56-57, Acts 20:1 - 21:16)

## INTERVENING HISTORY

In Chapter 19 it was noted that the apostle to the Gentiles was forced to quit his mission work in Ephesus due largely to the uprising of the silversmiths (Acts 19:21-29). However, word had come to him from Corinth that there was a division in the church there, and as Paul's plan called for another visit to Macedonia on his way to Greece (Achaia), he decided to write a letter to the members.

He stressed the oneness of the church in Christ, that the gospel was above human wisdom, that sainthood required high moral standards, and that our bodies are the temples of the Holy Spirit. He also discussed marriage and celibacy. The need for renunciation and self-discipline, the sacrament of the Lord's Supper, women's place in the church, gifts of the Spirit, resurrection of the dead, and the resurrected state.

After this letter known as First Corinthians was sent, perhaps by Timothy, word came back that the Judaizers had been there, casting doubt on Paul's apostleship, and many in the church were in open rebellion. It is probable that Paul made a hurried trip to Corinth, but had little success in winning back the defectors. Shortly after this and before starting for Macedonia, he wrote two or more epistles which were later edited and put together in what we call Second Corinthians. In this he defended his ministry and apostleship, warned against false leaders, spoke of his sacrifices and physical handicaps, his manner of giving ministry, the office work of the Spirit, faithfulness in tribulation, the effects of godly sorrow, and the virtue of aid to the needy.

## Back to Luke's Account in Acts 20

Luke's narrative takes up the account with Paul leaving Ephesus for Macedonia and moving on to Greece where he abode three months. Luke gave none of the details of this long and arduous trip which was mostly on foot. When Paul had gone over those parts and given them much exhortation, he came into Greece (Acts 20:2). This covers considerable history and geography. Doubtless he ministered to the churches in Philippi, Apollonia, Thessalonica, and Berea. He may have ministered at Illyricum (Rom. 15:19) on this tour.

While in Greece, most likely at Corinth, Paul wrote his epistle to the Romans. This will be considered later since it has little historical significance at this point.

## They Start for Jerusalem
(Acts 20:3-16)

Paul was about to start his journey to Jerusalem with the relief funds when he learned "the Jews laid wait for him" (v. 3). There may have been a plot to murder him on the high seas since he was "to sail into Syria." He went instead into Macedonia where he was joined by seven disciples representing the nations where the churches had contributed funds. Luke names Sopater, Aristarchus, Secundus, Gaius, Timotheous, Tychicus, and Trophimus. "These going before tarried for us at Troas. And we sailed away from Philippi after the days of unleaven bread" (v. 4, 5). The seven days immediately following the Passover are meant (Exodus 23:15; 34:18).

The "us" and "we" passages begin again at verse 5, indicating that Luke had joined Paul once more. "And we sailed away from Philippi . . . and came unto them to Troas in five days; where we abode seven days. And upon the first day of the week, when the disciples came together to break bread, Paul preached" (v. 6, 7). A characteristic of Dr. Luke's writing is his preciseness. It was "seven days," not about a week. The fact that Sunday was the day of worship and not Saturday, the Jewish Sabbath, is made clear.

A miracle was performed here at Troas under strange conditions. A "young man named Eutychus" went to sleep in a window of an upper chamber and "as Paul was long preaching . . . fell down from the third loft [story—R.S.V.], and was taken up dead. And Paul went down, and fell on him, and embracing him said, Trouble not yourselves, for his life is in him" (v. 8-10).

Inspired by this miracle, Paul continued preaching "till break of day, so he departed." They "sailed unto Assos" a coastal town twenty miles to the south in Lydia. The ship would have to sail around the Lectrum promontory and would take a long time, so Paul chose to go by land "afoot." He boarded the ship at Assos and sailed with his companions thirty miles south to Mitylene, the chief city on the island of Lesbos, heading for Ephesus and Jerusalem. He was desirous to get there before the Day of Pentecost (v. 11-16).

## Warned of Personal Danger
(20:17-38)

When the ship touched Miletus, Paul sent a messenger to call the elders of Ephesus to come there so he might talk to them. His purpose was to warn them against false teachers who threatened him in Corinth. This was a journey of thirty miles to the south of Ephesus. Paul doubtless was averse to

192

visiting Ephesus where his work had stirred up so much hostility.

Now . . . I go bound in the spirit unto Jerusalem, not knowing the things that shall befall me there; save that the Holy Ghost witnesseth in every city, saying that bonds and afflictions abide me. But none of these things move me. . . . I know that ye all, among whom I have gone preaching the kingdom of God, shall see my face no more.—V. 17-25.

Paul's knowledge did not cause him to avoid this danger; he was anxious to complete his mission and deliver the funds entrusted to him. His consolation was, "I have not shunned to declare unto you all the counsel of God" (v. 27). He had a concern for the work in Ephesus and exhorts the elders,

Take heed therefore unto yourselves, and to all the flock, over the which the Holy Ghost hath made you overseers . . . for I know this, that after my departing shall grievous wolves enter in among you, not sparing the flock. Also of your own selves shall men arise, speaking perverse things, to draw away disciples after them.—V. 28-30.

This prophecy of an apostasy recorded here by Luke is also in Paul's epistles. (See II Thess. 2:1-4; I Tim. 1:3-7; 6:20, 21; Jude 17-23; II Pet. 3:16, 17.) Paul then commends the elders to God "and to the word of his grace, which is able to build you up, and to give you an inheritance among all them which are sanctified." He reminds them in parting that he did not covet their money, but worked for his needs and so should they labor to sustain the weak, for "it is more blessed to give than to receive" (v. 32-35). Paul then prayed for them and, after a tearful farewell, he went aboard the ship.

## THE FINAL JOURNEY TO JERUSALEM
(Acts 21:1-16)

With careful detail Luke told of each stop on the journey from Miletus toward church headquarters, from Coos to Rhodes to Patara. Here they changed boats and took one sailing to Phoenicia, a distance of 350 miles. Luke's mention of coming in sight of the island of Cyprus brings out the fact that the longer route on the lee side to the north and east, usually taken, was avoided. Evidently the weather was more favorable than usual, so they put in at Tyre in Syria. "And finding disciples, we tarried there seven days" (v. 1-4). There is no record of a church having been founded in Tyre, but Paul evidently knew that there were disciples there and sought them out. The favorable weather and shortened journey enabled Paul's party to move more leisurely and still reach Jerusalem by Pentecost. A prophet in Tyre spoke "to Paul through the Spirit that he should not go up to Jerusalem." For some unexplained reason, Paul ignores the warning. It is presumed that he doubted its inspiration.

At the time for the ship's departure, the brethren with their families left the city to bid Paul and his party farewell. "And we kneeled down on the shore, and prayed." The next port was Ptolemais where they had a day to salute the brethren, and from there they sailed on to Caesarea where they were cared for in the home of "Philip the evangelist which was one of the seven" (Acts 6:3; 8:5, 40). He had four daughters "which did prophesy." After a few days the prophet Agabus (Acts 11:28)

came down from Judea. . . . He took Paul's girdle, and bound his own hands and feet, and said, Thus saith the Holy Ghost, so shall the Jews at Jerusalem bind the man that owneth this girdle, and shall deliver him into the hands of the Gentiles.

Both Paul's companions and the saints of Caesarea then pled with Paul that he change his destination, but the apostle was not to be dissuaded, "for I am ready not to be bound only, but also to die at Jerusalem for the name of the Lord Jesus." The group responded, "The will of the Lord be done" (v. 5-14).

The expression "we took up our carriages" is perhaps better translated in the American Standard Version as "our baggage." Certain disciples from Caesarea "[went with us

194

bringing us to the house of—R.S.V.] and Mnason of Cyprus, an old disciple, with whom we should lodge" went to Jerusalem with them (v. 15, 16). Thus the long and arduous journey for Paul and his companions ended without any untoward event, but with warnings and some misgivings on the part of the disciples.

At this point we shall break into Luke's narrative in Acts and present Paul's epistle to the Romans which was written from Corinth just before he started the long trek with the funds for the needy saints in Jerusalem.

## QUESTIONS FOR DISCUSSION

1. Why was this part of Luke's account (20:2) so fragmentary?
2. Why did Paul stay three months in Corinth?
3. What caused Paul to change his plans "to sail into Syria"?
4. Why did Paul take at least seven with him on his final journey to Jerusalem?
5. Tell of the conditions of Paul's preaching in Troas. Was Eutychus really dead or just unconscious?
6. What prophecy did Paul give to the Ephesians at Miletus, and how did the elders react?
7. When did the apostasy revealed here by the Holy Spirit actually occur and in what manner?
8. For what reason was Cyprus, which has been a world trouble spot recently, mentioned by Luke?
9. Who was Philip and how did he enter into Luke's account of this journey?
10. What was the prophecy given by Agabus and how did Paul respond to it?

# 30

# THE GOSPEL SPREADS TO ROME

(A.D. 57 or 58, Romans 1:1 - 3:20)

## INTRODUCTION

The epistle to the Roman saints is called the "longest letter of Paul which has survived . . . also the weightiest" and "comes nearer to being a systematic and inclusive statement of Paul's faith. It is thus the principal source book for the study of Paul's gospel, and in consequence it is unquestionably the most important theological book ever written."[1]

The reason Paul gave for writing the book is that he felt his work in Asia Minor and Greece was done and he wanted to push on to the west as a pioneer missionary rather than to "build upon another man's foundation" (Rom. 18:15; 15:19-28). He was an evangelist, and pastoral work burdened his spirit (II Cor. 11:27, 28). His letter was to prepare them for his visit. It was written in the home of Gaius, one of the few whom Paul baptized at Corinth (16:23; I Cor. 1:14).

The epistle has a typical Pauline salutation. He emphasized his calling as an apostle and stressed that his call was received from Jesus Christ. He had received his commission to preach to the Gentile world as a command from heaven (Acts 22:21). Besides his divine call, he emphasized that the gospel he preached had been promised by the prophets of old. He was presenting Jesus as God's Son, "the seed of David according to the flesh" (v. 1-6).

"I write to all who are in Rome, beloved of God [called to be saints—R.S.V.]" (v. 7). Note the future tense. All of us are "called to be," but are only saints in the making. Likewise all of us who have accepted the gospel by obedience to the initiatory principles anticipate salvation in celestial glory. But only "he that endureth to the end shall be saved" (Matt. 10:19; Phil. 2:12).

"I make mention of you always in my prayers, that you may be kept through the Spirit, in the gospel. . . . For I long to see you, that I may impart unto you some spiritual gift" (v. 9-11). Since Paul made no claim of ever having been in Rome, one wonders about his prayerful concern. We are sure that he knew Aquila and Priscilla whom he met in Corinth during the persecution of Emperor Claudius (Acts 18:2, 18). They went with him to Ephesus, but later returned to Rome (16:3). Twenty-six persons are named by Paul in the Roman epistle. How he made their acquaintance is not revealed.

## THE UNIVERSAL NEED OF THE GOSPEL
(1:16-32)

Oftentimes I purposed to come unto you (but was hindered hitherto,) that I might have some fruit among you also, even as among other Gentiles. . . . I am ready to preach the gospel to you that are at Rome also. For I am not ashamed of the gospel of Christ; for it is the power of God unto salvation to every one that believeth. . . . For therein is the righteousness of God revealed through faith.—V. 13-17.

This last sentence is called "the theme" of the Roman epistle. The Greek word *dynamis*, translated "power," is used throughout the New Testament to designate a miracle, a mighty work of God. From it comes our word "dynamic" and "dynamite."

"For the wrath of God is revealed from heaven against all ungodliness and unrighteousness of men; who love not the truth, but remain in unrighteousness." God is here pictured as angry with the sin and not the sinner. This declaration is followed by reminding the Romans that throughout the ages God has manifested himself "through his eternal power and Godhead; so that they are without excuse" (v. 18-20). Yet although they knew God they neither honored nor gave him thanks. "Professing themselves to be wise, they became fools." They worshiped idols (images) and animals. "Wherefore God also gave them up to uncleanness, through the lusts of their own hearts" (v. 21-24). This is supported by James, "Man is tempted, when he is drawn away of *his own* lust, and enticed" (Jas. 1:14).

Paul then indicates the nature of their sins: changed the truth into a lie, worshiped and served the creature more than the Creator. Both women and men practiced homosexual acts. Therefore God gave them over to a reprobate mind "and to improper conduct" (R.S.V.). To the sensual sins Paul adds many antisocial activities such as covetousness, envy, deceit, backbiting, boasting, disobedience to parents, and even murder. As a climax he charges that some who knew the "judgment of God . . . which commit such things are worthy of death." Yet instead of remorse in their practice they "have pleasure in them that do them" (v. 25-32).

## THE JEWS ALSO IN NEED OF SALVATION (2:1 - 3:20)

While Paul had in mind particularly the pagans or Gentiles, he now reaches out to others. "Thou art inexcusable, O man, whosoever thou art that thus judgest another . . . for thou . . . doest the same things." God's judgment is not based on race or nationality but on moral facts. The tendency to convince oneself that because no calamity has yet befallen him for his transgressions therefore none will is fatal. "There is

198

a way which seemeth right unto a man; but the end thereof are the ways of death" (Prov. 14:12) has been learned too late by many, for God "will render to every man according to his deeds; to them who by patient continuance in well doing seek for glory and honor and immortality, eternal life" (v. 1-7).

Some say that Paul has a conflict in his theology by affirming the reward of eternal life on the basis of one's deeds or works while having previously declared that "the just shall live by faith" (1:17). But in all his epistles, Paul makes clear that faith leads to works of righteousness. Any other kind of faith is dead (Titus 1:16; 3:8; Jas. 2:17). Works of the law of Moses have lost their value by the bringing in of a better hope through the gospel of Christ (Gal. 2:16; 3:21-25; Heb. 7:19).

"Tribulation and anguish" shall be visited upon "the Jew first" because of sinning against a greater light. But it shall come "also to the Gentile" that "doeth evil" for "there is no respect of persons with God" (v. 8-11). This was confirmed in the vision given to Peter in Caesarea (Acts 10:34). Men will be judged by the law under which they live. "Not the hearers of the law are just before God, but the doers of the law" (v. 12, 13).

Even though the Gentiles did not have the law and followed their own natures, that law was written on their hearts and consciences accusing or excusing them. But the Jew is without excuse who rests in ["rely upon"—R.S.V.] the law, and boasts of his relation to God, acting as "a guide of the blind, a light of them which are in darkness, an instructor of the foolish, a teacher of babes." They did not do the things which they taught and thus dishonored and blasphemed God. "He is not a Jew," wrote Paul, "which is one outwardly. . . . Circumcision is that of the heart, in the spirit, and not in the letter" (v. 14-29).

# Is There Any Virtue in Being a Jew?
(3:1-20)

There is an advantage in being of the house of Israel, for to them "were committed the oracles of God." While some disbelieved, this did not "make the faith of God without effect. . . . Let God be true, but [though—R.S.V.] every man a liar" (v. 1-4). The covenant of blessing was broken by the Jews but not by God. "Blindness in part is happened to Israel" (11:25), and they are no better off than the Gentiles; "Jews and Gentiles are all under sin" (Rom. 3:1-9). Verses 10-18 are selected passages from Psalms and Isaiah which support Paul's criticism.

"Now we know that what things soever the law saith, it saith to them that are under the law; that every mouth may be stopped, and all the world may become guilty before God." Since the Old Testament carried divine authority to the Jews, their protests were most likely to be silenced—every mouth is stopped. These scriptures ought to have created a conviction of guilt, and consequently should have awakened the sense of an impending judgment.

It may seem to us that Paul overdoes the point of justification through faith in Christ. However, two things of great significance enter into his treatment. First, he was under attack by the Jews who felt that only by obedience to the Mosaic ordinances could there be a proper foundation for Christianity. Second, there were disciples then, as now, who affirmed that faith was basically lip service—"by grace are ye saved." They were unwilling to subject themselves to moral and social disciplines.

"For by the law is the knowledge of sin; therefore by the deeds of the law shall no flesh be justified in his sight" (v. 20). Paul concludes this discussion on giving judgment by declaring that the purpose of the Mosaic law is to make men aware of the nature of sin. John wrote, "Sin is the transgression of the law" (I John 3:4). The Jews held that behind the code

200

was the divine presence. Likewise a new covenant has been given in latter days. In it the duty of the Saint is made clear. Ignorance of the law may dull one's conscience, but men will be held responsible for the opportunity of knowing. Jesus said, "This is life eternal, that they might know thee the only true God, and Jesus Christ, whom thou hast sent" (John 17:3). Many other versions omit the word "might." Yet the scripture seems clear that God will put no premium on being ignorant. Neither will the outward show of performing the deeds of the law bring a reward (Matt. 23:20-30).

1. *The Interpreter's Bible,* Vol. 9, p. 355.

## QUESTIONS FOR DISCUSSION

1. Why is the epistle to the Romans ranked so high among biblical scholars?
2. What is the implication of addressing his letter to those "called to be saints"?
3. Discuss the significance of the gospel as *power.*
4. In what respect were the Romans "left without excuse" for their sins?
5. Since God's judgment is not based on nationality, will the Jews and RLDS members be disadvantaged for having received the law and the new covenant?
6. John declared that God "lighteth every man who cometh into the world" (1:9). To what extent does this intelligence make him responsible for antisocial behavior?
7. Were the Jews worse off or did they have an advantage over the Gentiles?
8. What power does fear of eternal judgment have over the lives of men?
9. In what sense are men "saved by grace" or "justified by faith"?
10. What part does the conscience play in moral conduct and in eternal judgment?

# 31

# SALVATION THROUGH FAITH

(Romans 3:21 - 7:27)

Paul's epistle returns now to the theme so boldly set forth in 1:16, 17: The gospel is the power to salvation revealing righteousness through faith. This is quotable and acceptable to most Christians, but to those who are not familiar with New Testament language it may carry little motivation. The apostle tries to translate it so that the Romans, both the Gentiles and immature Christian Jews, will comprehend its significance.

"But now the righteousness of God . . . witnessed by the law and the prophets . . . is by faith of [in—R.S.V.] Jesus Christ unto all . . . them that believe" (v. 21, 22). "But now" brings us to the gospel era. It was predicted and anticipated by the prophets, but can be significant only through faith in the righteousness which was manifested in Christ. "The law of nature has not benefited the Gentile, nor has the law of Moses the Jew. Man's own powers leave him impotent."[1]

Since "all have sinned, and come short of the glory of God," man must look to another source of help. Justification, or salvation,

is by his grace through the redemption that is in Christ Jesus; whom God has set forth to be a propitiation ["expiation"—R.S.V.; "atone-

ment"—Standard Universal Dictionary] through faith in his blood.—
V. 23-25.

This is the first use Paul has made of the word "grace" to mean *unmerited* favor. "Where is boasting then? It is excluded. By what law? of works? Nay; but by the law of faith. Therefore we conclude that a man is justified by faith alone without the deeds of the law" (v. 26-28). When Paul said that works have nothing to do with salvation, he was talking about the law of carnal commandments and ordinances (Gal. 2:16, 17). Fleshly offerings served their purpose in pointing to Christ, "the Lamb slain from the foundation of the world" (Rev. 13:8). James made this very clear, "Faith without works is dead and cannot save you" (Jas. 2:18).

## The Old Covenant Is Fulfilled
(3:31 - 4:25)

God is a universal deity and not for the Jews alone. Faith in the Redeemer does not make void the law but upholds the law. "Abraham believed God, and it was counted unto him for righteousness" (v. 3). He was called the "father of all of them that believe" (v. 11). "Even as David also describeth the blessedness of the man, unto whom God imputeth righteousness without the law" and for evidence quoted Psalm 32:1, 2 (v. 6-8). Thus these two great patriarchs of the Hebrews are linked in justification of their faith. Paul assured the Romans that when God promised Abraham, "In thy seed shall all the nations of the earth be blessed," it was not to be by works of the law, "but through the righteousness of faith" (v. 12, 13). The blessing was not to be inherited through blood lineage but through faith that God would send "a leader and commander to the people" (Isa. 55:4), and that he did send the Messiah to save men from their sins.

"For if they which are of the law be heirs, faith is made void, and the promise made of none effect; because the law

worketh wrath; for where no law is, there is no transgression"
(v. 14, 15). "When the constraint of the commandment is
consciously felt, sin is 'provoked to opposition . . . and when
sin thus becomes conscious defiance, it incurs guilt and de-
serves punishment.' "[2]

Paul then cites the faith of Abraham that even in her old
age Sarah would bear a son (Gen. 17:23). "When he was
about a hundred years old . . . he staggered not at the promise
of God through unbelief, but was strong in faith, giving glory
to God" (v. 19, 20). Paul concludes with a comparison of
the faith which awakened Sarah's womb from the dead to the
faith we have that God "raised up Jesus our Lord from the
dead" (v. 21-25).

## Reconciliation and Justification through Christ
(5:1-21)

Paul here presents two aspects of justification, peace with
God because sin is pardoned and hope of the glory of God
because the believer is accepted as righteous. "Justification
thus means permanent reinstatement to favor and privilege,
as well as complete forgiveness of all sins."[3]

One having faith that he is justified in this sense can
glory in tribulation also, "knowing that tribulation worketh
patience" which leads to experience and hope. Then through
the ministry of the Holy Spirit the love of God is poured into
our hearts. We become conscious that "Christ died for the
ungodly" and that "while we were yet sinners, Christ died for
us" (v. 1-8).

Paul used the word reconciliation quite often. It connotes that there has been some degree of estrangement or hostility. Then by some act of grace a way is found to establish
peaceful and kindly relations again. Paul thus introduces this
logic:

204

For if, when we were enemies, we were reconciled to God by the death of his Son; much more, being reconciled, we shall be saved by his life. . . . Wherefore as by one man [Adam] sin entered into the world, and death by sin; so death passed upon all men . . . much more the grace of God, and the gift by grace, hath abounded by one man, Jesus Christ, unto many.—V. 10-15.

Paul repeats his reasoning in many ways so as to reinforce his teaching.

Moreover the law entered, that the offence might abound. But where sin abounded, grace did much more abound; that as sin hath reigned unto death, even so might grace reign through righteousness unto Jesus Christ our Lord.—V. 20, 21.

## DYING WITH CHRIST
(6:1-23)

Paul recognized the tendency man has to take an advantage and rationalize: "Why be in a hurry to obey or to learn the requirements of the gospel since man can depend on grace for justification or salvation?" Did he not write "Where sin abounded, grace did much more abound"? (5:20). So he anticipated this argument by asking, "Shall we continue in sin that grace may abound? God forbid. How shall we that are dead to sin, live any longer therein?" (6:1, 2). The only claim man has to grace is through Christlike righteousness (5:21).

Paul then connects two of the first principles (Heb. 6:1, 2) with Christ's death. "So many of us as were baptized into Jesus Christ were baptized into his death . . . buried with him by baptism into death; that like as Christ was raised up from the dead by the glory of the Father, even so we also should walk in newness of life . . . in the likeness of his resurrection" (v. 3-5). "Now if we be dead with Christ," he continued, "we believe that we shall also live with him. . . . Let not sin therefore reign in your mortal body, that ye should obey it in the lusts thereof" (v. 4-12).

The choice is ours. We may use our moral agency for spiritual life or for death. "Know ye not that to whom ye yield yourselves servants to obey, his servants ye are to whom ye obey; whether of sin unto death, or of obedience unto righteousness?" He concludes his discussion on the purpose of Christ's death with this memorable affirmation, "For the wages of sin is death; but the gift of God is eternal life through Jesus Christ our Lord" (v. 16, 23).

## He That Is Dead to the Law
(7:1-27)

To illustrate the limitation of the old law, Paul uses marriage customs. A woman is bound to her husband "till death do us part." When he is dead she is free from the marriage bond. The atonement of Christ marked the end (death) of the law. "The law and the prophets were until John; since then the good news of the kingdom of God is preached" (Luke 16:16—R.S.V.).

"But now we are delivered from the law wherein we were held, being dead to the law, that we should serve in newness of spirit, and not in the oldness of the letter" (v. 1-6). No one should say that the law itself is sin, but one is made aware of sin by the restrictions of the law. Paul uses the tenth commandment (Exod. 20:17) as a case in point: "For I had not known lust, except the law had said, Thou shalt not covet" (v. 7). "One would still have been subject to the same desires; but not only would one not have *known* that one was guilty of covetousness, but also one would not *in fact* have been guilty of it."[4]

"Once I was alive without transgression of the law [Acts 26:5], but when the commandment of Christ came, sin revived, and I died" (v. 9, 10). The law was holy and good until a better hope came and then that was "made death unto me. . . . But now I am spiritual . . . for what I know is not right, I would not do; for that which is sin, I hate. It is no more I that do sin; but I seek to subdue that sin which dwell-eth in me" (v. 12-18).

With open frankness Paul admits that he had to battle daily against his sinful nature (see Chapter 26, p. 174). "When I would do good evil was present with me; for I delight in the law of God after the inward man." Great characters are not afraid to express humility. "O wretched man that I am! who shall deliver me from the body of this death? I thank God through Jesus Christ our Lord, then, that so with the mind I myself serve the law of God" (v. 23-25).

1. *The Interpreter's Bible,* Vol. 9, p. 429.
2. A. E. Garvie, in *The Interpreter's Bible,* Vol. 9, p. 444.
3. *Baker's Dictionary of Theology,* p. 305.
4. *The Interpreter's Bible,* Vol. 9, p. 493.

## QUESTIONS FOR DISCUSSION

1. When did the carnal law die and what caused its death?
2. What did Paul mean by the word "justification"?
3. In what way can it truly be said that man is "saved by grace"?
4. Was the old covenant "by works of the law" through faith or without faith? Explain.
5. Why was Abraham called "father of the faithful"?
6. What was Paul's reasoning that the blessing to Abraham through his seed was not by heritage of the flesh?
7. Define reconciliation as used in Romans.
8. What did Paul mean by the "death of sin" and in what sense is sin dead in our day?
9. As here used does baptism refer to the burial of our sins or the atonement of Christ?
10. How was Paul "alive without transgression" as a Phari-see, but under the gospel "sin revived, and I died"?

# 32

# THE LIFE OF THE SPIRIT

(Romans 8:1-10:21)

In the last chapter Paul confessed that as a Pharisee he felt justified in doing many things which now troubled his conscience. The gospel set a higher spiritual standard and revealed him as a sinful man. Even when he would do good, the law of his nature was rebelling against his mind and bringing him into the captivity of sin. It is necessary for every man to know his weaknesses, but it is most important to know that no man will "be tempted above that ye are able; but will with the temptation also make a way to escape" (I Cor. 10:13)

## THE NEW RIGHTEOUSNESS
(8:1-13)

Without faith no one can be justified or please God (Heb. 11:6). Paul turned from this to a discussion of the victorious life.

"The law of the Spirit of life in Christ Jesus hath made me free from the law of sin and death" (v. 1, 2). It is important that we distinguish between the two laws Paul discusses. "The law of the Spirit" is the gospel; "the law of sin and death" is that of carnal commandments added in the wilderness of Sinai (Deut. 5:3), to lead Israel to Christ. But that law "made nothing perfect, but was only the bringing in of a better hope" (Heb. 7:16-19).

"For to be carnally minded is death; but to be spiritually minded is life and peace."

Both the old law and human flesh being weak, God did what these could not do by "sending his own son in the likeness of sinful flesh" (v. 3-6). By his living and teaching, and by the atonement, Christ made possible a life "after the Spirit, if so be that the Spirit of God dwell in you." Then to make the point more obvious, Paul added: "And if the Spirit of him that raised up Christ from the dead dwell in you, he that raised up Christ from the dead shall also quicken your mortal bodies by his Spirit that dwelleth in you."

## The Hope in Christ
(8:14-25)

In the life made possible through the gospel, a new heritage is brought into existence. "As many as are led by the Spirit of God, they are the sons of God." This new relationship is made evident to each individual by a self-revealed testimony. "The Spirit itself beareth witness, with our spirit, that we are the children of God; and if children, then heirs; heirs of God and joint heirs with Christ; if so be that we suffer with him" (v. 14-17). The Hebrews were conscious of a family relationship which might escape us entirely. Isaac was Abraham's son; Ishmael was just a child in the household. Thus a "son" of God was a real "heir." The son of bondage lived in the "spirit of adoption" which was a spirit of fear.

How may one know that he is a joint-heir with Christ? Because "the Spirit itself beareth witness with our spirit, that we are the children of God." No better evidence can be given than the living testimony of the Holy Spirit. "Creation waits with eager longing for the revealing of the sons of God"

(v. 19, R.S.V.).  The creature was made subject to tribulation (Gen. 3:22-25).  Paul pictured a time of misery and relief, for now "the whole creation groaneth and travaileth in pain together" (v. 18-22).  But this will not continue, for "we are saved by hope" and the "Spirit also helpeth our infirmities." "He that searcheth the hearts . . . maketh intercession for the saints according to the will of God" (v. 26, 27).

## TRIUMPH OF GOD'S LOVE
(8:28-39)

Speaking from a broad and turbulent experience, Paul gave a notable testimony which has brought comfort to Christians ever since.  "We know that all things work together for good to them that love God, to them who are the called according to his purpose" (v. 28).  This assurance is followed by a trend of thought which has proved difficult to interpret:

Whom he did foreknow, he also did predestinate to be conformed to his own image [to the image of his Son—K.J.V. and R.S.V.], that he might be the firstborn among many brethren.  Moreover, him whom he did predestinate, him he also called, him he also sanctified; and . . . glorified.—V. 28-30.

The King James and Revised Standard Versions put verses 29 and 30 in the plural so that they refer to mankind as called and predestinated rather than Christ.  Moffatt's and Weymouth's versions agree with the Inspired Version in verse 29 as pointing to Christ's preexistence.  The Inspired Version alone makes verse 30 refer to Christ.  "Those whom he predestinated, he also called" (R.S.V.) is the general idea they present.  This gave rise to Calvin's pronouncements that God chose those who were to be saved.

The rabbinical schools of Paul's day taught predestination, but with no denial of individual responsibility.  He cites Josephus as saying (*Jewish War* II, 8:14):  "They [i.e., the Pharisees] taught that everything is dependent upon Fate and God, but yet the choice of right and wrong lay for the most part with the individual."[1]

Still on the triumphant note, Paul asks, "If God be for us, who can prevail against us?" He continues with a series of inquiries: "Who shall lay anything to the charge of God's elect? It is God that justifieth" (v. 33). The "elect" are those who choose to serve God not, as John Calvin taught, that God did the choosing. This doctrine, however, is contrary to the law of agency and is not supported by Paul.

"Who is he that condemneth? It is Christ that died, yea rather, that is risen again, who is even at the right hand of God, who also maketh intercession for us" (v. 34). The love of Christ "is manifested not only in what Christ *did,* but also in what happened to him, or in what God did through him, i.e., in and through the entire event out of which the church was created."[2]

Paul was ever conscious that some gospel seed would fall on "stony places" and some "among thorns" and would not endure the heat of the sun nor bear grain or fruit. Thus some people would "depart from the faith, giving heed to seducing spirits, and doctrines of devils" (I Tim. 4:1). Thus he asked, "Who shall separate us from the love of Christ? shall tribulation, or distress, or persecution, or famine?" He then quoted Psalm 44:22, "For thy sake we are killed all the day long; we are accounted as sheep for the slaughter" (v. 35, 36). Doubtless this will remind some of Joseph Smith's statement as he left Nauvoo to ride to martyrdom in Carthage, Illinois, June 27, 1844 (D. and C. 113:4).

Then Paul answered in the negative,

Nay, in all these things we are more than conquerors through him that loved us. For I am persuaded that neither death, nor life [the things in them is meant], . . . shall be able to separate us from the love of God, which is in Christ Jesus our Lord.—V. 37-39.

211

## SORROW OVER ISRAEL'S REJECTION
(9:1-29)

"I have great heaviness and continual sorrow in my heart," and "I lie not" (v. 1, 2). This soberness doubtless arises from the fact that Paul, "the apostle to the Gentiles," had been accused of being disloyal to his race. He had hoped that by gathering funds and carrying them to Jerusalem for the needy Jewish Christians, this unkind accusation would be dispelled. He was a Jew, and his kinsmen were dear to him.

"They are not all Israel, which are of Israel. Neither, because they are all children of Abraham, are they the seed; but, In Isaac shall thy seed be called" (v. 6, 7). The term "Israel" means more than "Jew," as it indicates not only nationality but membership in a chosen people. Paul goes a step further and says the only true Israelite is the faithful servant of God. "Therefore hath he mercy on whom he will have mercy." Man shall not dictate to God the terms of his own salvation. So the apostle asked, "What if God, willing to show his wrath, and to make his power known, endured with much long-suffering the vessels of wrath fitted to destruction" (v. 18-22).

God has a purpose in this patience and will in due time show his glory and the calling "not of the Jews only, but also of the Gentiles" (v. 23, 24). Isaiah (10:22) is quoted, "Though the number of the children of Israel be as the sand of the sea, a remnant shall be saved; for he will finish the work and cut it short in righteousness . . . Except the Lord of Sabaoth had left us a seed," Israel would have perished. Christ, the seed, was the hope of Israel (v. 27-29).

## GOD'S CHOICE NOT ARBITRARY
(9:30-10:21)

Paul introduced a major change here in point of view. The Gentiles who did not have the law and cared not for the ways of the Lord "have attained to righteousness ... which is of faith. But Israel, which followed after the law . . . stumbled at that stumbling-stone, not by faith, but as it were by the works of the law" (v. 30-33).

To offset some of the discouraging things he had said, Paul gave reassurance of his loyalty; "Brethren, my heart's desire and prayer to God for Israel is, that they might be saved. . . . They have a zeal of God, but not according to knowledge. . . . For Christ is the end of the law . . . to every one that believeth" (11:1-4). He further contrasted the law of Moses and the gospel:

But the righteousness which is of faith speaketh on this wise, . . . If thou shalt confess with thy mouth the Lord Jesus, and shalt believe in thine heart that God hath raised him from the dead, thou shalt be saved. For with the heart man believeth unto righteousness; and with the mouth confession is made unto salvation.—V. 5-10.

The universal God is impartial in his love. Paul expressed this by saying: "There is no difference between the Jew and the Greek; for the same Lord over all is rich unto all that call upon him." However, they will not call on him unless the message is brought to them by "the preacher" who is sent by God with the "glad tidings of good things" (v. 11-15.)

The faith in the Messiah which the Jews lacked is their stumbling block, but "faith comes from what is heard, and what is heard comes by the preaching of Christ" (v. 17— R.S.V.). Paul concludes his argument on God's impartiality by quoting Isaiah (65:1, 2): "I was found of them that sought me not; I was made manifest unto them that asked not after me; but to Israel he saith, All day long I have stretched forth my hands unto a disobedient and gainsaying people" (v. 20, 21). This lays the premise for Paul's argument of Israel's rejection which he was soon to introduce.

---

1. *The Interpreter's Bible*, Vol. 9, p. 526.
2. *Ibid.*, p. 530.

## Questions for Discussion

1. What are the two laws Paul discusses and the nature or elements of each?
2. Tell about the new heritage mentioned in this chapter and who are included.
3. It was said that Ishmael was not Abram's son but only "a child of the household." Explain this.
4. How do you explain the statement, "We are saved by hope?"
5. What is meant by "predestination," and does the Bible teach it?
6. Paul infers that nothing can separate the saints from the love of Christ. Why then are there so many backsliders and cold church members?
7. Why was Paul accused of disloyalty to the Jews? Is there a difference between a Jew and an Israelite?
8. What prediction did Isaiah make about Israel being saved? Is modern Israel fulfilling this prophecy?
9. What did Paul say about Israel's zeal, and how may that apply to the Restoration?
10. Does Paul imply that salvation for the Gentiles depends on the preacher, and is what is implied true today?

# 33

## APOSTASY, LOVE'S LABOR
## FINAL COUNSEL

(Romans 11:1-16:27)

The preceding chapter closed on an affirmation of God's concern for both Jew and Gentile. By patient continuance and faith, the righteousness of God would triumph for the good of all mankind. Only those who call on him are heirs of the promise through Christ. Faith comes by hearing those whom God sends as his witnesses.

### JEWISH APOSTASY NOT FINAL
### (11:1-32)

"Hath God cast away his people?" To admit that, Paul would have to admit his own apostasy; "for I also am an Israelite . . . of the tribe of Benjamin." Then he recalled the experience of Elijah (I Kings 19:9-18), who complained that the Lord's prophets had been killed, and Israel had turned to the worship of Baal, and he was left alone. The Lord answered that there were seven thousand who had not bowed the knee to Baal. Likewise, Paul was not alone, and the faithful few can redeem the many (v. 1-5).

It is a distorted view which exalts the importance of one tribe or race but is blind to the outreach of God and the contribution of other people in the fulfillment of the plans and purposes of God. No matter how discouraging the conditions in one branch or district, God's arm is not shortened nor his power limited. "There is a remnant according to the election of grace"—that is, of those Jews who elected or chose to accept Christ. The rest were blinded to keep the works of the law. They had become insensitive and could not see nor hear the values and truths so obviously manifested through the gospel.

Then Paul pointed up his reasoning by a question concerning Israel, "Have they stumbled that they should fall? God forbid; but rather through their fall [trespass—R.S.V.] salvation is come unto the Gentiles," so as to make Israel jealous. Therefore if their limited failure brought riches to the world, "how much more will their full inclusion mean" (R.S.V., v. 6-12). By his work in creating a Gentile church, Paul is creating a still wider fellowship. Seeing the evidences of divine power in his work as "the apostle of the Gentiles," the Jews will desire for themselves the same benefits.

Paul adds on a significant clause, "I magnify mine office." He did not consider his apostleship an honor bestowed for work well done but a call to service. It is a challenge for each of us—church school officer, women's department leader, and priesthood member—to keep before us. Each person should dignify the office to which he or she is called to serve, and not accept the office as a badge of authority and honor. Paul hoped to stimulate others of his flesh (kindred) to emulate him to the saving of souls. Thus, their rejection as a chosen people would mean the reconciliation of the world to Christ (v. 13-15).

## A Branch Grafted In
(11:16-36)

Again the illustration of a graft on the wild olive tree is used. Nurserymen use the sturdy stock of the wild tree or shrub for growth and the tame branches for the fruit of superior quality. But Paul urges two points: (1) It is the root that supports the branches, not the branches supporting the roots. The Gentile Christians have no right to despise the Jews or to boast over the discarded branches. It was not because of their own merits but because of faith; therefore, they "be not high-minded, but fear," lest the same thing happen to them. If the Jews put away their unbelief, they shall be grafted in again, for with God this is possible (v. 16-24).

Only as each reader tries to put himself in the place of the people whom the apostle is trying to reach can his stress on this subject be appreciated. Israel was a proud race with a long and glorious history. It was not easy for them to conceive of "the God of Abraham, Isaac, and Jacob" rejecting them and adopting any other race or nation. Paul becomes repetitious, and perhaps to some Bible readers boring, as he belabors the point.

I would not, brethren, that ye should be ignorant of this mystery, lest ye should be wise in your own conceits, that blindness in part is happened to Israel, until the fulness of the Gentiles be come in. And then all Isarel shall be saved. . . . For this is my covenant unto them, when I shall take away their sins.—V. 25, 26.

What time is meant by "fulness of the Gentiles be come in"? It is a prophetic statement, but never fully explained. Some renditions by various scholars may help us, even though no time is fixed: "The final, sum-total of believing Jews and Gentiles"[1]; "Until the great mass of Gentiles has come in"[2]; "Until the full number of the Gentiles come in"—R.S.V. and Moffat's N.T.; "Until the full complement of nations enter into God's kingdom."[3]

Another question may arise about the clause "all Israel shall be saved." Does this lead to a belief in universal salvation? It offers some grounds for "a doctrine of salvation by pure grace [and] may lead to a doctrine of predestination;

but a doctrine of predestination (given that God loves all men) leads at least equally naturally to a doctrine of universal salvation."[4]

This must be rejected, for Paul's writings put too much stress on faith, unbelief, sin, agency, and eternal judgment to admit of that theology. Israel's salvation depends on a "doing" type of faith. For the gifts and calling of God are without repentance ["irrevocable"—R.S.V.].[5] Then Paul was led to exclaim, "O the depth of the riches both of the wisdom and knowledge of God! How unsearchable are his judgments, and his ways past finding out . . . to whom be glory for ever" (v. 29-36). "The problem is not solved; but the perplexity is overcome in an act of worship."[6]

## DIRECTIONS FOR CHRISTIANS
(12:1-14:23)

"Present your bodies a living sacrifice . . . which is your reasonable service." Sacrifices both of animals and money were then customary elements of worship. These are poor substitutes for the giving of one's heart and a willing labor of love for others. "Be not conformed to this world; but be ye transformed" to the will of God (v. 1, 2).

Paul next asked the saints to guard against pride. Man should not "think of himself more highly than he ought to think, but to think soberly," according to the faith God has given him. Each saint is precisely one member of the "body in Christ." The best contribution each is capable of giving should be placed on the altar of sacrifice. Paul lists many of the contributions which may be available: prophecy, ministry, exhorting, being kindly affectioned, hospitality, honesty, and living "peaceably with all men." "Let love be without dissimulation [genuine—R.S.V.]. Abhor that which is evil and cleave to that which is good" (v. 3-18).

These make for Christian unity and fellowship without which the church of Christ cannot function effectively. This

218

unity in diversity is possible through practice of the principles of the gospel.

"Let every soul be subject unto the higher powers. For there is no power in the church but of God." In the light of the conduct required as just stated, the saints should accept the church leaders, for they are God's agents. Then Paul writes concerning citizenship in the state. He may have had in mind the rebellious attitude of many toward Rome. His counsel should be taken with his background, which had a strong assurance of God's providential ordering of the world in mind. "Rulers are not a terror to good works, but to the evil" (13:1-3). They function by God's permission and tolerance. "Render to all their dues, according to custom," tribute, fear, and honor (v. 7). Then the apostle again reverts to saintly deportment. "Owe no man anything, but to love one another; for he that loveth another hath fulfilled the law" (v. 8). "Cast off the works of darkness, and let us put on the armor of light" (v. 12).

"Him that is weak in the faith receive ye, but not to doubtful disputations." Such matters as what to eat and the keeping of special days are mentioned. As one should not criticize the servant of another man, so we should withhold judgment of Christ's servants, either leaders or brethren. "For none of us liveth to himself, and no man dieth to himself." Our lives touch many others for good or ill (14:1-7).

Someday, as the Lord has said, "Every knee shall bow to me." Everyone then "shall give account of himself to God." Stewardship is obligatory. We will have to answer for our use of earth's bounties, our time, and our opportunities; whether we believe in God and want to confess his majesty, or whether we are atheists (v. 9-13).

If thy brother be grieved with thy meat, thou walkest not charitably if thou eatest . . . for the kingdom of God is not meat and drink; but righteousness, and peace, and joy in the Holy Ghost. . . . It is good neither to eat flesh, nor to drink wine, nor anything whereby thy brother stumbleth, or is offended, or is made weak.—V. 15-21.

## CHRIST OUR EXAMPLE
(15:1-16:27)

"We then that are strong ought to bear the infirmities of the weak . . . for even Christ pleased not himself; but, as it is written, The reproaches of them that reproached thee fell on me" (15:1-3). This, as in II Corinthians 8:9, is an incidental allusion to Christ's preexistence. (See also Phil. 2:6-8.)

"Now the God of patience and consolation grant you to be like-minded one toward another according as was Christ Jesus." Then Paul affirms that Jesus "was a minister of the circumcision [the Jews] . . . to confirm the promises made unto the fathers; and that the Gentiles might glorify God for his mercy" (v. 5-9).

On the note that Christ brought salvation to both Jew and Gentile, Paul brings his epistle to a close. To do so he introduces several quotations supporting his thesis from Psalm 18:49, Deuteronomy 32:43, Psalm 117:1, and Isaiah 11:10. He includes a mention of the "mighty signs and wonders" he wrought through the Spirit of God. "From Jerusalem, and round about unto Illyricum, I have fully preached the gospel of Christ" (v. 10-19). He was a frontier missionary, not wishing to "build upon another man's foundation." This, however, hindered his coming to Rome, but he was planning to go to Spain via Rome and would visit and labor there. "But now I go unto Jerusalem to minister unto the saints" (v. 20-32). This helps to establish the time and place of his writing the epistle.

In the conclusion Paul commended "Phoebe our sister" of Cenchrea, the seaport for Corinth. He sent greetings to twenty-two brothers and sisters whom he named and two unnamed individuals, two groups, and three churches. Certain ones joined in sending salutations. Among these are Timothy, Luke, and the scribe, Tertius.

1. *Baker's Dictionary of Theology*, p. 232.
2. Weymouth's New Testament.
3. *Peak's Commentary on the Bible*, p. 826.
4. *The Interpreter's Bible*, Vol. 9, p. 577.
5. "God never goes back upon his gifts and call"—Moffatt's N.T.
6. *The Interpreter's Bible*, Vol. 9, p. 578.

## QUESTIONS FOR DISCUSSION

1. How can one reconcile the scripture that "God is no respecter of persons" with the idea of Israel being "a chosen people"?

2. How did Israel's stumbling (fall) work to the favor of the Gentiles?

3. What was Paul's application of the saying, "the root supports the branches"?

4. Explain, "When the fulness of the Gentiles is come in," the Jews' blindness will be removed.

5. What is meant by "universal salvation" and "predestination"?

6. What did Paul say was "our reasonable service," and to what extent do members of our church give it?

7. Explain the terms "unity in diversity" and their application in this chapter.

8. Reconcile the counsel to "withhold judgment of Christ's servants" and "constructive criticism."

9. What did Paul mean by the statement, "The kingdom of God is not meat and drink"?

10. Discuss, "None of us liveth to himself, and no man dieth to himself."

# 34

# PAUL'S LAST DAYS
# IN JERUSALEM

(May A.D. 57—Acts 21:17-22:30)

In the last chapter Paul was telling the saints at Rome that he was contemplating a mission to Spain and would visit them en route. The scripture does not reveal any events of this journey, nor even that it was undertaken.

Clement of Rome, writing from Italy about A.D. 96, says that Paul "reached the bounds of the west," and the Muratorian fragment, written about A.D. 170, states explicitly that he went to Spain. This visit must have taken place after Paul's imprisonment in Rome which is recorded in Acts.[1]

Now our narrative returns to Luke's account of Paul's arrival in Jerusalem with the funds collected by the Gentile Christians for the needy saints in Judea. Chapter 29 ended with the arrival of Paul and the delegates from Asia Minor and Grecian churches. We continue the narrative from that point.

## PAUL'S LIFE THREATENED
(Acts 21:17-30)

The brethren of the church at Jerusalem received Paul and his group gladly. The group visited "James and all the

222

/ elders" the next day. This "James" was the brother of Jesus. The prominence given him on this and other occasions indicated that he was the leader of the church.[2]

2 Paul is given an opportunity to report on the "things God had wrought among the Gentiles by his ministry." They heard him gladly and "glorified the Lord." Luke included himself by saying "Paul went in with us." After this he drops out of the narrative for a time. The "we" passages begin again with Acts 27:1. Paul reported "particularly what things God had wrought among the Gentiles by his ministry" (v. 17-19).

The response was to praise the Lord for Paul's success and then inform him of the local situation, "Many thousands of Jews . . . believe, and they are all zealous of the law." These have learned of his teaching the Jews of the dispersion 3 "to forsake Moses, saying that they ought not to circumcise their children, neither to walk after the customs." A warning was added that the multitude would gather as soon as they heard that Paul had arrived.

A plan had been worked out and Paul was asked to follow it. "We have four men which have a vow on them. 4 . . . Purify thyself with them . . . that they may shave their heads." Paul was to pay the costs and thus evidence that "thou thyself walkest orderly, and keepest the law" (v. 20-24).

Apparently it was proposed that Paul should associate himself with the four in their vow, the phrase [purify yourself] being the equivalent of the Hebrew words, "to separate himself unto the Lord," which in Numbers 6:2 define the taking of a Nazarite vow.[3]

It was explained that the Gentiles did not need to observe these things, as the conference had so decided on a previous occasion (Acts 15:28, 29). "Then Paul took the men, and the next day, purifying himself with them entered into the temple" (v. 25, 26). Some problems arise here which are difficult to fully explain. Did Paul act hypocritically under pressure by carrying out the works of the old law, which he had written against so vigorously? Doubtless he did not want to antagonize the non-Christian Jews who used the temple, but the setting here was that of thousands of believing Jews (v. 20). Paul's statement, "Unto the Jews I became as a Jew, that I might gain the Jews" (I Cor. 9:20-22) is used by some to explain his philosophy. We know that he circumcised Timothy (Acts 16:3) as a matter of expediency. Yet his courage and defiance under stress among the Gentiles makes it hard to believe that he would sacrifice his convictions under any conditions. The best way to leave this enigma is to say that not enough of the facts are known to make a final judgment.

"And when the seven days were almost ended, the Jews which were of Asia, when they saw him in the temple, stirred up all the people, and laid hands on him" (v. 27). The seven days (Num. 6:9) must end before he could shave his head. The Jews of Asia were Orthodox Jews who came to Jerusalem periodically for temple rites. The attempt of the church leaders to conciliate the Jewish Christians only led to a clash with the Orthodox Jews. These were probably from Ephesus (v. 29) and had promoted the mob action in that city led by Alexander (Acts 19:33). They cried out that this man teaches everywhere against the Jews, their law, "and this place; and further brought Greeks also into the temple." This accusation came because Trophimus (Acts 20:4; II Tim. 4:20) was seen in Jerusalem with Paul (v. 28, 29).

## ARRESTED AND PUT IN CHAINS
(Acts 21:30-40)

The charge of profaning the temple was most serious.

A marble block . . . has been preserved with the inscription, "Let no foreigner enter within the screen and enclosure surrounding the sanctuary. Whosoever is taken so doing will be the cause that death overtaketh him." . . . Paul's expression "the middle wall of partition" (Eph. 2:14) is probably an allusion to this barrier.[4]

224

Paul was dragged from the temple and the gates were shut. "And as they went about to kill him" the chief captain heard of the uproar and came with his soldiers, rescued him from those who were beating him, and carried him to their barracks, which were probably in the Tower of Antonio at the northwest corner of the temple area. The captain ordered him chained to two soldiers for protective custody, as Peter was once (Acts 12:6). The people were not satisfied with his arrest and removal from the temple in chains; they followed crying, "Away with him." Luke must have been an eye-witness and he was able to point out many similarities to the last trial of Christ (v. 30-36).

Paul asked the captain for permission to speak. He replied, "Canst thou speak Greek?" Without waiting for an answer, he asked if he was "that Egyptian" who had led four thousand into the wilderness. Josephus is probably referring to the same incident in *Jewish War* II. 13.3,5. Paul identi-fied himself as a Jew of Tarsus in Cilicia. He asked permission "to speak unto the people." This was granted and Paul stood on the stairs, raised his hand for silence, and spoke in Hebrew (more likely Aramaic, the common language in Jerusalem at that time).

## Paul's Address to the People
(Acts 22:1-30)

"Men, brethren, and fathers, hear ye my defense." He said he had been "brought up in this city at the feet of Gamaliel [see 5:34], . . . and was zealous toward God, as ye all are this day." He then added a reference to persecuting the Christians ("this way") unto death. He told of his trip to Damascus with authority from the high priest to bring back Christians for punishment. He related the incident of the light from heaven and the voice of the Lord Jesus telling him what to do. The full account was given in Acts 9:1-18 (v. 1-16).

Variations made were doubtless due to the situation confronting Paul. In the current condition Ananias was said to be "a devout man according to the law" but nothing is said about his vision and the direction given by the Lord to go to the "house of Judas."

"When I was come again to Jerusalem, even while I prayed in the temple, I was in a trance" (v. 17). This may seem to be soon after his conversion; however, from Paul's own account, it was three years later (Gal. 1:16-18). A trance is "a state in which . . . the senses are suspended and the soul seems to be liberated from the body while it contemplates some extraordinary object."[5] Often the idiom is "fell into a trance" (Num 24:4, 16; Acts 10:10). It is not now in good repute as a religious term, being associated with the spiritualist movement which is not particularly religious. He was told "make haste, and get thee quickly out of Jerusalem; for they will not receive thy testimony concerning me" (v. 18).

Paul then reminded the Jews that he consented to the martyrdom of Stephen and "kept the raiment of them that slew him." Then returning to the account of his vision, he quotes the Lord as saying, "I will send thee far hence unto the Gentiles" (v. 19-21).

At the mention of the Gentiles, the mob began to clamor for his destruction: "It is not fit that he should live." Then the captain ordered that he "be brought into the castle . . . and examined by scourging." As he was bound with thongs, he asked a centurion standing by, "Is it lawful for you to scourge a man that is a Roman, and uncondemned?" He passed this question along to the captain with a warning, "Take heed what thou doest, for this man is a Roman." The chief captain asked Paul about it; he told Paul he had paid a great sum for his own freedom. "But I was free born," said Paul.

"It was customary for newly made citizens to adopt the

226

name of the emperor, and the tribune's name was Claudius Lysias (Acts 23:26)."[6]

Scourging with thongs (like a cat-of-nine-tails )was commonly used on slaves to extort a confession, but not on a free man. The next day the chief captain "commanded the chief priests and all their council [Sanhedrin] to appear, and brought Paul down, and set him before them" (v. 22-30).

1. *Westminster Dictionary of the Bible*, p. 577.
2. *The Interpreter's Bible*, Vol. 9, p. 302.
3. *Ibid.*, p. 282.
4. *Ibid.*, p. 286.
5. *Westminster Dictionary of the Bible*, p. 613.
6. *The Interpreter's Bible*, Vol. 9, p. 293.

## QUESTIONS FOR DISCUSSION

1. To whom did Paul and company report in Jerusalem and what office did he hold?
2. What evidence is there that Luke was with Paul and wrote the account?
3. What accusations were the Orthodox Jews making against Paul and was Paul guilty of them?
4. What plan was worked out by the brethren in Jerusalem to lessen antagonism against Paul?
5. Was Paul consistent with past teaching in following out this plan?
6. On what charges was Paul's arrest made?
7. In what ways was Paul's arrest and custodial treatment similar to that of Jesus?
8. What facts did Paul give of his life before his conversion in his address to the people?
9. Give some of the differences in Luke's account here and Paul's own account of his life and conversion.
10. Why did the chief captain countermand his order to examine Paul by scourging?

# 35

# PAUL'S HEARING
# BEFORE FELIX

(Acts 23:1-24:27)

The thing which the prophet Agabus had dramatized and foretold should happen to Paul at Jerusalem was now being enacted. The temple guard under Claudius Lysias brought the apostle into the barracks chained to two soldiers who planned to exact a confession by flogging him. But when they learned that he was a Roman, they gave up that plan and took him into protective custody. The next morning Lysias brought him before the "chief priests and all their council."

## PAUL ADDRESSED THE SANHEDRIN
(23:1-9)

Seeing an opportunity to give an effectual testimony he began, "I have lived in all good conscience before God until this day." This irritated Ananias the high priest, and he directed those standing nearby to "smite him on the mouth." Paul was vexed by this unjust treatment and said, "God shall smite thee, thou whited wall; for sittest thou to judge me after the law, and commandest me to be smitten contrary to the law?" This command fits Josephus' description of the high

228

priest who ruled from A.D. 48 to 58 when he was deposed:[1]
"A bold man in his temper, and very insolent; he was also
of the sect of the Sadducees, who are very stern in judging
offenders above all the rest of the Jews."[2]

When Paul was rebuked for reviling "God's high priest,"
he is said to have replied that he did not know he was the
high priest. It is possible that Ananias was summoned in such
short order that he was not wearing the robe and other regalia
of his office. Or he may have not known him personally and
did not know he was presiding. Since Luke was not present,
some scholars think he did not get all his details accurately,
though "it is in the main historical."[3]

When Paul noted that his audience was part Sadducee
and part Pharisee, he said, "Men and brethren, I am a Pharisee,
the son of a Pharisee; of the hope and resurrection of the dead
I am called in question." As anticipated by Paul, this set
one party against the other. "The Sadducees say that there
is no resurrection, neither angel, nor spirit; but the Pharisees
confess both [acknowledge them all—R.S.V.]." Paul was
not denying his Christian heritage, but he held that a Pharisee
could be a Christian by accepting Christ's teaching, and that
"circumcision is nothing, and uncircumcision is nothing, but
the keeping of the commandments of God" (I Cor. 7:19).
In latter days the Lord said, "He that keepeth the laws of
God hath no need to break the laws of the land" (D. and
C. 58:5 b). The inference is that he lives above the letter
of civil law.

"The scribes that were of the Pharisees" said, "We find
no evil in this man; but if a spirit or an angel hath spoken
to him, let us not fight against God" (v. 1-9). Many of the
scribes were Pharisees, though not all.

## THE JEWS PLOT PAUL'S DEATH
(23:10-35)

When it became evident that a part of the mob might

do violence to the apostle, the captain had his soldiers rescue him and take him into the castle of Antonio.

"The night following the Lord stood by him, and said, Be of good cheer, Paul; for as thou hast testified of me in Jerusalem, so must thou bear witness also at Rome."

About forty Jews took a vow the next day to "neither eat nor drink till they had killed Paul." They made this conspiracy known to the "chief priests and elders." They asked their cooperation in getting Lysias to bring Paul before them for further examination. However, their plot was overheard by Paul's nephew, who then informed Paul (v. 10-16). Paul called a centurion and then had his nephew taken to tell the chief captain about the plot on his life.

As a result the captain ordered two hundred soldiers, seventy horsemen, and two hundred spearmen made ready to leave for Caesarea at the third hour of the night. A horse was also provided for Paul's use, "Bring him safe unto Felix the governor" (v. 17-24).

Lysias sent a letter to the governor explaining the whole affair. His letter closed with these statements, "When it was told me how that the Jews laid wait for the man, I sent straightway to thee, and gave commandment to his accusers also to say before thee what they had against him. Farewell."

Leaving Jerusalem at 9:00 P.M. and arriving at Antipatris some forty miles west would be quite a ride for cavalry, but impossible for the infantry. The latter may have functioned only as an escort in getting away from the mob in Jerusalem. However, the "exact site [of Antipatris] is not known,"[4] therefore the distance might have been much shorter.

The governor read the letter, then asked Paul "of what province he was. And when he understood that he was of Cilicia; I will hear thee, said he, when thine accusers are also come" (v. 25-34).

## Paul before Felix
(24:1-27)

Antonius Felix was procurator of Judea from A.D. 52 to 58 when he was replaced by his brother Pallas. It was five days before "Ananias the high priest descended with the elders, and with a certain orator named Tertullus, who informed the governor against Paul." The "orator" was a lawyer hired by the Jews who knew Roman law and court procedure. His opening statements were the typical praise to ingratiate himself with the procurator.

"We have found this man a pestilent fellow, and a mover of sedition among all the Jews throughout the world, and a ring-leader of the sect of the Nazarenes; who also hath gone about to profane the temple" (v. 1-6). This last charge, if proved, "would have been legal ground for Paul's execution by the Romans."[5]

Tertullus added that the Jews would have dealt with him "according to our law, but the chief captain Lysias . . . with great violence took him away out of our hands" (v. 7-9).

When Paul was given an opportunity to defend himself he said that twelve days ago he

went up to Jerusalem for to worship. And they neither found me in the temple disputing . . . neither raising up the people. . . . Neither can they prove the things whereof they now accuse me. But this I confess unto thee, that after the way which they call heresy, so worship I the God of my fathers, believing all things which are written in the law and in the prophets . . . that there shall be a resurrection of the dead, both of the just and unjust.

He then added his testimony, I have "always a conscience void of offence toward God, and toward men" (v. 10-16).

Paul then made reference to his visit with relief funds to his nation after an absence of "many years." Some Asian Jews "found me purified in the temple" without multitude or tumult. "As the words read, the implication appears to be that Paul made an offering of alms to his nation and that the Jews found him doing this."[6]  Perhaps this purification claim was based on Acts 21:23, 24, in which Paul was to pay the charges for the four men who had taken the vow.  Had there been a tumult in the temple or city, he asked, why were not his accusers here to testify?  He inquired if the Sanhedrin members present had "found any evil doing in me, while I stood before the council."  Then he made a concession that on one point of doctrine, the resurrection, he might have spoken unwisely.  Of course, the Roman law had no interest in Jewish doctrine (v. 17-21).

Felix stopped the proceedings at this point, saying, "When Lysias the chief captain shall come down, I will know the uttermost of your matter."  He then told a centurion to keep Paul in custody and give him liberty to talk with his friends. Felix was married to a Jewess, Drusilla, who Josephus said was a sister of Herod Agrippa II.[7]  Felix had her with him a few days later and had Paul brought in

and heard him concerning the faith in Christ.  And as he reasoned of righteousness, temperance, and judgment, Felix trembled [was alarmed—R.S.V.], and answered, Go thy way for this time; when I have a convenient season, I will call for thee.—V. 22-25.

From what has been learned of the character of Felix, there was need for a drastic change in his life.[8]  Yet it is probable that a sudden change without deliberate thought and determination would not have long endured.  Luke reasoned that because the procurator saw Paul often during the next two years and talked with him, he was seeking money for Paul's release.

"The taking of money from prisoners as a bribe for release was expressly forbidden by law; but it was quite in keeping with what we know of Felix' character."[9]

"Willing to please the Jews, he left Paul bound for two years, when Felix was replaced, due to complaints of the Jews, by Festus.  Nero called him home in disgrace."[10]

232

Many in our time have been impressed by the gospel story but have put off a final decision until a more "convenient season." Procrastination is not only "the thief of time" but debilitates the will, and in the end may cause the loss of one's soul.

In 1950 the Lord told the church, "It is yet day when all can work. The night will come when for many of my people opportunity to assist will have passed" (D. and C. 142:5 b). "Convenient seasons" are not guaranteed to kings or peasants, to Saints or sinners. For many of us, it is later than we think.

---

1. "Assassinated by robbers—possibly the Sicarii or Zealots"—Josephus, *Jewish War*, II 17.6, 9.
2. *Antiquities*, XX 9.1, 2.
3. *The Interpreter's Bible*, Vol. 9, p. 297.
4. *Ibid.*, p. 305.
5. *Ibid.*, p. 286, 309.
6. *Ibid.*, p. 311.
7. *Antiquities*, XX 7.1, 2.
8. *The Interpreter's Bible*, Vol. 9, p. 313.
9. Josephus, *Jewish War* II, 14.1.
10. Josephus, *Antiquities*, XX 8.9.

## QUESTIONS FOR DISCUSSION

1. Why did Ananias order Paul slapped? Do you think Paul's reaction was justified?
2. How did the apostle cause a sharp division of the Sanhedrin members, and why did he claim that he was a Pharisee?
3. What divine message did Paul receive while he was a prisoner in the castle?
4. Tell of the vow of about forty Jews and what thwarted their murderous plan.
5. What was in the letter sent to Felix, and what was the procurator's first question to Paul?

6. Who came to Caesarea with the high priest and what accusations did he make against Paul?
7. How did Paul defend himself against these charges?
8. Paul conceded that he might have been unwise on one point in his defense in Jerusalem. What was it, and why do you think Paul mentioned it in Caesarea?
9. Give some possible reasons why Felix was lenient with Paul?
10. When is the "convenient season" for obedience to the gospel? Do you believe in "instant conversion"?

# 36 PAUL TRIED IN CAESAREA JOURNEYS TOWARD ROME

(Acts 25-27:44)

Paul was kept in custody by Felix for two years without a final decision on his guilt. Almost nothing has been written about his experiences during these twenty-four months. We are told that Felix had him brought before him often "and communed with him." It is intimated that he was trying to obtain money from Paul for his release. Instead of pleasing the Jews by keeping Paul in bondage, he infuriated them, and Rome replaced him by sending Festus as procurator.

The new Roman governor had been in Caesarea only three days when he left for Jerusalem. "The high priest and the chief of the Jews" immediately tried to gain his favor and have Paul brought there for examination. Secretly they planned to waylay him and kill him (v. 1-3).

Festus said, "Paul will be kept at Caesarea," and invited his accusers to return with him. He tarried in Jerusalem ten days; and the day following his return he "commanded Paul to be brought" before him. His accusers "laid many and grievous complaints against Paul, which they could not prove." When he had the opportunity to answer for himself, Paul said,

"Neither against the law of the Jews, neither against the temple, nor yet against Caesar, have I offended any thing at all." Festus, wishing to please the Jews, asked: "Wilt thou go up to Jerusalem, and there be judged of these things before me?" (v. 4-9).

"I stand at Caesar's judgment-seat where I ought to be judged. . . . If I have committed any thing worthy of death, I refuse not to die. . . . I appeal unto Caesar." Festus conferred with his chief officers, and then said, "Hast thou appealed unto Caesar? unto Caesar shalt thou go" (v. 10-12).

## AGRIPPA HEARS PAUL'S STORY
(25:13 - 26:32)

King Herod Agrippa II was the son of Herod Agrippa I, the first persecutor of the church (12:1). He did not rule over all Judea as did his father, but over some surrounding areas to which was added later "custody of the temple treasure and the appointment of the high priest."[1] With his sister Bernice, who was also a sister of Drusilla (24:24), he came to call on Festus. After a few days Agrippa was told about Paul who was "left in bonds by Felix." Festus told of the examination of Paul and that the Jews "brought none accusation of such things as I supposed; but had certain questions against him of their own superstition, and of one Jesus, which was dead, whom Paul affirmed to be alive" (v. 13-19). Festus said when he asked him to go to Jerusalem to be judged, he appealed to Emperor Augustus, and was being held till he could be taken to Caesar.

Agrippa asked to hear Paul and was promised the privilege on the morrow. "With great pomp" Agrippa and Bernice entered the judgment hall accompanied by "the chief captains, and principal men of the city." Festus reiterated the story adding, "I found that he had committed nothing worthy of death," but he had no grounds to support the send-

236

ing of the case to Caesar. He asked Agrippa to examine Paul and suggest what he might put in his letter to Augustus; "for it seemeth to me unreasonable to send a prisoner and not withal to signify the crimes laid against him" (v. 20-27).

Agrippa then invited Paul to speak. This pleased Paul and he launched into his life story from his youth "which was at the first among mine own nation² at Jerusalem" where he lived as a strict Pharisee. "And now I stand and am judged for the hope of the promise made of God unto our fathers . . . our twelve tribes" (26:1-7).

He then directed his questions and remarks to King Agrippa who also was a Jew. "Why should it be thought a thing incredible with you, that God should raise the dead?" While this is a general question, doubtless it had reference to Jesus' resurrection. He next related his experience in persecuting the saints, "and when they were put to death, I gave my voice against them" (v. 10). This is often taken to mean that he was a member of the Sanhedrin and cast a vote against the Christians. To others it merely means to give general approval to their persecution and death.

He told Agrippa of his vision on the Damascus road in which Jesus spoke to him and called him to the ministry, and particularly to carry the gospel of Christ among the Gentiles. After his conversion he went "first unto them of Damascus, and at Jerusalem, and throughout all the coasts of Judea, and then to the Gentiles," preaching "that they should repent and turn to God. . . . For these causes the Jews caught me in the temple, and went about to kill me." He quoted the prophets and Moses as saying that Christ (the Messiah) should suffer, rise from the dead, and "show light unto the people, and to the Gentiles" (v. 11-23). Perhaps this could refer to such passages as Isaiah 53:2-12; 55:3-11; Daniel 9:25, 26; Micah 5:2; Zechariah 9:9; 11:12; Genesis 49:10; and Deuteronomy 18:18.

In Christ the principles which were potentially present in the Jewish scriptures were explicitly applied and completely fulfilled. It was not the principles, therefore, to which the Jews objected, but the specific application of them in the revolutionary and redeeming figure of Jesus.[3]

Festus broke into the narrative at this point, "Paul, thou art beside thyself [are mad—R.S.V.]; much learning doth make thee mad." This was denied by the apostle, and he continued his appeal to Agrippa, "For the king knoweth of these things, before whom also I speak freely; for I am persuaded that none of these things are hidden from him. . . . King Agrippa, believest thou the prophets?" Agrippa answered, "Almost thou persuadest me to be a Christian." Paul replied that he wished that all who heard him "were both almost, and altogether such as I am, except these bonds" (v. 24-29).

Modern versions treat the king's reply as ironical, since he was a reprobate and living in incestuous relations with his sister. The Revised Standard Version says, "In a short time you think to make me a Christian." The Emphatic Diaglott and King James versions follow the *Vatican Manuscript,* which are similar to the Inspired Version as quoted above. History shows that the testimony of Paul had little power to change Agrippa's life.

The king, the governor, Bernice, "and they that sat with them" arose, and talking among themselves declared, "This man doeth nothing worthy of death or of bonds." Agrippa said he might go free had he not appealed to Caesar.

## THE VOYAGE TO ROME BEGINS
(Acts 27:1-44)

Luke's narrative again carries the "we" passages and has many indications of an eyewitness account. The officials determined when and how the prisoners, including Paul, should be carried to Rome. Julius, a centurion of Augustus' band, had them in charge. They boarded a ship going to Adramyt-

238

tium, a seaport just south of Troas in Asia Minor. Aristarchus (19:29; 20:4) went with them. Why he is mentioned is not explained, but it has been suggested that he acted as Paul's personal servant.

After a day's run the ship docked at Sidon in northern Phoenicia. Julius gave Paul the "liberty to go unto his friends to refresh himself." This suggests meeting with some brethren living there. The next port was Myra in Lycia. It is indicated that the ship could not take the usual route because of the adverse northwesterly winds. Myra was a port of call for larger ships such as hauled grain from Egypt to Rome. Here they were transferred to a ship coming from Alexandria, Egypt, and sailing to Rome (v. 1-6).

Now when much time was spent, and when sailing was now dangerous, because the fast was now already past,[4] Paul admonished them, . . . Sirs, I perceive that this voyage will be with hurt and much damage, not only of the lading and ship, but also of our lives.—V. 7-10.

The centurion took the advice of the captain and of the owner of the ship, disregarding Paul's warning, and they set out looking for a better port to spend the winter. Luke describes the battle of keeping the ship from being driven ashore, from breaking up, and from miring in quicksand. As conditions worsened, they lowered the sails and let the boat drift. "The next day they lightened the ship" by throwing out some of the cargo. The third day much of the gear, or tackle on deck, was cast out. For many days they did not see the sun or stars, and all hope was lost.

## Paul Gains Respect
(27:21-44)

Paul reminded them that they should have taken his advice and stayed in Crete; but now "be of good cheer; for there shall be no loss of any man's life among you, but of [only—R.S.V.] the ship." This he knew, for "an angel of God" had come to him the previous night, saying, "Fear not, Paul; thou must be brought before Caesar; and lo, God hath given thee all them that sail with thee." Yet they would be cast upon a certain island. After fourteen days they neared the coast of Malta and fearing that the boat would founder on the rocks, they cast anchors from the stern. When some of the crew let a small boat down to ride ashore, Paul told the centurion, "Except these abide in the ship, ye cannot be saved." His advice was respected, the ropes were cut, and the boat fell into the sea (v. 21-32).

They had been without food for two weeks at this time, so Paul spoke out again to avoid a crisis. "Take some meat; for this is for your health; for there shall not a hair fall from the head of any of you." Then he took bread and divided it among the 276 aboard. Then they cast out the rest of the cargo of wheat.

At daybreak they saw a creek which they thought might provide a safe harbor, so they pulled up the four anchors, "loosed the rudder bands . . . and made toward shore." However, they ran aground and the ship stuck fast. The stern was broken by the violence of the waves. The soldiers suggested that the prisoners be killed lest they make their escape by swimming. The centurion wished to save Paul, and so ordered those who could swim to cast themselves into the sea and get to land. The rest used boards and pieces of the ship to make shore so that all were saved (v. 33-44).

---

1. *The Interpreter's Bible*, Vol. 9, p. 319.
2. Most all other versions insert "and," thus allowing for his birth and childhood in Cilicia.
3. *The Interpreter's Bible*, Vol. 9, p. 329.
4. Day of Atonement, late September or early October.

## Questions for Discussion

1. Why was Paul kept as a prisoner for two years in Caesarea?
2. What was the plot of the chief of the Jews to kill Paul?
3. After Paul had appealed to Caesar, why did he submit to a further trial by Herod Agrippa II?
4. What evidence is there that Paul was ever a member of the Sanhedrin?
5. What did Moses and the prophets say about Christ's (the Messiah's) coming?
6. How did Paul's testimony affect Agrippa?
7. What evidence is there that Julius the centurion favored Paul while he had custody of the prisoners?
8. Why was sailing more dangerous after "the fast"?
9. Tell of Paul's prophetic utterances on this journey.
10. What happened to the ship and its crew and why did the soldiers want to kill the prisoners?

# 37 PAUL REACHES ROME; JAMES' LETTER ABROAD

(Acts 28:1-28; James 1:1-27)

The crew of the Egyptian grain ship reached an island which is called Melita, but is now known as Malta. It is fifty miles south of Sicily. The soundings of the modern entrance to the St. Paul Bay correspond to those mentioned in Acts 27:28. It is thought that the shipwreck occurred about December, A.D. 59. It was March 1 of A.D. 60 before Paul left for Rome.

## MARVELOUS EXPERIENCES ON MALTA
(Acts 28:1-10)

"The barbarous people showed us no little kindness; for they kindled a fire." The crew and prisoners were wet and cold. People who spoke any foreign tongue were often referred to as "barbarous." Paul helped by gathering some sticks for the fire. As the firewood became warm, a viper became active and bit his hand. The natives, who were of Phoenician descent, saw this and expressed the opinion that Paul must be a murderer and that he would meet the ven-

242

geance of death. But Paul "shook off the beast into the fire, and felt no harm." When they saw that no harm came to Paul, they "said that he was a god" (v. 1-6).

"The chief man of the island" was Publius. Two inscriptions have been found showing that this was an official title in Malta. Publius "received us, and lodged us three days courteously." His father "lay sick of a fever and of a bloody flux." Paul prayed for him with laying on of hands and healed him. Other sick people on the island, hearing of this, "came, and were healed." To show their gratitude the people "honored us with many honors; and when we departed, they laded us with such things as were necessary" (v. 7-10).

There is something deep in human nature that craves the miraculous and looks for God in the abnormal and unnatural. If Jesus had come down from the Cross, the crowd would have believed him and hailed him as the Son of God. But when Jesus endured the Cross, they mocked him and let him die.[1]

Since the ship had been wrecked and the men were forced to swim ashore and their personal possessions lost, doubtless the gifts provided by these grateful people were really "necessary" for their comfort and health. Ordinarily Paul would not accept gifts, preferring to labor at his trade for his own support. But his status as a prisoner had changed this.

## PAUL FINALLY REACHES ROME
(Acts 28:11-15)

"After three months, we departed in a ship . . . whose sign was Castor and Pollux." This would bring their sailing in early March, A.D. 60. The "Twin Brothers" as a figurehead were considered by sailors as a good luck charm. "And landing at Syracuse, we tarried there three days." This is one of the largest Greek cities on the southeast part of the island of Sicily. "And from thence we fetched a compass, and came to Rhegium." This means the ship made a circuit. This city is on the toe of Italy.

As they moved on toward Rome the ship put in at Puteoli some two hundred miles north of Rhegium. Here "we found brethren, and were desired to tarry with them seven days" (v. 11-14). It is not certain how the rest of the journey was made. It is known that a canal runs parallel to the road to Appii Forum which city is forty miles south of Rome. The Three Taverns are ten miles nearer Rome. The brethren who came out from Rome to meet Paul's group likely divided and part stayed in the Three Taverns, while the others went on to Appii so as to make more certain of a contact. Doubtless the rest of the journey was made by road on the Appian Way. When Paul saw these brethren waiting to receive him, "he thanked God, and took courage" (v. 15).

## Paul a Prisoner in His Own Hired House (28:16-31)

When Rome was reached, the centurion "delivered the prisoners to the captain of the guard; but Paul was suffered to dwell by himself with a soldier that kept him" (v. 16).

"After three days Paul called the chief of the Jews together." Since he could not go to the synagogue, he asked the local leaders to come to him. He explained why he was a prisoner, that he had committed no offense against the Jewish religion or people, that the Romans had declared him innocent and would have released him, but because of Jewish opposition he was compelled to appeal to Caesar to save his own life. "For the hope of Israel [the Messiah] I am bound with this chain" (v. 17-20).

They said to Paul,

We neither received letters out of Judea concerning thee, neither any of the brethren that came showed or spake any harm of thee. But, we desire to hear of thee what thou thinkest; for as concerning this sect, we know that everywhere it is spoken against.

A day was agreed upon when they would come to Paul's lodging. At that time many came, and "he expounded and testified the kingdom of God, persuading them concerning Jesus, both out of the law of Moses and out of the prophets, from morning till evening." Some believed but "some believed not." The term "kingdom of God" is here used as a synonym for the Christian church as it is in Acts 1:3; 8:12. Paul gave the usual argument that Jesus was the expected Messiah (v. 21-27). (See also Acts 13:30-39.)

Paul closed his talk by quoting Isaiah 6:9-10. Jesus used it also to explain why his hearers were not all convinced by his parabolic teaching (Mark 4:10-12; Luke 8:9, 10). "Be it known therefore unto you, that salvation of God is sent unto the Gentiles, and that they will hear it." The rest of the book of Acts is abrupt and unfinished.

The Jews departed, and had great reasoning among themselves. And Paul dwelt two whole years in his own hired house . . . preaching the kingdom of God and teaching those things which concern the Lord Jesus Christ, with all confidence, no man forbidding him.—V. 28-31.

Why would Luke leave his readers without explaining how the Roman officials disposed of Paul's appeal and imprisonment? What happened at the end of the two years in which they gave him such unusual liberties? All that historians and scholars can offer us is speculative.

## The Historical Setting

Luke starts his treatise to Theophilus, who was thought to be a Roman official, by explaining "all that Jesus began both to do and teach." He mentioned Jesus showing "himself alive after his sufferings," and his promise to the apostles that "ye shall receive power, after that the Holy Ghost is come unto you; and ye shall be witnesses unto me both in Jerusalem, and in all Judea, and in Samaria, and unto the uttermost part of the earth" (Acts 1:1, 8).

This pattern of history was followed, and Luke may have felt that his obligation to Theophilus was fulfilled. If he lived in Rome the rest of the story would be known to him as well as to Luke. Others have suggested that perhaps Luke planned to write another treatise telling of Paul's trial, missionary events, and finally of his death or acquittal, but that the author died before his work was completed.

Chrysostom is quoted on this matter as saying, "At this point the historian stops his account and leaves the reader thirsting so that thereafter he guesses for himself. This also non-Christian writers do. For to know everything makes one sluggish and dull."[2]

Emperor Claudius had expelled the Jews from Rome about A.D. 50 (Acts 18:2), but he died in A.D. 54 and evidently they had returned.

It is commonly assumed that Paul was kept in Rome for two years, and that during this period he wrote his pastoral epistles. These and others will be presented in the order of their writing to show the historical and doctrinal development of the church.

## THE GENERAL EPISTLE OF JAMES

Most scholars think this was written from Jerusalem about A.D. 60. Its authorship is not certain, but generally is conceded to be the work of "James the Lord's brother" (Gal. 1:19; Jude 1:1; Acts 12:17; 15:13). Josephus said that his death occurred in A.D. 62[3]

## SOME CHRISTIAN FUNDAMENTALS
(Jas. 1:1-27)

"To the twelve tribes which are scattered abroad, greeting. My brethren, count it all joy when ye fall into many

246

afflictions; knowing this, that the trying of your faith worketh patience." The phrase, "twelve tribes" doubtless means all of spiritual Israel and may be interpreted as written to Jewish Christians alone who live outside of Palestine.

"But let patience have its perfect work, that ye may be perfect and entire, wanting nothing" (v. 4). "Perfect" is used as a moralist's adjective, more or less equivalent to "satisfactory," to describe an ethical quality well within human attainment"[4] (see James 3:2; also chapters 13:1; 24:2).

The passage which served young Joseph Smith, Jr., in solving his problem of which church to join in 1820 comes next: "If any of you lack wisdom, let him ask of God." The promise is only to those who ask with unwavering faith (v. 5, 6).

The gospel is a leveler in that the poor shall be lifted up, while the rich shall be brought down. Material things have a way of slipping from us, or their glory and satisfactions perish. The stewardship program brings lasting joy to those who obey the gospel on either level.

Temptation is treated by James in a clear and helpful manner. "Blessed is the man that resisteth temptation." Only the person who has been tried knows himself. "I . . . will try them as gold is tried" (Zech. 13:9). But James will not permit anyone to use "temptation" as a crutch: "Man is tempted, when he is drawn away of *his own* lust, and enticed" (v. 12-14).

"Every good gift . . . cometh down from the Father of lights, with whom is no variableness, neither shadow of turning" (v. 17). This is a fundamental of our faith. If God were changeable, it would disprove his supreme light of intelligence (omniscience). His word and promises would be of little value. So James urges us to "receive with meekness, the engrafted word, which is able to save your souls" (v. 21). God expresses himself most always through human means, but the inspiration and virtue of the message has been tested and sustained by many generations of experience. Then a caution was added, "But be ye doers of the word, and not hearers only." Many convince themselves that they are virtuous when they verbally acknowledge a truth. But like those who look in a mirror and then forget or see only in part, so those who hear but fail to act are not profited (v. 22-25).

A helpful definition of "religion" closes the first chapter: "To visit the fatherless and widows in their affliction, and to keep himself unspotted from the vices of the world" (v. 27). Here is justification for an intensive home ministry program by those whose lives testify to having become Christlike.

---

1. *The Interpreter's Bible*, Vol. 9, p. 343.
2. *Ibid.*, p. 352.
3. *Antiquities* 20:9, 1; *The Interpreter's Bible*, Vol. 12, p. 5.
4. *The Interpreter's Bible*, Vol. 12, p. 22.

## QUESTIONS FOR DISCUSSION

1. What miracles were performed on Malta and how did they affect the natives?
2. Tell how Paul and his companions made the last forty miles of their journey to Rome.
3. Where was Paul imprisoned and what liberties were extended to him?
4. What was Paul's message to "the chief of the Jews" and how did he bring in his mission to the Gentiles?
5. Why does the book of Acts end inconclusively? Give some possible justification for this abruptness.
6. Who was Theophilus and what did Luke say he would explain to him?
7. Who was the author of the epistle of James and to whom did he write?
8. Is God's promise of wisdom to those who ask unconditional? Has it proved true in your experience?

9. How is the gospel a leveler? Can Satan be blamed for all evil temptations?
10. Is God the same in all ages—Old Testament and New Testament times and latter days? Explain. What is pure religion?

# 38 JAMES CONTINUES WRITINGS ON FUNDAMENTALS

(James 2:1-5:20)

The sound doctrines which James taught about the true follower of Christ will furnish a pattern for righteous conduct for all ages. The man who poses as a religious person but "bridleth not his tongue" is deceiving himself. It is often very difficult for one to see his own faults, or as Robert Burns wrote, "To see ourselves as others see us."

## THE INFLUENCE OF RICHES
(2:1-13)

"God is no respecter of persons," declared Peter (Acts 10:34). For Christians to show favoritism in their fellowship because of wealth or position is ungodly, and a denial of our faith. James said that this may show in the seating of a congregation; but in modern times, it more frequently appears in social clubs and in church organizations. It also protrudes into business and politics. "All men are created equal" is a high sounding phrase in our Declaration of Independence; but in reality, no two of us are precisely alike, and some have inborn advantages. To show favoritism, James wrote, we make ourselves "partial judges, and become evil in [our] thoughts" (v. 1-4).

250

"If ye fulfill the royal law according to the scripture, Thou shalt love thy neighbor as thyself, ye do well." Then James makes a sharp distinction: to fail to keep the whole law of love makes one guilty of violating all of the code God gave as judged by the "law of liberty" (v. 5-12).

## FAITH AND WORKS
(2:14-25)

"What profit is it . . . for a man to say he hath faith, and hath not works?" These works are not of the old covenant with Israel, but of the law of liberty—clothing and feeding a naked and destitute brother and sister. Intentions to do good are virtuous only as motivations which result in good works; but "faith, if it have not works is dead, being alone" (v. 14-18).

Abraham believed God, but was justified only after he offered his son Isaac on the altar. His faith was made perfect by his works. While he was not required to slay his son, his faith was "imputed unto him for righteousness; and he was called the friend of God" (v. 14-25).

## WISDOM THAT IS FROM ABOVE
(3:1-18)

The epistle of James is classed by many scholars as part of the "wisdom literature" of the Bible. "If any man offend not in word, the same is a perfect man, and able also to bridle the whole body." This observation is illustrated by putting bits in the horses' mouths, and the helms ["rudders"—R.S.V.] on ships. "Even so the tongue is a little member, and boasteth great things. Behold, how great a matter a little fire kindleth! . . . It defileth the whole body, and setteth on fire the course of nature; and it is set on fire of hell" (v. 1-6).

Man is able to tame or control every kind of beast and bird, "but the tongue can no man tame." Though we are made in the likeness of God, our tongue both blesses and curses. "These things ought not so to be. Doth a fountain send forth at the same place sweet water and bitter?" If man is wise he will "show out of a good conversation his works with meekness of wisdom" (7-13). Envying, strife, confusion, and every evil work is earthly, sensual, and devilish. "But the wisdom that is from above is first pure, then peaceable, gentle, and easy to be entreated, full of mercy and good fruits, without partiality, and without hypocrisy" (v. 14-17).

## Pursuit of Worldly Pleasures
(4:1-12)

"From whence come wars and fightings among you?" Human nature has changed little over the centuries. Some social progress has been made because men have learned that they can do better by forming organized systems and by giving support to governments by laws rather than by men. Yet the lust of men for property and social power remain our strongest motivations. Communism's advance shows how thin the wall of partition is between order and chaos. Men have willingly traded their birthright of intelligence, agency, and freedom for empty promises about a society of milk and honey, even though they know that these are to be obtained by deception, stealing, intimidation, and even murder. Under such labels as "the end justifies the means," "peaceful co-existence," and "better Red than dead" men are led into hopeless materialism.

"Ye lust, and have not; ye kill, and desire to have, and cannot obtain" is just as true today as in A.D. 60. "Ye ask, and receive not, because ye ask amiss, that ye may consume it upon your lusts" (v. 1-3).

"Ye adulterers and adulteresses" is admittedly a poor rendition of the Greek text. From the "imagery of Israel, the bride of God, who is unfaithful to her marriage vows,"[1] it means simply, "Ye unfaithful creatures" and it so reads

252

in the Revised Standard Version. "Friendship of the world is enmity with God." The desire for popularity has always been a strong motivation among men. And when this desire becomes too strong, character is sacrificed. "The spirit that dwelleth in us lusteth to envy." Human dignity suffers when we see our associates getting favors and promotions which we crave. However, "God resisteth the proud, but giveth grace unto the humble." This is not simply a religious proverb; it is life as we know it (v. 4-6).

"Resist the devil, and he will flee from you." The liberal mind is apt to deny the existence of a devil, but acknowledges the drawing power of lust and evil. It is not profitable to get into semantics or philosophy at this point; but experience teaches that prayer can dispel darkness, evil, and other human weaknesses. "Draw nigh to God, and he will draw nigh to you" (v. 7, 8). Spirit begets spirit.

## SINFUL SELF-CONFIDENCE
(4:12-17)

"Who art thou that judgest another?" Some evaluation and judgment must be exercised by us, but it is well to keep in mind that we see life from different angles each year. Society is a kaleidoscope. Only the Great Lawgiver can be an impartial judge. "Ye that say, Today or tomorrow we will go into such a city, and continue there a year, and buy and sell, and get gain," beware, for you have no guarantee of a tomorrow. Life is a vapor that easily vanishes. Some Bible literalists have followed the injunction, "Ye ought to say, If the Lord will, we shall live, and do this, or that" (v. 13-15).

Many people rejoice in their boastings. "All such rejoicing is evil." Usually the boaster fools only children and himself. The evil of it is that he loses the confidence of his peers and gets to the place where he doesn't really know what the truth is. "To him that knoweth to do good, and doeth it

253

not, to him it is sin" (v. 16, 17). Paul put it this way: "And even as they did not like to retain God according to some knowledge, God gave them over to a reprobate mind" (Rom. 1:28).

## ON LUXURY, FORBEARANCE, AND SICKNESS (5:1-20)

"Ye rich men, weep and howl for your miseries that shall come upon you. . . . Your gold and silver is cankered." Specifically James charged that they kept back the laborer's wages by fraud, they lived in pleasure, and condemned and killed the just. By depriving men of their livelihood when they were powerless to resist, the landlords of the fields became killers. Only in modern times have the wage earners found an effective weapon to defend themselves against industrial exploitation through labor unions. Now it may be that the pendulum has swung too far to the other side, and that the unions are exploiting the poor by keeping them out of their unions and causing high prices in consumer goods.

James urged forbearance and patience in faith "for the coming of the Lord draweth nigh" (v. 1-8). It is asking much of a man who needs food and raiment to wait for generations to have these necessities. But we are saved by hope, and so struggle on in expectancy. Grudge not one against another. "Take . . . the prophets . . . for an example of suffering affliction, and of patience." The "patience of Job" is cited as a case of the Lord's pity and mercy (v. 9-11).

"Swear not, neither by heaven, neither by the earth, neither by any other oath; but let your yea be yea; and your nay, nay." This also is followed literally by some religionists. In the courts of our land they are permitted to "affirm" instead of taking the usual oath.

"Is any among you afflicted? let him pray. Is any merry? let him sing psalms." "Affliction" may include any mental or physical distress or suffering. One's faith that God will

254

hear and answer should suffice. When relief comes, one's rejoicing should cause him to "sing praise" (R.S.V.)

Is any sick among you? let him call for the elders of the church; and let them pray over him, anointing him with oil in the name of the Lord; and the prayer of faith shall save the sick, and the Lord shall raise him up; and if he have committed sins, they shall be forgiven him.

Confess your faults and pray for one another "that ye may be healed" (v. 11-16).

Many of the healings described in the New Testament make no mention of anointing with oil. (See Matthew 8-13; Acts 9:33-40; 20:9-10.) Mark 6:14 and James 5:14 are exceptions. However, these carry more complete details, and establish a principle. Absence of these details are negative and do not disprove the principle.

"In what is now known as the Greek Orthodox Church the directions in James 5:14 were and still are followed literally."[2]

The "elders" are not just senior men but officers "of the church."

In Latin Christianity of the early Middle Ages the practice of anointing and prayer was the same, then

less and less emphasis was laid on the possibility of physical healing and more and more emphasis on spiritual healing. Consequently the meaning of the rite gradually shifted until it became regarded as primarily the means for obtaining remission of sins.

It eventually became "extreme unction," a rite for the dying.[3]

"The effectual fervent prayer of a righteous man availeth much." Elias (Elijah) is cited as an example (I Kings 17:1; 18:1, 40-45).

The epistle of James closes with this wisdom: "He which converteth the sinner from the error of his way shall save a soul from death, and shall hide a multitude of sins" (v. 17-20). Some think that this passage refers to the remission of sins of the one converted. However, most scholars interpret it as referring to the reward for missionary endeavor by any devout Christian. There is a reward even for one who gives "a cup of cold water only, in the name of a disciple" (Matt. 10:38).

1. *The Interpreter's Bible*, Vol. 12, p. 55.
2. *Ibid.*, p. 17.
3. *Ibid.*, pp. 17, 18.

## QUESTIONS FOR DISCUSSION

1. Tell why you think or do not think favoritism is shown where you worship because of individual wealth or vocation.
2. What does James call the "royal law," and why does showing partiality violate it?
3. Paul insists that the works of the Israelitic covenant profit nothing. How then was Abraham's faith made perfect by works?
4. What was James trying to prove by his illustrations of using bits in horses' mouths and rudders on ships?
5. Wars and fighting still come from selfish motives. Has better distribution of jobs and good wages through organizations changed men much in regard to human combativeness?
6. Give illustrations of "friendship with the world" and of some results of it.
7. In what ways does James say it is unjust to judge others?
8. Specifically what did James charge the rich men of doing that would condemn them, and would even make them murderers?
9. What evil do you see in taking an oath or predicting what you will or will not do?
10. Should the church make it easier for members to confess their faults and to seek administration in sickness? Defend your answer.

# 39

# EPISTLE TO THE PHILIPPIANS

Paul wrote seven letters during his two years of imprisonment. The most intimate of all his letters, and some regard it as the most beautiful of Paul's letters, is Philippians, containing several of his greatest religious utterances.

The apostle Paul had been cruelly treated on his first visit to Philippi (Acts 16:16-25). The church there later made up for that indignity by its affection and constant ministry to his temporal needs. In fact the occasion for the epistle seems to have been the arrival of Epaphroditus "with a generous gift. . . . The weary months were passing on, and he was obliged to rent a house of his own, and provide his own supplies, for the Roman government did not pay the expenses of its prisoners."[1]

## THANKSGIVING AND PRISON LIFE
(1:1-30)

Paul included Timothy in his salutation, and then speaks in first person, singular. "I thank my God upon every remembrance of you . . . for the steadfastness of you all, . . . your fellowship. . . . Inasmuch as both in my bonds, and in the defence and confirmation of the gospel, ye all are partakers of my

257

grace." The Revised Standard Version reads, "partakers with me of grace" (v. 1-7).

Paul continued in love and fatherly counsel. "And this I pray, that your love may abound yet more . . . that ye may approve things that are excellent; that ye may be sincere and without offence till the day of Christ." This day is when Christ is to return and claim his peoples (v. 8-10).

Philippians "was never intended to be the material for either a theological system or an ecclesiastical theory."[2] "Understand, brethren, that the things which happened unto me have fallen out rather [really served—R.S.V.] unto the furtherance of the gospel; so that my bonds in Christ are manifest in all the palace, and in all other places" (v. 12, 13). His imprisonment was a matter of public interest. Who was this Christ who inspired his followers with such willingness to suffer? The "palace" was probably the barracks of the military district.

The soldiers assigned to watch him would be always changing, and one man would talk about him to his comrades, so that Paul can say quite truly that the whole guard was now aware of why he was a prisoner—and not only the guard but all the rest.[3]

This in turn made "the brethren . . . much more bold to speak the word without fear" (v. 14). Some preach Christ from envy and rivalry, others from love, "and I therein do rejoice . . . for I know that this shall turn to my salvation [deliverance—R.S.V.]."

"For me to live, is to do the will of Christ; and to die, is my gain. Now I am in a strait betwixt two": a desire to depart and be with Christ, and a desire "to abide in the flesh" which is "more needful to you." Convinced of this, Paul declared, "I know that I shall abide and continue with you" (v. 15-26). Paul seemed to be quite certain of his acquittal and that he would pay another visit to Philippi. He admonished them, "Stand fast in one spirit, with one mind striving together for the faith of the gospel; and in nothing be terrified by your adversaries, who reject the gospel" (v. 27, 28).

## HUMILITY, EXALTATION, AND MINISTRY
(2:1-30)

"Be likeminded, having the same love, being of one accord. . . . Let each esteem other better than themselves. Look not every man on his own things [to his own interests—R.S.V.] but . . . on the things [interests] of others" (v. 1-4). These are more than lofty sentiments; they are Christian ideals. The Spirit of Christ does not come to people who are not of one accord. "Be one; and if ye are not one, ye are not mine" (D. and C. 38:6 a).

"Christ Jesus . . . being in the form of God, thought it not robbery to be equal with God." The Revised Standard Version reads, "did not count equality . . . a thing to be grasped." This translation seems more consistent with the verses which follow and is in harmony with most modern versions. "But made himself of no reputation [emptied himself—R.S.V.], and took upon him the form of a servant, and was made in the likeness of men . . . became obedient unto death, even the death of the cross" (v. 5-8).

"Once more, . . . Paul leaves the earthly history out of account, and falls back on something which he thinks of as happening in a heavenly pre-existence."[4] (See Genesis 1:27; John 1:2; 6:33; 7:29; 8:42; 16:28; 17:5; Jude 1:6.)

"God . . . hath . . . exalted him, and given him a name which is above every name; that at the name of Jesus every knee should bow . . . and . . . every tongue should confess that Jesus Christ is Lord, to the glory of God the Father" (v. 9-11). This passage must refer to the return of Christ in glory and to his millennial reign which was to be followed by the great day of judgment. Then some of the worldly people will want to hide, even to have the mountains and rocks fall on them (Rev. 6:14-17).

259

> Wherefore, my beloved, . . . work out your own salvation with fear and trembling; . . . do all things without murmurings and disputings; that ye may be blameless and harmless, the sons of God . . . holding forth the word of life; that I may rejoice in the day of Christ, that I have not run in vain.

The matter of faith and works is again introduced in Paul's theology. Perhaps he is suggesting that now he can help but little; it is up to them to serve with humble mind. Nevertheless, he emphasizes that Christian works, by serving in Christ's stead, will have influence on one's eternal life. "God . . . worketh in you both to will and to do of his good pleasure" (v. 12-17).

Because Paul is unable to come to Philippi himself as he would like, he is sending two trusted servants. Timothy, who labored with him there as a son, and naturally ["genuinely"— R.S.V.] cares about them will depart as "soon as I shall see how it will go with me; but I trust in the Lord that I also myself shall come shortly" (v. 19-24). He could not tell how soon his trial would be held and Timothy could start; therefore, he considered it necessary to send Epaphroditus at once. This man had been their messenger to bring funds to Paul (4:18) and then became ill "nigh unto death, not regarding his life, to supply your lack of service toward me." Paul asked them to "receive him therefore in the Lord with all gladness" (v. 25-30).

"This declaration was to prove a momentous one in the history of the church. The age of persecution was now opening, and Paul seemed here to sanction the principle that those who suffered martyrdom in any form were thereby vested with authority."[5]

## Paul's Loss to Gain Christ
### (3:1-21)

"Finally, my brethren, rejoice in the Lord." The word "rejoice" was also the Greek word for "farewell." Being preceded by the word "finally" indicated that Paul had this meaning in mind. He mentioned that his repetition in writing doesn't bother him and is "safe" for them. Reiteration might contribute to their protection against apostasy. He may have intended to end his letter with this farewell; but then something changed his mind, and he started off in forcible terms, warning them of dangers.

"Beware of dogs," . . . evil workers . . . concision ["those who mutilate the flesh"—R.S.V.]. Doubtless Paul had in mind those who were trying to seduce Christians into a garbage heap, "without any discrimination of clean and unclean meats."[6]

"We are the [true—R.S.V.] circumcision, which worship God in the spirit" is in contrast to the practice in Judaism which was a poor symbol of inward consecration (v. 1-4).

Paul then told of his heritage in the tribe of Benjamin and his being a Pharisee. "I count all things but loss for the excellency of the knowledge of Christ Jesus my Lord." Some people like to brag about their lineage and achievements, but he considered that they were "but dung" to him in comparison with the gospel.

Then in moderation he added,

Not as though I had already attained, either were already perfect . . . but this one thing I do, forgetting those things which are behind, and reaching forth unto those things which are before, I press toward the mark for the prize of the high calling of God in Christ Jesus.—V. 5-14.

This is a favorite text of many Christians.

"Brethren, be followers together of me, and mark them which walk so as ye have us for an ensample" (v. 17). How could a person who had acknowledged his imperfections set himself up for an example? Surely he was not referring to his own goodness, for he disclaimed "having mine own righteousness, . . . but that . . . which is of God" (v. 9).

"What he wanted others to imitate was the sense of falling short."[7]

With a sad heart he mentioned those who are "enemies of the cross of Christ . . . whose God is their belly, and who glory in their shame, who mind earthly things" (v. 19). He may have referred to unworthy members of the Philippian church; but it is more likely that he meant professing Christians in general who had disgraced the name of Christ.

1. *Book of Life*, Vol. 7, p. 279.
2. *The Interpreter's Bible*, Vol. 11, p. 14.
3. *Ibid.*, p. 30.
4. *Ibid.*, p. 47.
5. *Ibid.*, p. 71.
6. *Ibid.*, p. 73.
7. *Ibid.*, p. 93.

## QUESTIONS FOR DISCUSSION

1. What indignities did Paul suffer on his first visit to Philippi?
2. What did Paul mean by "the day of Christ"?
3. What are the evidences that Paul did proselyting while a Roman prisoner?
4. Explain the statement "for me to die is gain."
5. Are Christians expected "to esteem others better than themselves"? Explain and compare with Leviticus 19:18, Romans 13:9.
6. How did God exalt Christ? Under what conditions will all men, at the name of Jesus, bow the knee?
7. Explain "work out your own salvation." When will it be done?
8. Whom did Paul send to Philippi and why did he select these two men?
9. Who were the "dogs" Paul warned against, and why did he say "we are the true circumcision"?
10. How did Paul express the objective toward which he was pressing? Did he set himself up as an example?

# 40

# PHILIPPIANS CONCLUDED; EPISTLE TO COLOSSIANS

Paul's practice was to close each epistle with a section of practical counsel, personal notices, and greetings. This last chapter contains some excellent material of this character.

## FINAL ADMONITION
## (4:1-9)

"My brethren, dearly beloved and longed for, my joy and crown, so stand fast in the Lord." This and many other passages show that the apostle to the Gentiles had a great affection for the church at Philippi. He admonished Euodias and Syntyche to resolve their differences in the spirit of the Lord. Some quarrels had broken out in this congregation; but this one in particular had grieved him, since the women concerned were both very dear to Paul. He entreats an unnamed yokefellow to help reconcile these women who worked with him and Clement (v. 1-3).

"Let your moderation [forbearance—R.S.V.] be known unto all men. The Lord is at hand." The word "moderation" implies a willingness to give and take and not stand rigidly on one's rights or on so-called "principle." Then Paul adds what had become the watchword of the early Christians, "The

Lord is at hand." This was the hope which sustained these early day saints through their growing pains and persecutions.

"Be afflicted for nothing; but in everything by prayer and supplication with thanksgiving let your requests be made known unto God." The King James Version translated this "Be careful for nothing," while the Revised Standard Version reads, "Have no anxiety about anything." Prayer and thanksgiving often do relieve anxiety.

This chapter contains the oft quoted "Whatsoever" text.

Finally, brethren, whatsoever things are true . . . honest . . . just . . . pure . . . lovely . . . of good report; if there be any virtue, and if there be any praise, think on these things. Those things, which ye have both learned, and received, and heard, and seen in me, do; and the God of peace shall be with you.—V. 8, 9.

It is as difficult as it is important for one to control his thoughts. It is wise, however, to use great care in selecting one's environment including his close companions. "For as he thinketh in his heart, so is he" (Prov. 23:7). But mere contemplation is not enough, Paul continued; what you have learned, received, heard, and seen in me, that you should do. This alone will bring the peace of God.

## PHILIPPIAN GENEROSITY—GREETINGS EXCHANGED (v. 10-22)

He expressed his joy in the revival of their care for him as opportunity had opened to them. He did not say this because he had unsupplied wants, for he had "learned, in whatsoever state I am, therewith to be content." He had tasted both the bitter and the sweet in life, and had learned to trust God. This he expressed very beautifully: "I can do all things through Christ which strengtheneth me" (v. 10-13).

Paul then mentioned that on his first journey, after leaving Macedonia, the only church which inquired after and ministered to his need was Philippi. "Not because I desire

a gift; but I desire fruit that may abound to your account."
He was paid in full with the gift which Epaphroditus brought
from them. In turn he could assure them "my God shall
supply all your need according to your riches in glory by
Christ Jesus" (v. 15-19).

He closes his letter by saluting every saint. "The brethren
which are with me greet you. All the saints salute you,
chiefly they that are of Caesar's household" (v. 21, 22).
Doubtless Paul had in mind that after the brethren in leadership had read the epistle, it would be read aloud at a public
meeting and so transmit these greetings to all the saints.
"They . . . of Caesar's household" might refer to some converts close to the emperor. Yet it was also "a general term
for those who worked in the government service. Many of
them were slaves; others held minor offices in the civil and
military administration."[1]

# THE EPISTLE TO THE COLOSSIANS
Written by Paul, about early A.D. 62

The time and place of writing this letter has been questioned. Some have argued that it was written from Caesarea
during his two years of imprisonment there. The important
thing is, what does it say?

The epistle to the Colossians was called forth by the necessity of
guarding the truth of the gospel against an insidiously attractive per-
version of its fundamental principles—a syncretism of Judaic and
pagan doctrines and practices which tended to obscure and diminish
the glory of Christ while professing to set forth a higher knowledge
and a more severely ascetic morality.[2]

## SALUTATION AND MYSTERY OF THE GOSPEL
(1:1-29)

Again Paul associates Timothy with him in the salutation
to the saints. "We give thanks to God . . . praying always
for you, since we heard of your faith in Christ Jesus, and of

265

your love to all the saints" (v. 1-4). This reflects "that Paul had never had any personal contact with the church to which he is writing [See 2:1]; he knew of their state only at second hand."[3] This concern extends to "the hope which is laid up for you in heaven, whereof ye heard before in the word of the truth of the gospel." Epaphras had taught them and told Paul of their "love in the Spirit" (v. 5-8).

Paul also expressed thanks and prayers for their "spiritual understanding" and that they be

fruitful in every good work . . . unto all patience . . . giving thanks unto the Father . . . who hath delivered us from the power of darkness, and hath translated us into the kingdom of his dear Son; in whom we have redemption through his blood, even the forgiveness of sins.—V. 9-14.

These statements are better understood against the background of 2:8; 16-18. The Gnostic philosophy (discussed in chapters 21:4; 22:4) has deceived some in the church by claims of superior revealed knowledge, mystic formulas, secret initiations, and ceremonial rites. Paul assured them that God had delivered them from this darkness and redeemed them from their sins by the sacrificial offering of his Son on the cross. Christ is

the image of the invisible God . . . for by him were all things created, that are in heaven, and that are in earth. . . . All things were created by him, and for him . . . and he is the head of the body, the church . . . that in all things he might have the pre-eminence.—V. 13-18.

Some who may fail to see the basic function of the church in the plan of salvation interpret this position of Christ in transcendental terms as "head" of an eternal or heavenly "body." However, Paul emphasized, "It pleased the Father that in him should all fulness dwell; and, having made peace through the blood of his cross, by himself to reconcile all things unto himself; by him, I say, whether they be things in earth, or things in heaven." Even as the Colossians were once alienated "by wicked works, yet now hath he reconciled, in the body of his flesh through death, to present you holy and unblamable" (v. 19-22).

Paul followed this by once more expressing his joy in sufferings in the flesh for "his body's sake, which is the church." His ministry is

to fulfil the word of God; even the mystery which hath been hid from ages and from generations, and now is made manifest to his saints; to whom God would make known what is the riches of the glory of this mystery among the Gentiles; which is Christ in you, the hope of glory.—V. 23-27.

Though the saints at Colossae were not known to Paul, yet he suffered for them as part of Christ's body, the church.

## ABIDE IN THE VICTORIOUS CHRIST
(2:1-22)

The city of Laodicea, a thriving commercial city in the Roman province of Asia Minor lying ten miles west of Colossae, was to receive the letter also, as they were being troubled by the Gnostic heresy. Paul wanted their hearts also to be comforted "to the acknowledgment of the mystery of God and of Christ, who is of God, even the Father, in whom are hid all the treasures of wisdom and knowledge. And this I say, lest any man should beguile you with enticing words" (v. 1-4). This states plainly the purpose of the letter. An alien philosophy, making false claims to hidden wisdom and secret knowledge, inaccessible to man except by revelation, was making inroads on these churches. "Beware lest any man spoil you through philosophy and vain deceit, after the traditions of men . . . and not after Christ. . . . Ye are complete in him which is the head of all principality and power" (v. 9-11).

"Erroneous ideas can have a high degree of fascination, especially where they offer a short cut to truth for undisciplined minds, or an assurance of knowledge beyond human reach."[4]

The churches are admonished to put off

the body of the sins of the flesh by the circumcision of Christ; buried with him in baptism, wherein also ye are risen with him through the faith of the operation of God, who hath raised him from the dead . . . blotting out the handwriting of ordinances that was against us, . . . nailing it to his cross. . . . Let no man therefore judge you in meat, or in drink, or in respect of a holyday, . . . the new moon, or of the sabbath days; which are a shadow of things to come; but the body is of Christ. Let no man beguile you of your reward in a voluntary humility and worshipping of angels, intruding into those things which he hath not seen, vainly puffed up by his fleshly mind.—V. 11-18.

The rest of the chapter continues in condemnation of Gnostic heresies.

It might be well for us of the Restoration to examine our claim to superior knowledge of the gospel because of the revelations given to the church. There is no denying that godly wisdom has been received by those who have asked in faith, but we must be considerate of those who doubt the virtue of our claim unless they see a superior type of light and life shining out of Zion.

---

1. *The Interpreter's Bible,* Vol. 11, p. 128.
2. *Ibid.,* p. 134.
3. *Ibid.,* p. 151.
4. *Ibid.,* p. 189.

## QUESTIONS FOR DISCUSSION

1. What trouble in the church at Philippi did Paul first mention, and what remedy did he propose?
2. What meaning was attached to the word "moderation" and the expression, "The Lord is at hand"?
3. Quote the "whatsoever text" and point out the elements of most value to us as Saints.

4. What did Paul recommend for guidance in saintly life?
5. Does it seem that Paul's praise for the saints' generosity was to encourage more giving to him? Why or why not?
6. State the main purpose of the letter to the church in Colossae. What other church had a similar problem?
7. How had Paul learned of their "love in the Spirit," and what remedy did he offer for their problem?
8. What are the teachings of the Gnostics and why would these doctrines appeal to believers in the gospel?
9. For what reason did Paul bring in baptism and what relation had it to Judaism and Gnosticism?
10. What relationship has the Restoration message to the Gnostic doctrines? *revelation?*

# 41

## COLOSSIANS CONCLUDED; PHILEMON

(3:1 - 4:18)

In our last chapter much was said about heretical doctrines of the Gnostics. Yet it may seem strange that this name was not used by Paul nor any other writer in the scriptures. The name is coined from the Greek word *gnosis* which means "knowledge." It was

a very dangerous heresy which came into the church like a flood in the second century. By the beginning of the third century nearly all of the more intellectual Christian congregations in the Roman Empire were affected by it. Its errors are clearly referred to in the New Testament, e.g., I John 2:22; 4:2, 3, where reference is made to those who deny that Christ had come in the flesh. The system was eclectic [selective] and its materials were drawn from many quarters such as the mythologies of Greece, Egypt, Persia, and India, and from the philosophies and theosophies of these lands.[1]

John refers to this philosophy as "that spirit of antichrist." Perhaps the movement had not grown to sufficient importance in the first century to have a name which was commonly used. Paul was outspoken against this heresy, but a little more specific against the Judaizers (see Chapter 11:1) who gave him more direct opposition and were more aggressive.

# Put Off the "Old Man"—Family Counsel
(3:1-25)

"If ye then be risen with Christ, seek those things which are above." This presumes the death and burial of the "old man with his sins" (2:11, 12), and then the coming out of the sacramental water to face a new life with Christian ideals to guide the way. "When Christ, who is our life, shall appear, then shall ye also appear with him in glory" (v. 1-4). This may imply, though not necessarily, that Paul thought some of his readers would be alive to share in that glorious return of Christ to this earth as "king of kings." (Compare with I Thessalonians 4:15-17.)

"Mortify [put to death—R.S.V.] therefore your members [practices] which are upon the earth." Then he lists some of them: fornication, covetousness, malice, and blasphemy. "Lie not one to another, seeing ye have put off the old man with his deeds; and have put on the new man, which is renewed in knowledge . . . where there is neither Greek nor Jew . . . but Christ is all, and in all" (v. 5-11).

From warning against the vices of pagan life, Paul turned to the character of new life open to

the elect of God . . . kindness . . . meekness . . . forbearing . . . and forgiving one another . . . even as Christ forgave you. . . . Put on charity, which is the bond of perfectness. . . . Let the word of Christ dwell in you richly in all wisdom; teaching . . . one another in psalms and hymns . . . and whatsoever ye do in word or deed, do all in the name of the Lord Jesus.—V. 12-17.

Christian work is to be undertaken only after prayer.

The letter then was directed toward the homelife of the saints, which instruction was both timely and timeless. "Wives, submit yourselves unto your own husbands, as it is fit in the Lord." Two aspects of this counsel need consideration. (1) Jesus placed loyalty to family ties as subordinate to allegiance of the individual to Christ and to God (Matt.

10:31-33; Luke 14:26). (2) How should wives subordinate themselves to their husbands? In the Hebrew law and custom and those of many other nations of the pre-Christian era wives were considered as the husband's property. He could demand her labor or divorce her at will. Jesus would not tolerate such partiality. With him every soul was precious and to be accorded human dignity. Note that the passage Paul wrote about submission is qualified, "as it is fit in the Lord" (v. 18, 19; see also Eph. 5:25).

Paul added some instruction for the children. "Obey your parents in all things; for this is well pleasing unto the Lord. Fathers, provoke not your children to anger, lest they be discouraged" (v. 20, 21; see also Matt. 18:5).

"Servants [slaves—R.S.V.], obey . . . your masters . . . in singleness of heart, fearing God."

Slaves constituted a great part—perhaps the majority—of the early Christian communities; even more, it [this admonition] is occcasioned by the need to check the tendency to rebellion which the Christian gospel of freedom was bound to quicken in the mind of the slave.[2]

The New Testament does not condone slavery, but neither does it encourage rebellion nor immediate or radical shifts in social mores without regard to consequences. They are to be treated "just and equal" (4:1).

"He that doeth wrong shall receive for the wrong which he hath done; and there is no respect of persons." This is far different from the dividing "sheep from goats" doctrine in which the sheep go to heaven and the goats go to hell. Judgment and reward is based on man's work, his total life (Rev. 20:12-14). This applies to priest or slave, male or female.

## EXHORTATION TO PRAYER—FINAL GREETINGS (4:1-18)

Prayer and thanksgiving should characterize their worship; but specifically, he asks that they pray for him. This is not a formal request, as we sometimes use as terminal thought in prayer meeting, nor does he ask them to pray that his chains may be removed. The greatness of his soul is again manifested as he asks, "that God would open unto us a door of utterance, to speak the mystery of Christ, for which I am also in bonds . . . as I ought to speak" (v. 2-4). There is no self-pity here. He wishes only better opportunity to preach Christ.

"Walk in wisdom toward them that are without, redeeming the time." The Revised Standard Version makes it a little clearer, "toward outsiders, making the most of the time" (v. 5). He may have had in mind the time before the return of Christ.

"Let your speech be always with grace, seasoned with salt." This suggests pleasantness and good humor. Every person is different—and should be treated as an individual rather than one of the mass of humanity.

The rest of the epistle contains personal references. Tychicus, a Gentile convert, accompanied Paul to Jerusalem with the aid fund (Acts 20:4), and was with Paul in Rome. Onesimus was a runaway slave (Philemon 1:10-13) who had been converted by Paul. These two brethren were to carry the epistle and "make known unto you all things which are done here" (v. 6-9).

Those named as sending greetings from Rome include Mark, author of the second Gospel, and "Luke, the beloved physician," author of the third Gospel and the book of Acts.

## The Letter to Philemon
(1:1-25)

This letter is addressed to individuals and to a church which met in their home. "Though brief, it was composed with extraordinary care and . . . is one of the most skillful letters ever written." This may seem to be greatly exaggerated to the casual reader. "It contains no explicit theological or ethical teaching. And yet it is one of the most interesting and illuminating documents in the New Testament and in some ways one of the most important."[3]

## MASTER AND SERVANT RELATIONSHIP

"Paul, a prisoner of Jesus Christ, and Timothy our brother, unto Philemon our dearly beloved, and fellow-laborer, and to our beloved Apphia, and Archippus our fellow-soldier, and to the church in thy house" (v. 1, 2). Some have concluded that Apphia was the wife of Philemon and Archippus (Col. 4:17) was their son.[4]

"Hearing of thy love and faith, which thou hast toward the Lord Jesus, and toward all saints." Not much is known of Philemon as this is the only mention of him in the Bible. That he was a believer in Christ and served the saints in Colossae is certified here.

"For love's sake I rather beseech thee, being such a one as Paul the aged, and now also a prisoner of Jesus Christ; I beseech thee for my son, Onesimus, whom I have begotten in my bonds" (v. 5-10). This man was a servant (slave) of Philemon, but had run away. He came in contact with Paul at Rome and was baptized by him ("begotten").

Onesimus had formerly been

to thee unprofitable, but now profitable to thee and to me. . . . Receive him . . . whom I would have retained with me, that in thy stead he might have ministered unto me in the bonds of the gospel; but without thy mind [consent—R.S.V.] would I do nothing.—V. 11-14.

This comes directly to the purpose of the letter. As a Christian, the slave should return to his master. Paul would have been happy to keep him as a servant, but that was not lawful without the consent of the slave's owner. Paul tries to reconcile the situation of each by saying,

Perhaps he . . . departed for a season, that thou shouldest receive him for ever; not now as a servant [slave—R.S.V.], but above a servant,

274

a brother beloved, specially to me, but how much more unto thee, both in the flesh, and in the Lord.—V. 15, 16.

Even as a slave, with Christian ideals he would be a better servant. Then Paul makes a more direct appeal, "Receive him as myself. If he hath wronged thee, or oweth thee aught, put that on mine account." This suggests to some scholars that Onesimus had taken with him some of Philemon's money.[5] "I will repay it," Paul declared, and calls attention that this promise is valid since it is in his own handwriting.

It is presumed that Philemon had been baptized at Ephesus by Paul, since the apostle had never been in Colossae (Col. 1:4). As a beneficiary of Paul's ministry he owed something to Paul. "Yea, brother, let me have joy in thee. . . . Having confidence in thy obedience I wrote unto thee, knowing that thou wilt also do more than I say." As an apostle, Paul hoped that his request would be respected. "Prepare me also a lodging; for I trust that through your prayers, I shall be given unto you" (v. 17-22).

The epistle closes with an exchange of greetings.

---

1. *Baker's Dictionary of Theology*, p. 387.
2. *The Interpreter's Bible*, Vol. 11, p. 227.
3. *Ibid.*, p. 555.
4. *Westminster Dictionary of the Bible*, p. 477.
5. *Ibid.*

## QUESTIONS FOR DISCUSSION

1. What did John mean by "that spirt of antichrist"?
2. What is meant by the "old man" and the "new man"?
3. What function do psalms and hymns perform in the church? How do they differ?
4. Was Paul inspired to direct wives to submit themselves to their husbands? Explain your answer.
5. Was he inspired to command children to obey their

parents? Does this apply until they are twenty-one years old?

6. Was he inspired to command servants and slaves to obey their masters? Defend your answer.

7. What aspect of eternal judgment is given here? How do the terms "sheep and goats" apply here?

8. For what specific reason did Paul solicit the prayers of the Colossian saints?

9. Who were Philemon and Onesimus and how were they connected with Paul?

10. What two purposes might Paul have had for writing to Philemon? Did he condemn slavery?

# 42

# EPISTLE TO THE EPHESIANS

Modern scholars seem in unanimous agreement that the writings and teachings of Paul are the substance of this epistle but that it was not actually written by him. However, most all versions retain the heading, "The Epistle of Paul the Apostle to the Ephesians."

The writer is a great theologian in his own right. Less gifted than Paul in some respects . . . he is at the same time a far more systematic thinker; and he has attempted, as Paul never did, to reduce Paul's bold and brilliant ideas to a system, to correlate them one with another, to bring them under the dominion of a single ruling theme— the eternal purpose of God to unite all things in heaven and on earth in Christ; and so to demonstrate their significance, not alone for the particular social situation which first called forth their expression, but for the life of the church in all ages.[1]

While this view of authorship of Ephesians may not be acceptable to some, it will not be discussed here since the contents rather than the authorship of the book is our chief interest. "No book in the Bible is more pertinent to the life of our own times, when mankind faces the challenge now presented to it with compelling urgency: *Unite or perish*."[2]

"A recent expositor speaks of it as 'at once the most "modern" in many ways, of all books of the New Testament and the richest record of Christian experience.' "[3]

277

# The Supremacy of Christ
## (1:1-23)

"To the saints which are at Ephesus, and to the faithful in Christ Jesus" (v. 1). "The evidence of our earliest authorities [manuscripts] shows unmistakably that the words rendered 'at Ephesus' are not original."[4] While they may have been added by a later scribe, this does not change their significance but only broadens their appeal. The letter has been known in Christian history as a church epistle.

Blessed be the God and Father of our Lord Jesus Christ . . . according as he hath chosen us in him before the foundation of the world, that we should be holy and without blame before him in love; having predestinated us unto the adoption of children by Jesus Christ to himself.—V. 3-5.

This indicates that Jesus has a secondary position to God. The mystery in the next part quoted has been discussed through many centuries. If the ones addressed were chosen by God before their physical creation, it may seem that they were predestined individually to accept the gospel. The fallacy in this interpretation is its individual application. As a general statement it has validity. But when applied to any individual, it violates agency. The Revised Standard Version translates it, "He destined us in love to be his sons in Jesus Christ" (v. 5).

The key passage seems to be this: "That in the . . . fulness of times he might gather together in one all things in Christ, both which are in heaven, and which are on earth; even in him" (v. 10). Christ "is the focal point of the universe, of all history, and of all being."[5]

In whom ye also trusted, after that ye heard the word of truth, the gospel of your salvation; in whom also, after that ye believed, ye were sealed with that Holy Spirit of promise, which is the earnest of our inheritance until the redemption of the purchased possession, unto the praise of his glory.—V. 13, 14.

278

The climax of Christ's supremacy comes in the concluding verses of this first chapter. Here we are told that the greatness of God's power is manifested in Christ through us who believe. This was

wrought in Christ, when he raised him from the dead, and set him at his own right hand in the heavenly places, far above all principality, and power, and might, and dominion, . . . not only in this world, but also in that which is to come; and hath put all things under his feet, and gave him to be the head over all things to the church, which is his body.—V. 19-23.

## THE IMPLICATIONS OF CHRIST'S SUPREMACY (2:1-22)

In time past ye walked according . . . to the prince of the power of the air . . . but God, who is rich in mercy, for his great love . . . even when we were dead in sins, hath quickened us together with Christ . . . that in the ages to come he might show the exceeding riches of his grace . . . through Christ Jesus.—V. 2-7.

The Ephesians and others addressed were once pagans serving Satan, the prince of the air. They had been raised to a new life through the gospel. "For by grace are ye saved through faith; and that not of yourselves; but it is the gift of God; not of works, lest any man should boast" (v. 8, 9). The Revised Standard Version reads, "For by grace you have been saved." Most modern texts agree with it, starting with the American Revised Version of 1901. This gives color to the interpretation of a past tense salvation, "once in grace, always in grace." This, however, contradicts the doctrine of Christ and Paul that the Christian must deny himself, take up his cross, and follow Christ. Jesus declared, "He that endureth to the end shall be saved" (Matt. 10:19; Mark 13:13). Paul wrote, "Work out your own salvation with fear and trembling" (Phil. 2:12), and "to us who are being saved" (I Cor. 1:18, R.S.V.). Jesus' parable of "the sower of the word" (Matt. 13:3-7; Mark 4:13-17) makes this very clear.

279

Man cannot save himself by good deeds, or various sacrifices (the works of the law of Moses); but neither will the grace of Christ save him without the gospel ordinances and the works of righteousness and service (see Chapter 30:3).

"For we are his workmanship, created in Christ Jesus unto good works" (v. 10). As Gentiles they were without Christ,

being aliens . . . having no hope, and without God in the world; but now in Christ Jesus . . . having abolished in his flesh the enmity, even the law of commandments contained in ordinances . . . that he might reconcile both unto God in one body by the cross.—V. 11-16.

"And are built upon the foundation of the apostles and prophets, Jesus Christ himself being the chief corner stone . . . in whom ye also are builded together for an habitation of God through the Spirit" (v. 19-22). Note, the foundation is not apostles and prophets but the same foundation they built upon.

## Paul Reveals the Mystery of Christ (3:1-21)

"As ye have heard that by revelation he made known unto me the mystery of Christ . . . which in other ages was not made known unto the sons of men, as is now revealed unto his holy apostles and prophets by the Spirit" (v. 3-5). The Revised Standard Version reads "assuming that you have heard"; while Moffatt reads "for surely you have heard." The point at issue is whether Paul ever had seen or written those addressed. The words, "As I wrote before in few words," with which verse 3 concludes, seem to answer the problem in part. More significant is the fact that the knowledge came to Paul by revelation, which has been shared by other apostles and prophets.

By authority of the Spirit, he assured the Gentile Christians that they should be fellow-heirs . . . and partakers of his promise in Christ by the gospel; . . . and to make all men see what is the fellowship of the mystery, which from the beginning of the world hath been hid in God, who created all things by Jesus Christ . . . that now . . . might be known by the church the manifold wisdom of God.—V. 6, 9, 10.

Modern versions omit the phrase "by Jesus Christ" found in the King James Version and Inspired Version. The significant part of the text is that the redemptive plan of the gospel which was made "from the beginning . . . according to the eternal purpose . . . in Christ Jesus our Lord" is now revealed and "known by the church" (v. 10, 11). The church is the instrumentality through which "other forms of spiritual life are to be found."[6]

The writer then prays,

That Christ may dwell in your hearts by faith; that ye, being rooted and grounded in love . . . which passeth knowledge, that ye may be filled with all the fulness of God. . . . Unto him be glory in the church by Christ Jesus throughout all ages.—V. 17-21.

## EXHORTATION TO UNITY OF THE CHURCH (4:1-16)

Paul appeals to his readers to walk worthy of their calling, "forbearing one another in love; endeavoring to keep the unity of the Spirit . . . one Lord, one faith, one baptism" (v. 1-6). He then is diverted from the unity theme momentarily with a quotation from Psalm 68:18, "When he ascended up on high, he led captivity captive, and gave gifts unto men." It is explained parenthetically that to ascend one must first descend, and it was Christ who came to earth as the Redeemer and then "ascended up into heaven to glorify him who reigneth over all heavens" (v. 8-10). See also I Peter 3:18-20.

And he gave some, apostles; and some, prophets, and some, evangelists; and some, pastors and teachers; for the perfecting of the saints, for the work of the ministry, for the edifying of the body of Christ;

till we, in the unity of the faith, all come to the knowledge . . . of the stature of the fulness of Christ; that we henceforth be no more children, tossed to and fro, and carried about with every wind of doctrine . . . but speaking the truth in love, may grow up into him in all things, which is the head, even Christ.—V. 11-15.

In verse 7 it is said that each is given a gift through the grace of Christ. Now he shifts from the organic functioning of the church to its corporate life—the various ministries. But it is through Christ, the head of the church,

from whom the whole body fitly joined together and compacted by that which every joint supplieth, according to the effectual working in the measure of every part, maketh increase of the body unto the edifying of itself in love.—V. 16.

---

1. *The Interpreter's Bible,* Vol. 10, p. 604.
2. *Ibid.,* p. 605.
3. *Ibid.,* p. 610.
4. *Ibid.,* p. 608.
5. *Ibid.,* p. 620, 621.
6. *Ibid.,* p. 671.

## QUESTIONS FOR DISCUSSION

1. Is there anything wrong with crediting the epistle to the Ephesians to the authorship of Paul?  Explain.
2. Name all who were addressed in the epistle.
3. Does the first chapter teach predestination?  Explain.
4. What is meant by "The earnest of our inheritance"?
5. What specifically shows Christ's supremacy?
6. In what ways do good works affect our salvation?
7. What is the "foundation of the apostles and prophets"?
8. What was the mystery hid from the beginning in God, and to whom was it hid?
9. When did Christ "descend," where to, and why?
10. What ministers are mentioned in Chapter 4, and what is their function in the church?

# 43

# EPISTLE TO EPHESIANS CONCLUDED

Paul stressed that "the manifestation of the Spirit is given to every man to profit withal" in writing to the Corinthians (I Cor. 12:7; I Tim. 4:14; see also Acts 2:38, 39). In this Ephesian letter he gave emphasis to the gift of the several ministries in the church (see also I Cor. 12:27-31). It would be a mistake to conclude that either is excluded because one is emphasized to the neglect of the other. His climax in our last chapter was "Till we in the unity of the faith, all come to the knowledge of the Son of God, unto a perfect man [to mature manhood—R.S.V.]," as a fellowship, not individually.

## Break with Gentile Ways— Put On the New Man
(4:17-32)

"Henceforth walk not as other Gentiles" refers here to pagans, not the non-Jews who have become Christians. Specifically Paul warned against vanity, ignorance, lasciviousness, and greediness. "Put off the old man, which is corrupt according to the deceitful lusts; and be renewed in the mind of the Spirit; . . . put on the new man, which after God is created in righteousness and true holiness" (v. 17-24).

This putting "on" and "off" is not like the garments one wears, but is a continuing process "renewed day by day" (II Cor. 4:16). He exhorted them to put away "lying, speak every man truth with his neighbor; for we are members one of another." The author then gave some special injunctions: "Can ye be angry and not sin? let not the sun go down upon your wrath; neither give place to the devil" (v. 25-27). The King James and American Revised Version put this in the declarative mood: "Be ye angry, and sin not." The Diaglott and Weymouth versions are more cautious, using the subjective moods, "If angry, beware of sinning."

"Neither give place to the devil." The Old Testament uses the name "Satan." Both refer to the supreme evil spirit (Gen. 3:7; Matt. 4:2). He is also referred to as "the prince of the devils" (Matt. 9:40) and as "Beelzebub" (Matt. 12:22). Paul was more specific in his letter to the Romans: "Know ye not, that to whom ye yield yourselves servants to obey, his servants ye are . . . whether of sin unto death, or of obedience unto righteousness?" (Rom. 6:16). James made it quite clear, "Resist the devil, and he will flee from you" (Jas. 4:7).

"And grieve not the Holy Spirit of God, whereby ye are sealed unto the day of redemption." The Inspired Version usually follows the King James using the term "Holy Ghost." There are only three places where the third part of the Godhead is referred to as "Holy Spirit": Luke 11:14; Eph. 1:13; and I Thess. 4:8. In all modern versions the term "Spirit" has superseded "Ghost" wherever it occurs. The latter has taken on an odious connotation. Note also the impersonal aspect of the phrase, "Spirit of God."

The fourth chapter concludes with admonitions against stealing, corrupt communication, bitterness, wrath, anger, and malice. Then in fatherly counsel, Paul closed with these beautiful lines, "Be ye kind one to another, tender-hearted, forgiving one another, even as God for Christ's sake hath forgiven you" (v. 28-32).

## An Appeal to All Readers
(5:1-6:20)

The epistle continues in a hortatory strain to be followers of God and avoid sin. "Walk in love, as Christ also hath loved us, and hath given himself for us an offering and a sacrifice to God." In order to be such a follower the author warns against fornication, covetousness, filthiness, foolishness, jesting and things "which are not convenient [fitting—R.S.V.]; but rather giving of thanks" (v. 1-5).

"Let no man deceive you with vain words [with empty words—R.S.V.]." "This warning clearly implies that specious arguments were being advanced in some quarters to justify immorality, or to persuade Christians that licentious living had no significant relation to the life of the spirit."[1] It seems easy to get people to believe in things which justify lustful desires and their fulfillment. No strata of society, rich or poor, learned or ignorant, priesthood or laity, white, black, or brown are immune to the philosophy which gives license to human passions.

"For ye were sometime darkness, but now are ye light in the Lord; walk as children of light . . . for it is a shame even to speak of those things which are done of them in secret" (v. 6-12). This counsel seems apropos also for this age. There is hardly anything that men and women do in private that they are ashamed to mention in their parlor talk. This is often accompanied by the wearing of suggestive dress and by exhibitionism in modern, popular dances. Christians should not indulge in such pagan customs. Perhaps the chief difference between our present-day customs and those of Paul's day is that then the religious rites of pagan (non-Christian) society held that the immoral acts were practiced as a part of their religion.

The whole warning is important as evidence of the existence of sects which practised rites of such a character that they can, rightly or wrongly, be accused of the vilest secret vices, although they cannot be accused simply of idolatry.[2]

"Wherefore be ye not unwise, but understanding what is the will of the Lord. And be not drunk with wine, wherein is excess; but be filled with the Spirit." The phrase, "wherein is excess," has been translated by the Diaglott and by Revised Standard Version "for that is debauchery." Moffatt's translation is, "that means profligacy." These translations do not give any license to moderation which seems so popular today (v. 17-20).

## COUNSEL FOR THE FAMILY
(5:22-6:20)

Wives, submit yourselves unto your own husbands, as unto the Lord. . . . Husbands, love your wives, even as Christ also loved the church, and gave himself for it. . . . So ought men to love their wives as their own bodies. He that loveth his wife loveth himself.—V. 22-30.

Too often men use this and other scripture by selecting such portions as best suit their purpose. It should be read as a whole to get the real intent.

The virtue of submission is not popular in modern times. The ideals of democracy have pretty well broken the hold over the minds of men which rank and degree once possessed. "All men are created free and equal." This today is dogma almost throughout the world. . . . Nevertheless, Christian insight brings criticism to bear upon the doctrine of democratic equalitarianism in its turn. Abolish inequality of inherited rank or status or caste, and you may merely have substituted for it the inequality of wealth. Abolish the inequality of wealth, and you may have left the inequality of power. . . . A communist utopia turns into a slave state![3]

There should be some mutual submission in a household, a city, or a state to avoid anarchy and maintain an ordered social life. Yet such authority should not be wielded as by a domestic or institutional tyrant. All of this counsel was based on the premise, submitting "yourselves one to another in the fear of God" (v. 21). Using the parallel of the marriage state and Christ's union with the church, the apostle uses the scriptural language, "For this cause shall a man leave his father and mother, and shall be joined unto his wife; and they two shall be one flesh" (Gen. 2:30; Matt. 19:5).

Children, obey your parents in the Lord; for this is right. Honor thy father and mother; which is the first commandment with promise. . . . Ye fathers provoke not your children to wrath; but bring them up in the fear and admonition of the Lord.—6:1-4.

This injunction circumscribes the absolute dominion accorded to the head of the family in Roman law, which entitled him to expose an unwanted infant, to sell a grown child into slavery, to disinherit him, to scourge or imprison him, or even put him to death.[4]

The scripture continues:

Servants, be obedient to them that are your masters according to the flesh . . . not with eye-service, as men-pleasers; but as the servants of Christ . . . knowing that whatsoever good thing any man doeth, the same shall he receive of the Lord, whether he be bond or free. And, ye masters, do the same things unto them, forbearing threatening; knowing that your Master also is in heaven; neither is there respect of persons with him.—V. 5-9.

These injunctions to slaves and masters do not imply either approval or condemnation of this economic system. It merely recognized the sociological framework within which the Christian community then lived. "Finally, my brethren, be strong in the Lord, . . . put on the whole armor of God . . . for we wrestle not against flesh and blood, but against principalities, against powers . . . against spiritual wickedness in high places . . . and having done all, to stand." Like the good soldier, who is trained and well equipped, take a stand against your enemy and hold your ground. Having your "feet shod with the preparation of the gospel . . . taking the shield of faith . . . the helmet of salvation . . . the sword of the Spirit, which is the word of God; praying always" (v. 10-18). It is quite likely that the soldiers of Christ most commonly fail at these last two points: they lack the sword of the Spirit in knowledge of the word of God, and they do not pray in faith, "nothing wavering."

The epistle is closed by relating that its bearer, Tychicus, "shall make known unto you all things . . . that ye might know our affairs, and that he might comfort your hearts" (v. 21-24).

---

1. *The Interpreter's Bible,* Vol. 10, pp. 707, 708.
2. *Ibid.,* p. 710.
3. *Ibid.,* pp. 716, 717.
4. *Ibid.,* p. 731.

## QUESTIONS FOR DISCUSSION

1. What is meant by "the old man" and "the new man"?
2. How may anger be connected with sin?
3. Is there a difference between "the Holy Ghost" and "the Holy Spirit"?
4. How may one "resist the devil"?
5. Discuss the present trends concerning modesty, indulgence, and frankness. Do the virtues exceed the dangers?
6. Is there justification for drinking wine in moderation?
7. To what extent does God ask wives to be submissive to their husbands?
8. To what extent can the Saints expect to be equal?
9. Should parents demand unquestioning obedience of their children? At what age should children be encouraged "to learn by experience"?
10. Does Ephesians justify slavery? In what way does it compare the life of the saint and the life of the soldier?

# 44

# THE FIRST EPISTLE
# TO TIMOTHY

(Written about A.D. 63)

This is the first of three letters called "pastoral epistles" because they are addressed to the two most intimate friends of Paul as leaders[1] and pastors of the churches. . . . It is supposed that the first Epistle to Timothy and the Epistle to Titus were written after Paul's first imprisonment [in Rome]; and the Second Epistle to Timothy after his second arrest, shortly before his death.[2]

Some modern biblical scholars, including those who wrote the introduction to *The Interpreter's Bible,* Volume Eleven, page 343 ff., hold to the theory that Paul's name was added to the pastorals by a writer of the second century. The arguments introduced by them do not seem to me to be conclusive. For our purpose we shall follow the lead of the great majority of New Testament translators—Moffatt, Weymouth, and the Revised Standard, Diaglott, American Revised, and the King James versions which in their titles credit these epistles to Paul.

Professor E. E. Stringfellow, after stating several arguments for a later authorship, concludes that the weight of reasons for the genuine Pauline authorship overbalances those against the later authorship. While the books are not in Marcion's canon (A.D. 140), they are in three other versions he named written in the second century. He added that these pastorals are "quoted as Paul's by Irenaeus, by Clement of Alexandria, by Tertullian, and are classified by Eusebius as among the 'accepted books.' "[3]

## TIMOTHY TO REBUKE FALSE TEACHERS (1:3-20)

"Unto Timothy, my own son in the faith." The scriptures do not reveal that Timothy was baptized by Paul (Acts 16:1, 2), but he may have been confirmed by him (II Tim. 1:5, 6). In the Philippian epistle, Paul wrote, "as a son with the father, he hath served with me in the gospel" (2:22). Paul reminded Timothy that he had asked him to stay in Ephesus, rather than go with him into Macedonia, that Timothy might guard the saints there against false teachers and doctrines. He added, "Neither give heed to fables and endless genealogies, which minister questions, rather than godly edifying" (v. 1-4).

The epistle does not elaborate on the nature of these false teachings, but it does reveal that some "have turned aside with vain jangling, desiring to be teachers of the law, understanding neither what they say, nor whereof they affirm" (v. 6, 7).

Some who fit this description are still teaching and writing. They give conjectures and affirmations as if they were established facts. Any wise student, including those in religion, has a right and duty to ask, "What evidence do you have to support that?" Every learner needs to be humble, but never gullible. The teacher or speaker may have the advantage of an extensive education, and may make one feel inferior, but he should never assume to exercise another's agency to choose ideas and decide for himself.

"The law is not made for a righteous man, but for the lawless and disobedient." More recent scripture reads, "He that keepeth the laws of God hath no need to break the laws of the land" (D. and C. 58:5 b). Paul then listed a number of sins, and also immoral and unlawful acts (v. 5-11).

He thanked Christ "who hath enabled me, for that he counted me faithful, putting me into the ministry." In humility Paul acknowledged that Christ "came into the world to save sinners; of whom I am chief. Howbeit for this cause I obtained mercy, that in me first Jesus Christ might show forth all long-suffering, for a pattern to them which should hereafter believe on him" (v. 12-16).

He charged Timothy, according to the prophecies, to "war a good warfare, holding faith, and a good conscience; which some having put away, concerning faith have made shipwreck." He mentioned "Hymeneus and Alexander, whom I have delivered unto Satan, that they may learn not to blaspheme" (v. 18-20. See also II Timothy 2:17, 18).

## Regulations of a Christian Church (2:1-3:16)

"I exhort . . . that . . . prayers . . . and giving thanks be made for all men; for kings, and for all that are in authority; that we may lead a quiet and peaceable life in all godliness and honesty." Christians had been persecuted for their refusal to observe the edicts for emperor worship. This counsel is not that they should pray to the emperor, but for him; for God "is willing to have all men to be saved, and to come unto the knowledge of the truth" (v. 1-4). This refutes the doctrines of predestination, that God selects a few to be saved; and of universal salvation, that all will accept of God's grace and eventually be guests of heaven. The initiative is with man. When he uses his agency to righteous ends, he can take advantage of God's willingness.

"For there is one God, and one mediator between God and men, the man Christ Jesus." The relationship and subordination of Father and Son is here clearly stated (v. 5-7).

The epistle then states some rules for public worship pertaining to women. They should dress in modest apparel, avoid ostentation with gold and pearls, but adorn themselves with good works. They should not usurp administrative authority over the men (v. 9-15).

The instruction next turns to the character of bishops and deacons. While God is no respecter of persons, he does call men with special qualifications for the ministry. The bishop must be blameless, monogamous, sober, hospitable, an apt teacher, not given to wine or violence, nor be greedy for money. He should rule well his own house and care for the church. "Moreover he must have a good report of them which are without." What people of the community think of the ministry means much to the progress of the church (3:1-7).

"Deacons likewise must be serious, not double-tongued, nor addicted to much wine, not greedy for gain" (v. 8, R.S.V.). Their wives are to be grave, temperate, and faithful. They should rule their children and households well (v. 9-12).

At the time of this writing, Paul was hopeful of seeing them soon; but if this was impossible, his letter would guide them. "The pillar and ground of the truth is . . . God was manifest in the flesh, justified in the Spirit, seen of angels, preached unto the Gentiles, believed on in the world, received up into glory" (v. 13-16).

## PERSONAL COUNSEL TO TIMOTHY
(4:1-6:2)

Paul prophesies of an apostasy

in the latter times. Some shall depart from the faith, giving heed to seducing spirits, and doctrines of devils; speaking lies . . . forbidding to marry, and commanding to abstain from meats. . . . Every creature of God is good, and nothing to be refused . . . for it is sanctified by the word of God and prayer.—4:1-5.

Paul advises the church to refuse profane and silly myths. Bodily exercise has some value, but godliness has value in every way. "These things command and teach" (v. 7-11).

Let no man despise thy youth; but be thou an example . . . in word . . . in charity, in spirit, in faith, in purity. Till I come, give attendance to reading, to exhortation, to doctrine. Neglect not the gift that is in thee, which was given thee by prophecy, with the laying on of the hands of the presbytery.

The Revised Standard Version reads, "by prophetic utterance when the elders laid their hands upon you" (see 1:18; Acts 13:2-4).

## TREATMENT OF AGED AND WIDOWS
(5:1-24)

"Rebuke not an elder [an older man—R.S.V.], but entreat him as a father; and the younger men as brethren; the elder women as mothers; the younger as sisters, with all purity. Honor widows that are widows indeed."

"A real widow is one without children or grandchildren who can support her."[4] The widow without descendants should trust in God as manifested by her religious devotions. Paul warned against taking into membership widows under sixty years old, and then only those known for their good works. The younger widows are apt to marry again, cast off their faith, thus inviting damnation (v. 1-15).

The descendants of widows in the church are to look after their needs so that the church will not be charged. "If any provide not for his own [household] . . . he hath denied the faith, and is worse than an infidel" (v. 16 and v. 8).

"Against an elder receive not an accusation [charge—R.S.V.], but before two or three witnesses" (v. 19). "Being in administrative positions, elders are naturally subject to persistent criticism. They therefore need protection from malicious and unfounded charges."[5] (See Deuteronomy 19:15; Matthew 18:15-17; II Corinthians 13:1.)

"Do nothing by partiality. Lay hands suddenly on no man, neither be partaker of other men's sins; keep thyself pure." Some men's sins, and good works, go "before to judgment, and some . . . follow after." Physically, socially, and spiritually men's conduct affects them in this life, but they will also be held to account for their deeds and records hereafter (Rev. 20:12, 13).

## Contrasting the False and the True Teacher (6:3-19)

Paul again exhorts the Christian masters to treat the believing slaves as brethren. He warns against any who teach otherwise because of pride, "doting about questions and strifes of words" (v. 1-4).

> Godliness with contentment is great gain . . . and having food and raiment, let us be therewith content. But they that will be rich fall into temptation and a snare, . . . for the love of money is the root of all evil; which while some coveted after, they have erred from the faith.—V. 6-10.

The warning then, as now, is not to the men of the world but to those in danger of losing their faith who pierce "themselves through with many sorrows" by coveting wealth.

This first epistle is concluded by charging Timothy to "lay hold on eternal life" keeping this commandment without spot, unrebukable, until Christ's appearing in God's own time. Here the title "King of kings, and Lord of lords" is applied to God "whom no man hath seen . . . only he who hath the light and hope of immortality dwelling in him."

He praises those who are "rich in good works, ready to distribute, willing to communicate . . . that they may lay hold on eternal life" (v. 13-19).

1. The Greek word for "bishop" is *episcopos* and means overseer.
2. *The Book of Life*, Vol. 7, p. 315; also *Westminster Dictionary of the Bible*, p. 608.
3. E. E. Stringfellow, *Acts and the Epistles*, p. 238.
4. *The Interpreter's Bible*, Vol. 11, p. 435.
5. *Ibid.*, p. 443.

## QUESTIONS FOR DISCUSSION

1. Name the "pastoral epistles." Why were they called that?
2. Why did Paul call Timothy "my own son"?
3. Why should or should not class members question the teacher on things taught in the class?
4. In what respect could Paul say he was "the chief" of sinners?
5. What is the difference in God's willingness that all men be saved and in "universal salvation"?
6. Were the rules of public worship more favorable for men than women? Defend your answer.
7. What were some of the requirements for bishops and deacons? How did they differ?
8. What are the conditions predicted that show an apostasy in latter times? When is this to be?
9. What were the gifts conferred on Timothy by prophecy and the laying on of hands?
10. Why would Paul refuse church membership to widows under sixty? Was this just a local and temporary rule?

# 45

# THE EPISTLE TO TITUS;
# II TIMOTHY, PART I

As explained in the introduction to First Timothy, this pastoral letter was probably written by Paul during his first imprisonment. Some hold that it was put together by Luke or some other companion from Paul's notes after his death.

Titus was a Greek convert of Paul, who accompanied him to Jerusalem. Paul resisted efforts made there to compel Titus to be circumcised (Titus 1:4; Gal. 2:3). He accompanied Paul on his third missionary journey and aided in collecting the offerings in Greece for the saints in Jerusalem (II Cor. 8:6-24). Titus was sent by Paul to Corinth with a severe letter and was able to handle a delicate situation there with success (II Cor. 7:6-16).

## DIRECTIONS TO THE ELDERS OF THE CHURCH (1:5-16)

Paul identified himself as "a servant of God, and an apostle of Jesus Christ." He addressed his letter "to Titus, mine own son after the common faith" (v. 1-4).

Paul had accompanied Titus to Crete where they had made converts in the Jewish communities of several cities. Paul had left before these converts were organized into churches. Titus was given the task of completing these

296

branch organizations and to "counteract the influences of Jewish mercenary teachers."[1]

Paul gave instructions as to the kind of elders to be used as overseers (bishops). This duplicated the counsel given to Timothy (I Tim. 3:1 ff.). To this he urged him to hold fast "the faithful word as he hath been taught, that he may be able by sound doctrine" to "convince the gainsayers; for there are many unruly and vain talkers and deceivers, specially they of the circumcision." These false teachings, which were upsetting whole families, were given by men who received money for their preaching. "Wherefore rebuke them sharply . . . that turn from the truth" (v. 9-14).

"Unto the pure, let all things be pure; but unto them that are defiled and unbelieving, nothing is pure; but even their mind and conscience is defiled." They profess to know God but their works deny him (v. 15, 16).

## Counsel to Various Classes of the Family (2:1-15)

The aged men and women should be good examples to the younger men and women. The younger women are exhorted to love their husbands and children, and the younger men are counseled to be "a pattern of good works; in doctrine showing uncorruptness, gravity, sincerity" (v. 1-7).

Servants and slaves are exhorted to obey their masters and not to talk back or steal, "but showing all good fidelity."

All this is to be in anticipation of the "glorious appearing of the great God and our Savior Jesus Christ . . . a peculiar people, zealous of good works" (v. 9-14).

## Saintly Attitude toward Others (3:1-11)

"Be subject to principalities and powers, to obey magistrates, to be ready to every good work." Christians should be men of goodwill and respect those in authority. When Peter defied the Jewish leaders who had imprisoned him for preaching in the name of Christ, he declared, "We ought to obey God rather than man" (Acts 5:29). This is not intended to give a license for civil disobedience. Man's right to the free practice of his religion is protected by the basic laws of all free governments. A situation similar to Peter's is not likely to confront Christ's ministers today.

"Speak evil of no man" is especially applicable to our leaders. The Greek word for this translation is *blasphemein,* the word from which we get "blaspheme," which means to speak profanely of sacred things. "For we ourselves also were sometimes foolish, disobedient, deceived, serving divers lusts and pleasures." When tempted to speak harshly of others, it is well for us to ask ourselves, "Haven't we ever done these things?" Since God's mercy was meted out to us, and our salvation was not earned by our good works alone, we should be tolerant, "showing . . . meekness unto all men." It is only by divine grace that we are made heirs to eternal life (v. 1-7).

Lest some might get the impression from this that salvation is by grace alone, Paul added, "I will that thou affirm constantly that they which have believed in God might be careful to maintain good works. . . . But avoid foolish questions, and genealogies, and contentions" (v. 8-11). The epistle is concluded with a few personal instructions. Paul proposed to send either Artemus or Tychicus to relieve Titus. As soon as his successor arrived, Titus was to come promptly to Nicopolis where Paul would meet him.

## II TIMOTHY—WRITTEN IN ROME LATE A.D. 67

This is more of a personal letter than a pastoral message. It was intended to give Timothy a final word of counsel, to help him recall some previous instructions, and to give a farewell message.

298

# A Heritage of Faith and Doctrine
(1:5-18)

"When I call to remembrance the unfeigned faith that is in thee, which dwelt first in thy grandmother Lois, and thy mother Eunice; I am persuaded that [it is] in thee also." These women were born Jewesses and were converts to Christianity. Timothy's father was a Greek (Acts 16:1). Paul may have wished to convey the idea that Christianity is the legitimate continuation of Judaism. He also may have wished to show his faith in a third-generation minister. "New converts are not to be trusted too far: they bring too many alien ideas and attitudes with them" (see I Tim. 3:6).[2]

"Wherefore I put thee in remembrance, that thou stir up the gift of God, which is in thee by the putting on of my hands. . . . Be not thou therefore ashamed of the testimony of our Lord, nor of me his prisoner" (v. 5-8).

The power of God, Paul declared, "is now made manifest by the appearing of our Savior Jesus Christ, who hath abolished death, and hath brought life and immortality to light through the gospel." To this Paul added one of his great affirmations of faith:

For I know whom I have believed, and am persuaded that he is able to keep that which I have committed unto him against that day. Hold fast the form of sound words, which thou hast heard of me, in faith and love which is in Christ Jesus. That good thing which was committed unto thee keep by the Holy Ghost which dwelleth in us.—V. 10-14.

Some commentary is of interest here.

These last two verses furnish the foundation of the Catholic teaching relative to the tradition [ministers or church officials are especially endowed]. The apostles have received the Christian truth from the Lord; they themselves have transmitted it orally, especially to their co-workers and successors in the ministry. . . . But this conservation and this transmission cannot be sufficiently guaranteed by human forces. It is the Holy Spirit which preserves them from all alteration and all deviation.[3]

"All they which are in Asia be turned away from me." But he named only two, then blessed the household of Onesiphorus who had befriended him (v. 15-18).

## BE READY TO SUFFER FOR CHRIST (2:1-26)

Timothy is admonished to pass along to faithful men, who shall be able to teach others also. Thou therefore endure hardness, as a good soldier of Jesus Christ. No man that warreth entangleth himself with the affairs of this life. . . . Remember that Jesus Christ of the seed of David was raised from the dead, according to the gospel; wherein I suffer trouble, as an evil doer, even unto bonds; but the word of God is not bound [fettered—R.S.V.]. Therefore I endure all things for the elect's sake.—V. 1-10.

Paul asks Timothy to remind his hearers of those things, and that they "strive not about words to no profit. . . . Study to show thyself approved unto God, a workman that needeth not to be ashamed, rightly dividing the word of truth" (v. 14, 15). This counsel given to a young minister in the first century is good for all time and for all who love truth.

Then Paul warns against heresies, "But shun profane and vain babblings" which will eat as does a canker; "of whom is Hymeneus and Philetus; who concerning the truth have erred, saying that the resurrection is past already; and overthrow the faith of some. Nevertheless the foundation of God standeth sure" (v. 16-19).

"Flee also youthful lusts; but follow righteousness, faith, charity, peace, with them that call on the Lord out of a pure heart. . . . The servant of the Lord must not strive; but be gentle unto all men, apt to teach, patient" (v. 22-24).

Doubtless Timothy was by now of mature age, but to Paul, who was not far from his "three-score and ten," he was still a boy, "my son." "Let no man despise thy youth" (I Tim. 4:12). "The energies of youth require direction. The passions of youth demand self-control. The loyalties of youth cannot be satisfied without an adequate object."[4] This can best be found in the gospel and life of Christ.

1. Stringfellow, *Acts and the Epistles*, p. 243.
2. *The Interpreter's Bible*, Vol. 11, p. 463.
3. *Ibid.*, p. 473.
4. *Ibid.*, p. 494.

## QUESTIONS FOR DISCUSSION

1. What previous acquaintance with Titus do we find in the scriptures?
2. In what way are "all things pure" to the pure and undefiled?
3. Are young people as apt to follow the example of older men and women as of that of their contemporaries?
4. In what ways are Saints to be "a peculiar people"?
5. Should men support bad laws and wicked magistrates? Defend your answer.
6. Reconcile these scriptures: "Speak evil of no man" and "Judge not unrighteously" (Matt. 7:2).
7. Upon what does one's salvation depend?
8. Why did Paul write his second epistle to Timothy?
9. What heritage did Timothy get from his ancestors?
10. What do Saints commit to Christ that he will keep till the final day?

# 46

# SECOND TIMOTHY, PART II; PETER'S LETTERS, PART I

Paul's last letter to his son in the gospel, Timothy, manifested a deep concern that he keep his spiritual heritage strong and maintain unchanged the doctrines as they had been taught to him. The rest of the epistle contains a warning of trials to come and a prediction of Paul's death.

## APOSTASY FORESEEN—USE OF SCRIPTURE
(II Tim. 3:1-17)

In the last days perilous times shall come, for men shall be lovers of their own selves, covetous, boasters, proud, blasphemers, disobedient to parents . . . without natural affection, truce-breakers . . . despisers of those that are good, traitors . . . lovers of pleasures more than lovers of God; having a form of godliness, but denying the power thereof; from such turn away.—V. 1-5.

Questions may be raised as to whether this social corruption fits a particular age or period, or if these conditions are so general as to have no particular application. One commentator says that the

description of verses 2-5 is applicable to any revolutionary period in history when belief in the mores or traditional restraints is weakened, when there is widespread repudiation of tradition and law, whether

302

of God, parents, society, or natural affections, in favor of an arbitrary and extreme individualism.[1]

It would not be helpful to dogmatize on this issue, even though one had strong convictions. Some of these evil conditions were probably present among some of the human race at most any period of history. It seems clear, however, that Paul was exercising a prophetic gift, and the phrase "In the last days" indicated not the first century, or the near future, but near the coming of the Son of God in glory.

As Jesus sat with his disciples on the Mount of Olives, they asked him, "When shall these things be . . . and what is the sign of thy coming; and of the end of the world, or the destruction of the wicked?" He answered, in part, "In those days, shall be great tribulations on the Jews . . . such as was not before sent upon Israel . . . nor ever shall be sent again upon Israel. . . . And ye also shall hear of wars, and rumors of wars . . . but the end is not yet." Mine elect shall "be gathered from the four quarters of the earth. . . . This gospel of the kingdom shall be preached in all the world for a witness unto all nations, and then shall the end come, or the destruction of the wicked" (Matthew 24:4, 18, 25, 28, 32).

Christ's prophecy just quoted seems to parallel Paul's, and when they are put together they seem to be quite significant. A strong argument can be made that many of these signs of the times indicate this present age. Let us consider the closing statement of Paul's prophecy. The people of these "last days" who were religious ("having a form of godliness") would "deny the power" of godliness. Many liberal theologians seem to have lost faith in a God of miracles and gifts, not only for our age; they rationalize the supernatural aspect of New Testament Christianity on a broader scale now than ever before.

"Ever learning and never able to come to a knowledge of the truth." One of our philosophers has emphasized our situation by saying, "The trouble with the world today is that the ignorant are so cocksure and the intelligent are so full of doubt."

All that will live godly in Christ Jesus shall suffer persecution; for evil men and seducers shall wax worse and worse, deceiving, and being deceived. . . . From a child thou hast known the holy Scriptures, which are able to make thee wise unto salvation through faith which is in Christ Jesus.—V. 12-15.

This promise is contingent on faith. But the scriptures need not be accepted in blind faith. Isaiah gave a consistency test which should be applied, "To the law and the testimony; and if they speak not according to this word, it is because there is no light in them" (Isa. 8:20).

"All Scripture given by inspiration of God, is profitable for doctrine, for reproof, for correction, for instruction in righteousness; that the man of God may be perfect, thoroughly furnished unto all good works" (v. 16, 17). Some versions read "All scripture *is* given" or "All scripture is inspired by God" (such as K.J.V., Moffatt, R.S.V.); however, the American Revised, Westcott and Hort, and the Diaglott are in harmony with the Inspired Version rendering. Some of that which is included as scripture in the Bible is admittedly the language of men and even of the devil or Satan, therefore it is not of God.

Much has been said about Christ's appearing and the judgment. Paul indicated that these events are related, even if not simultaneous (4:1). See also 1:10; I Timothy 6:14; Titus 2:13. He exhorts Timothy to "preach the word," for a time of apostasy will come when men "will not endure sound doctrine" but seek out "teachers, having itching ears." Such persons will "summon teacher after teacher, in great numbers—teachers without ecclesiastical accreditation, who will 'pander to their desires by telling them what they long to hear.' "² Paul wrote that these will "turn away their ears from the truth, and shall be turned unto fables" (4:2-4).

Following this prediction, Paul wrote the sad words of his expected demise. "I am now ready to be offered, and the time of my departure is at hand." Then with stoical composure he added, "I have fought a good fight, I have finished my course, I have kept the faith." He looked forward with joyful anticipation for "the crown of the righteousness" which he would share with "all . . . that love his [Christ's] appearing." He then gave some personal items: "Do thy diligence to come shortly unto me, for Demas hath forsaken me. . . . Only Luke is with me. Take Mark, and bring him with thee" (v. 5-11). In his farewell other persons are mentioned for some comment or greeting.

## First Peter—A.D. 65

This book has been described as the "Epistle of Hope." "Among the shorter writings of the New Testament there are few more attractive than this." B. H. Streeter, in *The Primitive Church*, p. 124, 1929, wrote that this "is one of the finest things in the New Testament."[3] It is quoted by Clement of Rome, A.D. 95; by Polycarp, who died A.D. 155; by Irenaeus, A.D. 185; and accepted by the historian Eusebius.

The epistle is addressed to the Christian churches in Asia Minor and urges them to stand fast in the faith against the impending persecution.

## Blessings of the Redeemed
(1:3 - 2:10)

"Peter, an apostle of Jesus Christ" not only identifies the writer but also gives his authority for what he wanted to impart to them. "Blessed be the God and Father of our Lord Jesus Christ which . . . hath begotten us again unto a lively hope by the resurrection of Jesus Christ from the dead" (v. 3). This was not intended as a theological teaching, as Peter assumed that these dispersed Christians, "the elect," accepted the Father and Son as divine, and also the historicity of Jesus' death and resurrection.

"Though now for a season" your faith be tried as with fire "might be found unto praise . . . and glory at the appearing of Jesus Christ; whom having not seen, ye love" (v. 6-8). While Peter does not say so here, he had seen Jesus and companied with him (Luke 1:2; Acts 10:39). Those of the dispersion who had not seen Jesus could believe on the testimony of others (John 20:29). "For a season" means the waiting till Christ should appear in the glory of his kingdom. The apostles had good reason to assure the faithful of this coming event.

The prophets . . . prophesied of the grace bestowed upon you . . . searching what time, and what manner of salvation . . . unto whom it was revealed, that not unto themselves, but unto us they did minister the things, which are now reported.—V. 10-12.

Peter addressed them,

as obedient children . . . be ye holy in all manner of conversation. . . . Call on the Father, who without respect of persons judgeth according to every man's work. . . . Ye were not redeemed with corruptible things . . . but with the precious blood of Christ, as a lamb without blemish and without spot; who verily was foreordained before the foundation of the world, but was manifest in these last times for you.—V. 14-20.

The statements are pregnant with doctrinal teachings of great significance: The Resurrection, Ascension, rebirth, God's enduring word, and the frailty of human existence. Chapter 2 continues with admonition for righteous conduct. Christ is the "living stone" rejected of men but chosen of God. As we partake of his nature, we become "lively stones" in a spiritual house, a holy priesthood offering up acceptable sacrifices unto God. Isaiah's prophecy (28:16) is used to support the theme that Jesus is the one who has the honored cornerstone position in the temple in Zion (2:1-6).

Peter's statement that these lively stones are also "an holy priesthood" has been used to shift the New Testament doctrine of a priesthood called and chosen of God (Heb. 5:4; John 15:16; 5:45). In the past the Israelites were not a people—that is, a strong nation—but were part of the Greek and Roman empires. Now they are "the people of God" (v. 7-10).

## CHRISTIAN ATTITUDE TOWARD THOSE IN AUTHORITY
(2:11-25)

Peter asked those of the dispersion to set a good example before the Gentiles that "they may by your good works, which they shall behold, glorify God." To do this they must submit to "every ordinance of man," those of kings and governors. While they are free, they are not to use their "liberty for a cloak of maliciousness" (v. 11-16). Servants should "be subject to your masters." He then makes a good point for us to remember: When we are "buffeted for" our faults, and take it patiently, this is pleasing to God. But if we are persecuted without cause and are patient, it results in greater glory, since we, like Christ, will leave a worthy example (v. 17-24).

He closed this chapter by reminding them that, like sheep, all had gone astray, "but are now returned unto the Shepherd and Bishop [overseer] of your souls" (v. 25).

---

1. *The Interpreter's Bible,* Vol. 11, p. 498.
2. *Ibid.,* Vol. 11, p. 509.
3. *Ibid.,* Vol. 12, p. 77.

## QUESTIONS FOR DISCUSSION

1. Is Peter's prediction of an apostasy based on known conditions of his day or was it prophetic? Why?
2. What signs of the times of Christ's appearing can you name which are peculiar to "the latter days"?

3. Is a desire to know "the truth" the basic motive of today's students? What other motives have they?
4. Timothy's knowledge of the scriptures is cited as a worthy heritage. Is this necessarily an asset?
5. In what ways has knowing God's word helped you?
6. What definition of sacred scripture is given? Is this a clear and positive identification?
7. What is meant by "the judgment day"? Will all our sins and works be appraised at one time?
8. Who was Peter and to whom did he write his first epistle?
9. What advantage did Peter claim as one who knew Jesus personally? Was there any disadvantage to those who never saw him? What was it?
10. Most Protestants accept the doctrine of a universal "priesthood of all believers." Tell why you do or do not.

# 47

# EPISTLES OF PETER, PART II

## ADVICE TO HUSBANDS, WIVES, AND OTHERS
(I Peter 3:1-12)

Peter had been admonishing the saints to follow the example of Christ. Those who had strayed from the fold of faith were urged to return to the Good Shepherd.

"Likewise, ye wives, be in subjection to your own husbands." If the husbands do not follow after the gospel, the conduct of the wives may win them back, not with the outward adorning but with a "meek and quiet spirit." He then cited Sarah's respect and dutifulness to Abraham (Gen. 18:12) as a worthy example (v. 1-6).

Husbands should honor their wives "being heirs together of the grace of life [eternal]; that your prayers be not hindered" (v. 7).

Finally, be ye all of one mind, having compassion . . . be pitiful, be courteous; not rendering evil for evil . . . for he that will love life, and see good days, let him refrain his tongue from evil. . . . Let him seek peace and ensue it. For the eyes of the Lord are over the righteous, and his ears are open unto their prayers.—V. 8-12.

## Suffering and Its Reward
(3:13 - 5:11)

"If ye suffer for righteousness' sake, happy are ye . . . and be ready always to give an answer with meekness and fear to every man that asketh of you a reason for the hope that is in you" (v. 14, 15).

It is better . . . that ye suffer for well doing, than for evil doing. For Christ also once suffered for sins, the just for the unjust, being put to death in the flesh, but quickened by the Spirit, that he might bring us to God. For which cause also, he went and preached unto the spirits in prison; some of whom were disobedient in the days of Noah . . . while the ark was preparing, wherein . . . eight souls were saved by water.—V. 17-20.

Concerning Christ's preaching to the spirits in prison, we read,

The passage is one of the darkest in the New Testament, and the exegetes [commentators] have differed about the meaning of every word. . . . The simplest meaning is that our Lord descended between his passion and resurrection, to preach to certain spirits imprisoned in Hades.[1]

When Jesus came to Nazareth and read in the synagogue from Isaiah 61:1, the people were astounded; for he declared that he was the one that fulfilled this scripture which said, "The Spirit of the Lord is upon me, because he hath anointed me to preach the gospel to the poor, he hath sent me to heal the broken-hearted, to preach deliverance to the captives" (Luke 4:17-19). The Jews then rose up against him and thrust him from the city.

So that this passage might not be "spiritualized" or applied as a figure of speech, Peter made a specific application: "Some of whom were disobedient in the days of Noah." The saving of those who believed Noah's warning by entering the ark is then likened to baptism as a symbol of Christ's atonement and ascension.

310

"Forasmuch then as Christ hath suffered for us in the flesh," Peter argued, we should be like-minded and cease from sin, and do the will of God. For all of us

shall give account to him that is ready to judge the quick and the dead. Because of this, is the gospel preached to them who are dead, that they might be judged according to men in the flesh, but live in the spirit according to the will of God.—4:1-6.

This passage reinforces the prophecies of Isaiah and Christ to which Peter had previously referred. Other versions of I Peter 3:19 omit the modifying phrase "some of whom," thus making Christ's mission to Hades serve alone the disobedient who perished in the flood. The wording in 4:6 makes no such limitation. Since Peter could have known of Christ's mission only by the inspiration of the Holy Spirit, now as in times past, it would favor the rendition of the Inspired Version.

"Have fervent charity among yourselves; for charity preventeth a multitude of sins" (v. 8). Other versions have "covereth" for "preventeth." Moses warned Israel that disobedience would bring guilt, therefore "be sure your sin will find you out" (Num. 32:23). There is no suggestion that one may cover his sin by acts of charity.

Those who speak with authority or who minister are to do so that God may be glorified through Christ (v. 8-11).

If any man suffer as a Christian, let him not be ashamed; but let him glorify God on this behalf. For the time is come that judgment must begin at the house of God. . . . And if the righteous scarcely be saved, where shall the ungodly and the sinner appear?—V. 16-18.

Peter next directs his epistle to the elders. "Feed the flock of God which is among you, taking the oversight thereof, not by constraint, but willingly; not for filthy lucre, but of a ready mind; neither as being lords over God's heritage, but being ensamples to the flock" (5:1-3). This is sound counsel for administrative officers and others. Jesus spoke of the shepherds who are not as much concerned for the sheep as for the wages. When the wolf comes they run away. Jesus, the good Shepherd, knows his sheep and they know him, "but he who is a hireling fleeth, because he is a hireling, and careth not for the sheep" (John 10:11-14).

Let no one say that ministers who receive money for their services are hirelings in a bad sense, for Jesus also said, "The laborer is worthy of his hire" (Luke 10:7). One who gives all his time to his calling as a minister must be supported, but if he deserts his calling for a more lucrative pulpit or vocation, he will have to answer to God for that.

Peter concluded his first epistle with an exhortation to be vigilant and to resist "your adversary the devil," knowing that the same afflictions are required of your brethren throughout the world, and that by suffering they shall be stabilized and strengthened through the grace of God (v. 8-11).

The epistle was probably written by and entrusted to Sylvanus for delivery. "They at Babylon, elected together with you, salute you, and so doth Markus my son." "Babylon" is thought to designate Rome (v. 12, 13).

## SECOND PETER—PERHAPS WRITTEN FROM ROME ABOUT A.D. 68

Most modern scholars regard it as the work of an unknown author who about A.D. 150 wrote in the name of the great apostle Peter in order to secure a wider hearing. . . . It was written . . . to rebuke nascent Gnosticism creeping into the churches.[2]

Although the objections to authenticity are sufficiently weighty, so as to preclude dogmatism, they are not absolutely conclusive. As has been said by Sanday, "While it is difficult to resist a total impression which is against the genuineness of the epistle, every prima facie view is not necessarily the true one; and if the writer of this were to commit himself definitely to the negative conclusion, he would feel that he was leaving behind arguments on the other side which he had not fully answered, and combinations which he could not say were impossible."[3]

312

However, II Peter is in the Bible! It is in the canon, or list of approved writings regarded by the church as the word of God. And it is so in spite of the fact that no other New Testament writing won so limited and hesitating a recognition.[4]

Since the value of the epistle rests on what it says, rather than who said it, we prefer to leave the question of authorship at this point, and accept the text for what it is worth. It surely contains some gems of great truth.

"Simon Peter, a servant and an apostle of Jesus Christ . . . according as his divine power hath given unto us all things that pertain unto life and godliness . . . whereby are given unto us exceedingly great and precious promises," and an escape from the corruptions of the world through lust (v. 1-4).

## Progress in Christian Life
(1:5-21)

Having partaken of the divine nature, Peter wrote, "Add to your faith virtue." Then keep on adding such qualities as knowledge, temperance, patience, godliness, brotherly kindness, and charity. "He that lacketh these things is blind, and . . . hath forgotten that he was purged from his old sins" (v. 5-9).

"I think it meet, as long as I am in this tabernacle [flesh], to stir you up by putting you in remembrance; knowing that shortly I must put off this my tabernacle, even as our Lord Jesus Christ hath showed me" (v. 10-14). Peter may have had in mind his age and the impending persecution. But the fact that he was shown this by Christ may indicate a special revealment as mentioned in John 21:18, 19.

Peter then referred to the voice from heaven on the Mount of Transfiguration (Matt. 17:1-13). As a result of this experience, he claimed to

have . . . a more sure knowledge of the word of prophecy . . . knowing this first, that no prophecy of the scriptures is given of any private

313

will of man . . . but holy men of God spake as they were moved by the Holy Ghost.—V. 13-21.

## Beware of False Teachers and Gnosticism
(2:1-22)

Some would privily "bring in abominable heresies, even denying the Lord that bought them . . . by reason of whom the way of truth shall be evil spoken of." This description fits the evils of antinomian Gnosticism. They taught that "the moral law was not binding upon Christians as a rule of life . . . and refuse to recognize any law but their own subjective ideas which they usually claim were from the Holy Spirit."[1]

"God spared not the angels" which were cast down with Satan, nor the wicked from the flood, nor the corrupt from Sodom and Gomorrah, "making them an ensample unto those that after should live ungodly" (v. 4-6). Peter continued to warn against "them that walk after the flesh in the lust of uncleanness, and despise government." These

speak evil of the things they understand not . . . count it pleasure to riot in the day-time . . . having eyes full of adultery, and that cannot cease from sin. . . . For . . . they speak great swelling words of vanity, they allure through the lusts of the flesh . . . while they promise them liberty.—V. 10-19.

Peter wrote concerning these wicked heretics. "It had been better for them not to have known the way of righteousness, than, after they had known it, to turn from the holy commandment delivered unto them" (v. 21).

## The Delay of the Lord's Coming
(3:1-17)

"In the last days there shall come scoffers, walking after their own lusts; denying the Lord Jesus Christ, and saying, Where is the promise of his coming? . . . All things . . . have

314

continued as they are from the beginning of the creation" (v. 3, 4). Peter's answer was, "One day is with the Lord as a thousand years. . . . The Lord is not slack concerning his promise and coming, . . . but is long-suffering toward us, not willing that any should perish" (v. 3-9).

A common weakness men have is lack of patience. They want action now. Only when some disaster is upon them do they turn to God. Peter warns that "the day of the Lord will come as a thief in the night." There will be earthquakes, mountains melted with fervent heat. Therefore we ought to be "preparing for . . . the coming of the Lord. . . . Nevertheless, if we shall endure, we shall be kept according to his promise. And we look for a new heavens, and a new earth wherein dwelleth righteousness" (v. 12, 13). "So also our beloved brother Paul wrote to you according to the wisdom given him" (v. 15, R.S.V.). Peter then added, "Therefore, beloved, seeing ye know before the things which are coming, beware lest ye also being led away with the error of the wicked, fall from your own steadfastness" (v. 17).

---

1. *The Interpreter's Bible,* Vol. 11, p. 132.
2. *Westminster Dictionary of the Bible,* p. 475.
3. E. E. Stringfellow, *op. cit.,* p. 255.
4. *The Interpreter's Bible,* Vol. 12, p. 166.
5. *Baker's Dictionary of Theology,* p. 48.

## QUESTIONS FOR DISCUSSION

1. Can a devoted wife win an unbelieving husband to faith in the gospel? Give examples.
2. Does God punish men to make them repent? Defend your answer.
3. What could Christ preach to the spirits of the disobedient in Hades which would help them?
4. In what manner can charity cover or hide a multitude of sins?

5. What is the problem which concerned Peter about salaried ministers? Does our church have that problem?

6. Why is there disagreement among scholars about the authorship of II Peter?

7. What did Peter mean by saying, "Shortly I must put off this tabernacle"?

8. Who were the false teachers that Peter warned against, and what heresies were they teaching?

9. Why did he say, "It had been better for them not to have known the way of righteousness"? Does this apply to us also?

10. Why did the backsliders of Peter's day say that God was slack concerning his promises? What are men saying about Christ's coming today?

# 48
# EPISTLE TO THE HEBREWS, PART I

This epistle does not identify its author. "Ancient church opinion was divided. . . . The Early Eastern Church received it as Pauline, though it was felt to be unlike the rest of Paul's epistles."[1] Tertullian (A.D. 210) "assigned it to Barnabas; Origen (A.D. 250) expressed the view which many would express even now, 'who wrote it God only knows'. . . . The one point upon which scholars are quite generally in agreement is that it is not Paul's."[2]

It was probably written about A.D. 69 or 70. Professor Stringfellow pointed out that it was "extensively used by Clement of Rome in his letter to the Corinthians written in A.D. 95."

The epistle is a magnificent setting forth of the right of Jesus to the leadership of humanity, based on his victorious suffering and sacrifice. The great "Faith Chapter" [11] is one of the loftiest flights of sustained eloquence in literature.[3]

## Jesus Christ the Perfect Revelation of God (1:1 - 2:18)

God, who at sundry times . . . spake . . . unto the fathers by the prophets, hath in these last days spoken unto us by his Son; . . . who being the . . . express image of his person . . . when he had by himself purged our sins, sat down on the right hand of the Majesty on high; being made so much better than the angels, . . . obtained a more excellent name than they.—V. 1-4.

"But to which of the angels said he at any time, Sit on my right hand, until I make thine enemies thy footstool? Are they not all ministering spirits, sent forth to minister for them who shall be heirs of salvation?" (v. 13, 14). The first part of this quotation, from Psalm 110:1, emphasizes the superiority of Christ over the angels who are sent out to serve.

"Therefore we ought to give the more earnest heed to the things which we have heard, lest at any time we should let them slip" (2:1). Most other versions read, "lest we drift away from it." Apostasy is always a gradual process, whereas letting something slip from our grasp connotes a sudden loss.

For if the word spoken by angels was steadfast . . . how shall we escape, if we neglect so great salvation . . . spoken by the Lord, and . . . confirmed unto us . . . God also bearing them witness, both with signs and wonders, and with divers miracles, and gifts of the Holy Ghost, according to his own will? For unto the angels hath he not put in subjection the world to come. . . . What is man that thou art mindful of him? . . . Thou madest him a little lower than the angels; thou crownedst him with glory and honor, and didst set him over the works of thy hands.—V. 2-7.

From this point on the "Son of Man," as Jesus referred to himself, is associated with man for his salvation. "Thou hast put all things in subjection under his feet" (v. 8). Jesus told the eleven, "All power is given unto me in heaven and in earth" (Matt. 28:17).

For it became him, for whom are all things, and by whom are all things [God, the Father], to make the captain of their salvation perfect through sufferings. For both he that sanctifieth and they who are sanctified are all of one [God]; for which cause he [Jesus] is not ashamed to call them brethren. . . . Forasmuch then as the children are partakers of flesh and blood, he also himself likewise took part of the same; that through death he might destroy him that had the power of death, that is, the devil.—V. 10-14.

He took not on him the likeness of angels [who did not need salvation]; but he took on him the seed of Abraham . . . made like unto his brethren, that he might be a merciful and faithful high priest in things pertaining to God. . . . For in that he himself hath suffered being tempted, he is able to succor them that are tempted.—V. 16-18.

## SALVATION COMES NOT THROUGH MOSES AND JOSHUA, BUT THROUGH JESUS THE SON OF GOD (3:1 - 4:14)

Wherefore, holy brethren, . . . consider the Apostle and High Priest of our profession, Christ Jesus; who was faithful to him that appointed him, as also Moses was faithful in all his [God's] house. . . . For every house is builded by some man; but he that built all things is God.—V. 1-4.

The faithfulness of Moses over his house was as a servant; while "Christ as a son over his own house; whose house are we, if we hold fast the confidence and the rejoicing of the hope firm unto the end" (v. 5, 6).

Our heritage in the household of God is not by grace alone then, but on a steadfast endurance. Israel's unfaithfulness during the forty years in Sinai grieved God, so "I sware in my wrath, They shall not enter my rest" (v. 8-11). Then the author warned against "an evil heart of unbelief. . . . Exhort one another daily . . . lest any of you be hardened through the deceitfulness of sin" (v. 12-19).

"Unto us was the rest [gospel—K.J.V. See also Gal. 3:8] preached, as well as unto them; but the word preached did not profit them, not being mixed with faith in them that heard it" (4:2, 3).

For he spake in a certain place of the seventh day on this wise, And God did rest the seventh day from all his works. And in this place again, If they harden not their hearts they shall enter into my rest. . . . There remaineth therefore a rest to the people of God. For he that is entered into his rest, he also hath ceased from his own works, as God did from his.—V. 4-10.

319

"Seeing then that we have a great high priest, that is passed into the heavens, Jesus the Son of God, let us hold fast our profession." This high priest can be "touched with the feeling of our infirmities"; for he was "on all points tempted like as we are, yet without sin" (v. 14, 15).

## A BETTER PRIESTHOOD THAN JUDAISM
(5:1 - 7:28)

Every high priest taken from among men is ordained for men in things pertaining to God, that he may offer both gifts and sacrifices for sin. . . . And no man taketh this honor unto himself, but he that is called of God, as was Aaron. So also Christ glorified not himself to be made a high priest; but he that said unto him, Thou art my Son, to-day have I begotten thee. As he saith also in another place, Thou art a priest for ever after the order of Melchizedek. . . . And being made perfect, he became the author of eternal salvation unto all them that obey him.—Hebrews 5:1, 4-6, 9.

## PRINCIPLES OF THE GOSPEL AND RESTITUTION
(6:1-18)

Therefore not leaving the [elementary—R.S.V.] principles of the doctrine of Christ, let us go on unto perfection; not laying again the foundation of repentance from dead works, and of faith toward God. Of the doctrine of baptisms, of the laying on of hands, and of the resurrection of the dead, and of eternal judgment.—6:1, 2.

For he hath made it impossible for those who were once enlightened, and have tasted of the heavenly gift, and were made partakers of the Holy Ghost, . . . if they shall fall away, to be renewed again unto repentance; seeing they crucify unto themselves the Son of God afresh, and put him to an open shame.—V. 4-6.

"The impossibility of a second repentance—which is, with the exception of the priesthood of Jesus, the most significant teaching of Hebrews—was to have important consequences in the practice and teaching of the church."[4]

This does not forever bar the backslider from returning to the fold of Christ by God's grace, but applies only to those

320

who were enlightened and partakers of the Holy Spirit; who have lost the desire and hence the ability to repent. As long as a man repents we are to forgive him, not just "seven times" but until "seventy times seven" (Matt. 18:21, 22). Surely God would not ask man to be more merciful than he is.

"For God is not unrighteous, therefore he will not forget your work and labor of love, which ye have showed toward his name, in that ye have ministered to the saints, and do minister" (v. 10).

God promised Abraham to bless and multiply him, "and so, after he had patiently endured, he obtained the promise." We who have fled to God for refuge should "lay hold upon the hope set before us; which hope we have as an anchor of the soul, both sure and steadfast" (v. 13-18).

## THE TWO PRIESTHOODS
(7:1-28)

The priesthood of Jesus was "after the order of Melchizedek" who was once "king of Salem, priest of the most high God" (6:20; 7:1). "By Salem, Jerusalem is probably meant."[9] The extended discussion of Melchizedek (5:11 - 6:20) "serves only one purpose: to prove the existence of another order of priesthood, older, superior, and so superseding both the Levitical priesthood and the law which rests on it."[6]

"Melchizedek is not *inferior* to the Son; he is the prototype of the Son. . . . He [the author] has established proof that Jesus is the Son; he must now show that he is Priest."[7]

To whom also Abraham gave a tenth part of all . . . for this Melchizedek was ordained a priest after the order of the Son of God, which order was without father, without mother . . . having neither beginning of days, nor end of life. *And all those who are ordained unto this priesthood are* made like unto the Son of God, abiding a priest continually.—V. 2-3.

The words in italics are Inspired Version only. It broadens the scope considerably and lays a heavy responsibility on the elders of the church. The first part of the quoted material is similar to Genesis 14:20, 21.

The author then wrote that members of the Levitical priesthood were commanded "to take tithes of the people according to the law," but Melchizedek not only took tithes of the patriarch Abraham but blessed him.

If therefore perfection were by the Levitical priesthood (for under it the people received the law,) what further need was there that another priest should rise after the order of Melchizedek, and not be called after the order of Aaron? For the priesthood being changed, there is made of necessity a change also of the law. . . . For it is evident that our Lord sprang out of Juda, of which tribe Moses spake nothing concerning priesthood—V. 11-14.

The matter of priesthood here discussed should be of special interest to the Saints since most Christians think of it as a dead letter law. They infer that every man is his own priest ("priesthood of all believers"). Thus the sacraments of the church lose much of their significance (see Doctrine and Covenants 83:3).

"For the law was administered without an oath and made nothing perfect, but was only the bringing in of a better hope" (v. 19). The priests of the Aaronic order died, "but this man [Christ], because he continueth ever, hath an unchangeable priesthood. Wherefore he is able also to save them to the uttermost . . . seeing he ever liveth to make intercession for them" (v. 22-24).

1. *Westminster Dictionary of the Bible*, p. 231.
2. E. E. Stringfellow, *op. cit.*, p. 258.
3. *Book of Life*, p. 352.
4. *The Interpreter's Bible*, Vol. 11, p. 651.
5. *Westminster, op. cit.*, p. 388.
6. *The Interpreter's Bible*, Vol. 11, p. 660.
7. *Ibid.*, p. 661.

## QUESTIONS FOR DISCUSSION

1. Give at least one difference in the introduction of this epistle and the others we have studied.
2. What are the differences between the ascended Christ and the angels cited in the first chapter? between angels and men?
3. What purpose is served by "suffering" according to the epistle? Is this equally true of man and Christ?
4. What comparisons are made of Moses and Christ (Chapter 3)?
5. What evidence is given in this epistle that the gospel was given before Christ, and even before Moses?
6. How was the "great high priest . . . touched with the feeling of our infirmities"?
7. Are the principles of the doctrine of Christ contained in Hebrews 6:12? Are any omitted? If so, which?
8. Who are those that it will be impossible to renew unto repentance?
9. What are the three priesthoods mentioned and how do they differ?
10. Why do RLDS members attach more significance to priesthood than do the Protestants?

# 49

# EPISTLE TO THE HEBREWS, PART II

Our last chapter closed with a discussion to convince the Jews that the priesthood brought in by Jesus Christ was superior to the Aaronic priesthood under which Judaism was functioning. This chapter continues in the same general direction, but with different emphases.

## JESUS MINISTERS, SACRIFICES, AND A BETTER COVENANT
### (8:1-13)

"For every high priest is ordained to offer gifts and sacrifices; . . . therefore while he [Christ] was on the earth, he offered for a sacrifice his own life for the sins of the people" (v. 3, 4). Every priest must offer sacrifices under the law as a shadow of heavenly things, but Jesus has "a more excellent ministry . . . [as] the mediator of a better covenant, which was established upon better promises" (v. 5, 6). Had that first covenant been faultless, there would have been no need for a second one, but God said,

Behold, the days come, saith the Lord, when I will make a new covenant with the house of Israel and with the house of Judah; not according to the covenant that I made with their fathers. . . . For . . .

324

I will put my laws into their mind, and write them in their hearts. . . . And they shall not teach every man his neighbor, and every man his brother, saying, Know the Lord; for all shall know me, from the least to the greatest.—V. 8-11.

This quotation is taken from Jeremiah 31:31-34.

The author's use of this prophecy, according to Peake, is to emphasize three points: (1) It ensured that man's obedience to God should be a matter of inward choice, not merely a law imposed from without. By their spontaneous obedience to God, men were to be recognized as indeed his children. (2) Their knowledge of God was to be immediate and personal, no longer dependent on what they had learned from others. (3) They were to receive the assurance that all their sins were forgiven.

"The covenant that carries with it these great promises is described in the prophetic passage as a new one" (v. 13).[1]

## Some Contrasts between the Old and the New Covenants
(9:1-28)

The old covenant had "ordinances of divine service, and a worldly sanctuary" with candlestick, the table and showbread; the second veil was before the Holy of Holies, and behind this curtain was the golden censer, the ark of the covenant, the golden pot that had manna, Aaron's rod that budded, and the tables [stone] of the covenant. Above it was the cherubim of glory shadowing the mercy-seat. The priests went into the first tabernacle (Holy Place), but only the high priest entered the Holy of Holies once every year to offer blood "for himself, and for the errors of the people . . . which was a figure for the time then present, in which were offered both gifts and sacrifices, that could not make him that did the service perfect as pertaining to the conscience" (v. 1-9). See also Exodus, chapters 25 and 26.

Then the author refers to Christ who entered a more perfect tabernacle not made with hands. His offering is not "the blood of goats and calves, but by his own blood he entered in once into the holy place, having obtained eternal redemption for us" (v. 11, 12). Therefore "he is the mediator of the new covenant, that by means of death . . . they which are called might receive the promise of eternal inheritance. For where a covenant is, there must also of necessity be the death of the victim" (v. 15-17). The King James uses "testament" and "testator" for "covenant" and "victim." The Revised Standard Version reads: "For where a will is involved, the death of the one who made it must be established."

"Almost all things are by the law purged with blood; and without shedding of blood is no remission." But Christ did not use the blood of others, but "once in the meridian of time hath he appeared to put away sin by the sacrifice of himself . . . and he shall appear the second time, without sin unto salvation unto them that look for him" (v. 22-28).

## THE EFFICACY OF CHRIST'S SACRIFICE
(10:1-39)

The law was only a symbol of good things to come, "which they offered continually year by year" and could not make the worshipers perfect; so there was "a remembrance again made of sins every year, for it is not possible that the blood of bulls and of goats should take away sins" (v. 1-4).

The author of the epistle then quoted from Psalm 40:6-8. When Christ came into the world he said, "Sacrifice and offering thou wouldst not, but a body hast thou prepared me; in burnt offerings and sacrifices for sin thou hast had no pleasure. . . . I come to do thy will, O God." In this manner he took "away the first [covenant], that he may establish the second." Thus "after he had offered one sacrifice for sins forever, sat down on the right hand of God; from henceforth to reign until his enemies be made his footstool . . . whereof the Holy Ghost also is a witness to us" (v. 5-15).

In a summary statement the author declared, "where remission of these [sins] is, there is no more offering for sin." Christ entered into the holiest of places, through the veil of death, therefore "Let us draw near with a true heart in full assurance of faith." Then he further exhorted his Hebrew brethren, "And let us consider one another to provoke [stir up—R.S.V.] unto love and to good works; not forsaking the assembling of ourselves together, as the manner of some is" (v. 18-25). This touches a basic doctrine of the gospel. Fellowship in worship is the root of right relations. Those who claim they "can worship just as well out in the woods as in church" on Sunday are overlooking the need of others, and generally are trying unsuccessfully to convince themselves.

If we sin wilfully after that we have received the knowledge of the truth, there remaineth no more sacrifices for sins. . . . Vengeance belongeth unto me, I will recompense, saith the Lord. . . . It is a fearful thing to fall into the hands of the living God.—V. 26-31.

Cast not away therefore your confidence, which hath great recompense of reward, for ye have need of patience, that after ye have done the will of God, ye might receive the promise. For yet a little while, and he that shall come will come. Now the just shall live by faith.—V. 35-38.

The assurance to those facing persecution and even death, the promises of the change through Christ's coming given by most writers of the New Testament, were comforting. Luther built his theology largely on the last clause in the quotation, "The just shall live by faith." By "just" he meant those who live righteous lives.

## The Triumph of Faith
(11:1 - 12:3)

"This chapter [11] is a rhetorical masterpiece ranking with the great New Testament passages. . . . Its force lies in the cumulative and massive testimony of assembled witnesses."[2]

"Now faith is the assurance of things hoped for, the evidence of things not seen," it begins. The King James Version says "the substance of things"; however, the Revised Standard Version uses "assurance," but instead of "evidence" it uses "conviction." To the extent that one has a functioning conviction it is evidence to him and others.

Then follows a list of instances where faith had triumphed. By it the elders obtained a good report, men understood the plan of creation, Abel's sacrifice was accepted. Enoch did not die, for God took him. See Genesis 5:7; 7:78. The author then breaks into his narration with a significant and much quoted parenthetical statement: "But without faith it is impossible to please him [God]; for he that cometh to God must believe that he is, and that he is a rewarder of them that diligently seek him" (v. 1-6).

There is a likelihood that many oversimplify this promise. They do not receive a satisfactory reward because they only believe or assent. But the faith required must be wrought out of experience, having both assurance and evidence.

Other incidences of faith were then added: By it Noah prepared an ark and saved his household; Abraham left his homeland and dwelt in a strange country. "He looked for a city which hath foundations, whose builder and maker is God. Sarah conceived and bore Isaac when she was ninety (Gen. 17:23); Abraham offered up Isaac; Isaac blessed Jacob and Esau; Jacob blessed the sons of Joseph; Moses' life was spared when he was hid for three months. Moses "refused to be called the son of Pharaoh's daughter; choosing rather to suffer affliction with the people of God, than to enjoy the pleasures of sin for a season" (v. 7-25).

By faith Moses led his people from Egypt, the walls of Jericho fell, and Rahab's life was spared. The prophets subdued kingdoms and stopped the mouths of lions. Women received their dead raised to life again, and others received

328

bonds and imprisonment. Some were stoned and sawed asunder. But God "provided some better things for them through their sufferings, for without sufferings they could not be made perfect" (v. 27-40).

Seeing we also are compassed about with so great a cloud of witnesses, let us lay aside every weight . . . and let us run with patience the race that is set before us, looking unto Jesus . . . who . . . endured the cross, despising the shame, and is set down at the right hand of the throne of God.—12:1, 2.

## Chastening, Purity, and the Kingdom (12:4-29)

My son, despise not thou the chastening of the Lord, nor faint when thou art rebuked of him; for whom the Lord loveth he chasteneth, and scourgeth every son whom he receiveth. If ye endure chastening, God dealeth with you as with sons.—V. 4-8.

This is hard for children (and some parents) to understand. "Now no chastening for the present seemeth to be joyous, but grievous; nevertheless, afterward it yieldeth the peaceable fruit of righteousness" (v. 11).

The author of the epistle then recalls the mistakes made by Esau, and by others at Sinai. "But ye are come unto mount Sion, . . . the heavenly Jerusalem, . . . to the general assembly and church of the first-born . . . see that ye refuse not him that speaketh" (v. 16-25).

"Wherefore we receiving a kingdom which cannot be moved, should have grace, whereby we may serve God acceptably" (v. 28).

## Exhortations to Charity and Faithfulness (13:1-25)

"Let brotherly love continue. Be not forgetful to entertain strangers; for thereby some have entertained angels unawares." Then he commends marriage, generous giving, consecration without covetousness, respect for those who rule over you [church leaders]. For "consecrations" (v. 5) the King James Version uses "conversation." Most versions agree with the Inspired Version.

He assured the Hebrews of Christ's unchangeability (v. 8) and warned against apostasy (v. 9). "Here we have no continuing city, but we seek one to come" (v. 14). "Obey them that have the rule over you . . . for they watch for your souls. . . . Pray for us . . .that I may be restored to you the sooner" (v. 17-19). "Know ye that our brother Timothy is set at liberty; with whom, if he come shortly, I will see you." This indicates that the writer was not imprisoned.

---

1. *Peake's Commentary on the Bible,* p. 894, 895.
2. *The Interpreter's Bible,* Vol. 11, p. 718.

## QUESTIONS FOR DISCUSSION

1. Explain "The law required sacrifices as a shadow of heavenly things."
2. Jeremiah prophesied of a new covenant. Give one of the three points drawn from the prophecy.
3. Which historical relics are named as belonging to tabernacle and temple worship?
4. What comparisons are made between the high priest and the tabernacle and Christ and the heavenly tabernacle?
5. The covenant is compared to a will (testament). What parallels can you name?
6. Which passage is used to encourage regular church attendance?
7. What significance do you get from the statement, "The just shall live by faith"?
8. What definition is given for faith? How can it be applied to your daily life?
9. What are the rewards of faith which are promised to believers?
10. What is the purpose of God's chastening? How has your life been made better by it?

# 50

# JUDE, AND JOHN'S EPISTLES

The short epistle of Jude is addressed to "them who are sanctified of the Father; and preserved in Jesus Christ." The writer is "the servant of God, called of Jesus Christ, and brother of James" (v. 1).

This is generally interpreted as referring to Jude, the brother of Jesus (Mark 6:3) [6:4, I.V.] for the following reasons: (1) He does not claim to be an apostle. (2) The designation, "brother of James," is in accord with the manner of designating James, the Lord's brother (Mark 6:3; Acts 12:17; Gal. 1:19). (3) It is the sort of letter to be expected from the Lord's brother. (4) It is in the Muratorian Fragment, the earliest church canon, presumably on the grounds that it was written by the Lord's brother; Eusebius, however, places it among the disputed books, and Jerome (A.D. 400) said that it was rejected by many.[1]

The date is "perhaps about A.D. 80." In the introduction, Jude wrote that he had planned to discuss "the common salvation . . . and exhort you that ye should earnestly contend for the faith which was once delivered to the saints" (v. 3). Instead he found it necessary to warn against "ungodly men, turning the grace of our God into lasciviousness, and denying the only Lord God, and our Lord Jesus Christ." He reminded his readers of their deliverance from Egypt with the destruction of the unbelievers. He went back into pre-creation days when the "angels . . . kept not their first estate, but left their own habitation" (see D. and C. 28:10 c). He mentioned the corruption of Sodom and Gomorrah which brought them to "suffering the vengeance of eternal fire" (v. 4-7).

Likewise also these filthy dreamers defile the flesh, despise dominion, and speak evil of dignities, . . . [and] of those things which they know not. . . . Woe unto them! for they have gone in the way of Cain . . . after the error of Balaam.—V. 8-11. (See also Numbers 22:24; Nehemiah 13:2.)

"Jude expressed the determined opposition of the Roman church to Docetism, a heretical doctrine of the person of Christ that denied his real humanity."[2] He was "merely a phantom." He employed five metaphors to further emphasize the errors of this heresy. They were "spots in your feasts of charity"; "clouds without water"; "trees with withered, dead fruits"; "raging waves of the sea, foaming with shame"; and "wandering stars to wander forever in blackness" (v. 12, 13).

"Enoch also, the seventh from Adam prophesied . . . Behold, the Lord cometh with ten thousand of his saints, to execute judgment upon all." Especially upon the ungodly who made hard speeches against him, "the murmurers, complainers, walking after their own lusts," using favors for advantage. Jude asked his readers to remember the apostle's words that "there should be mockers in the last time, who . . . separate themselves, sensual, having not the Spirit" (v. 14-19).

The epistle is concluded by an admonition to build "up yourselves on your most holy faith . . . and of some have compassion, making a difference; and others save with fear, pulling them out of the fire." Jude's benediction is majestic:

Now unto him that is able to keep you from falling, and to present you faultless before the presence of his glory with exceeding joy, to the only wise God our Savior, be glory and majesty, dominion and power, both now and ever. Amen.—V. 20-25.

The first epistle of John was First John, probably written A.D. 97. This is one of the nine books in the New Testament which do not identify their authors. Tradition and scholars are almost unanimous that the apostle John, "the beloved disciple," wrote the Gospel and the three epistles.

## God Is Manifested in Christ

The introduction is John's testimony of things he heard, saw, and handled. "Eternal life, which was with the Father, . . . was manifested unto us" (v. 1, 2; John 17:3).

The same fellowship which he enjoyed is available to us. John declared that Christ's message was "that God is light. . . . If we say that we have fellowship with him, and walk in darkness, we lie . . . but if we walk in the light, as he is in the light, we have fellowship one with another, and the blood of Jesus Christ his Son cleanseth us from all sin."

This is straightforward language and sound logic. "If we say that we have no sin, we deceive ourselves, and the truth is not in us. . . . We make him a liar, and his word is not in us." But if we confess our sins he will forgive and cleanse us from all unrighteousness (v. 3-10).

## Fellowship Requires Obedience and Love (2:1-17)

John was now an old man. This shows in his manner of addressing his readers: "My little children."

If any man sin and repent, we have an advocate with the Father, Jesus Christ the righteous. . . . He that saith, I know him, and keepeth not his commandments, is a liar. . . . But whoso keepeth his word, in him verily is the love of God perfected.—V. 1-5.

Again a new commandment I write unto you, which thing was of old ordained of God. . . . He that saith he is in the light, and hateth his brother, is in darkness even until now. He that loveth his brother abideth in the light, and there is none occasion of stumbling in him.—V. 7-10.

333

I write unto you, little children, because your sins are forgiven you. . . . Unto you, fathers, because ye have known him that is from the beginning. . . . Unto you, young men, because ye have overcome the wicked one. . . . Ye are strong, and the word of God abideth in you.—V. 12-14.

Love not the world, neither the things that are of the world. . . . The world passeth way, and the lust thereof; but he that doeth the will of God abideth for ever.—V. 15-17.

## Beware of Many Antichrists
(2:18-28)

"Little children, it is the last time; and as ye have heard that antichrist shall come, even now are there many antichrists. . . . They went out from us, but they were not of us." Some today point to atheistic Communism as our antichrist. This is a distorted religious judgment. These persons here mentioned are Christian apostates who "went out from us." However "communism in its ideological form has been called a Christian heresy, 'a leaf taken from the book of Christianity—a leaf torn out and misread.' "[3]

Doubtless John was aiming his arrows at the Gnostics and particularly the group teaching Docetism. "Who is a liar . . . that denieth that Jesus is the Christ [anointed] . . . that denieth the Father and the Son" (v. 22, 23). Later John made this more clear, "Every spirit that confesseth not that Jesus Christ is come in the flesh is not of God; and this is that spirit of antichrist" (4:3).

"Little children, abide in him; that, when he shall appear, we may have confidence, and not be ashamed before him at his coming" (v. 28).

## Brotherly Love Fulfills the Law
(3:1 - 4:21)

Behold what manner of love the father hath bestowed upon us, that we should be called the sons of God. . . . It doth not yet appear

334

what we shall be; but we know that, when he shall appear, we shall be like him; for we shall see him as he is. And every man that hath this hope in him, purifieth himself, even as he is pure.—V. 1-3.

See also Romans 8:14; Matthew 5:9. This is a beautiful passage and very challenging.

He that continued in sin is of the devil; for the devil sinneth from the beginning. For this purpose the Son of God was manifested, that he might destroy the works of the devil.—V. 8.

Marvel not, my brethren, if the world hate you. We know that we have passed from death unto life, because we love the brethren. . . . Whosoever hateth his brother is a murderer; and ye know that no murderer hath eternal life abiding in him. . . . Whoso hath this world's good, and seeth his brother have need, and shutteth up his bowels of compassion from him, how dwelleth the love of God in him? . . . If our heart condemn us, God is greater than our heart, and knoweth all things. . . . And whatsoever we ask, we receive of him, because we keep his commandments, and do those things that are pleasing in his sight. . . . And hereby we know that he abideth in us, by the Spirit which he hath given us.—V. 13-24.

Try the spirits whether they are of God; because many false prophets are gone out into the world. And every spirit that confesseth not that Jesus Christ is come in the flesh is not of God.—4:1-3.

Beloved, let us love one another; for love is of God. . . . He that loveth not, knoweth not God; for God is love. . . . Herein is love, not that we loved God, but that he loved us, and sent his Son to be the propitiation for our sins. Beloved, if God so loved us, we ought also to love one another. . . . There is no fear in love; but perfect love casteth out fear. . . . We love him, because he first loved us. . . . And this commandment have we from him, That he who loveth God love his brother also.—V. 7-21.

"Whatsoever is born of God overcometh the world; . . . he that believeth that Jesus is the Son of God. . . . This is he that came by water and blood, even Jesus Christ. . . . And it is the Spirit that beareth witness" (5:4-6). Jesus asked for baptism in the waters of Jordan to set the example of the new birth. His blood on the cross, which we memorialize in the Lord's Supper, made atonement for sins. This atonement was denied by the Docetists.

Three bear witness in heaven: Father, the Word, and the Holy Ghost. Three bear witness on earth: the Spirit, the water, and the blood (v. 6-9).

"All unrighteousness is sin; and there is a sin not unto death." Paul wrote, "For to be carnally minded is death" (Rom. 8:6); and most sins become sins of the flesh and are therefore mortal. "The whole world lieth in wickedness," but with the understanding given us we know that Christ is the true son of God (v. 17-21).

## John's Second and Third Epistles,
### about a.d. 98

"The elder unto the elect lady and her children, whom I love in the truth." This is a gracious reference to the church.

I rejoice greatly that I found of thy children walking in truth. . . . Many deceivers are entered into the world, who confess not that Jesus Christ is come in the flesh. . . . Whosoever transgresseth, and abideth not in the doctrine of Christ, hath not God. He that abideth in the doctrine of Christ, he hath both the Father and the Son. If there come any unto you, and bring not this doctrine, receive him not into your house, neither bid him God-speed.— II John. v. 1, 4, 7, 9, 10.

Third John was written about the same time as Second John. It is largely personal and addressed to Gaius. This was a common name of that time. He was a prominent member of the church, but nothing further is known. John rejoiced when some brethren testified that "thou walkest in the truth." The main purpose of the letter was to commend Gaius for his previous hospitality. Some missionary elders are soon to visit his church and he solicits Gaius to care for them (III, v. 1-8).

A brother by the name of Diotrephes (Di-ot're-phes) who desired preeminence "receiveth us not." Instead he prates "against us with malicious words." He would not receive the traveling elders, forbade others to receive them, and cast them out of the church (v. 9-10).

"Demetrius hath good report of all men, and of the truth itself." The contrast between these two men is intense. John closed his letter by expressing the hope to see and speak to Gaius shortly (v. 12-14).

1. Stringfellow, *op. cit.*, p. 269; see also *Westminster Dictionary of the Bible*, p. 337.
2. *The Interpreter's Bible*, Vol. 12, p. 317.
3. Arnold Toynbee, quoted in *The Interpreter's Bible*, p. 244.

## QUESTIONS FOR DISCUSSION

1. What is known of Jude's background?
2. What did he mean by "angels that kept not their first estate"?
3. Jude warned the saints against a heretical group now called Docetists. What errors did they teach?
4. John's testimony is that "God is light." We are to "walk in the light." We are to be "the light of the world." What is the meaning of light in each quotation?
5. Explain, "He that doeth the will of God abideth forever."
6. Who are the "antichrist"? Are they in Russia?
7. John wrote that we shall be like Christ. When is this to be? What is to make us worthy of this?
8. John infers that one who "hates his brother is a murderer," and no murderer has eternal life dwelling in him. Can one who hates have eternal life?
9. Explain, "Perfect love casteth out fear." Do you have any fear? Can you name someone without phobias?
10. Have we an obligation to give hospitality to traveling ministers for Christ? How far does this duty extend?

# TOPICAL INDEX

339